LONDON POSTAL WORKERS – A TRADE UNION HISTORY 1839–2000

Norman Candy

This book is dedicated to the memory
of Derek Walsh (1935–2014)
and all those Postal Workers who have the courage
to fight for a better life.

ABOUT THE AUTHOR

Norman Candy is 65 and works as a Policy Advisor to Dave Ward the Deputy General Secretary (Postal) of the Communication Workers Union. He started working in 1965 and became an activist in the Building Craft Section of the Transport and General workers Union. In the early 1970s he was blacklisted as a result of his trade union activities and in 1976 obtained employment with Royal Mail as a postman. In the following years he held various positions within the London Division of the CWU before being elected to the Union's Executive in 2002. In 2007 he began work as a Policy Advisor at the Union's Headquarters in Wimbledon.

Published by Blue Collar

CONTENTS

INTRODUCTION

History is constantly moving forward; the further away we get the more detailed it becomes. More events, more discoveries of our past.

Too often the past is told to us by people who focus on the great and the good. The account by common people is often overlooked and all too often written by uncommon folk. History written and told by people who were there and help shape it; this is even rarer still.

Such is the value of this book on London Postal Workers. It tells both of the stories of what went on before and during events in which the author took part and helped shape.

London is a city with about 300 spoken languages; a diverse and exciting place. The voice of struggle shouts out from the pages of this book.

Thanks to Norman Candy for putting on paper, those who went before us and giving them a place in our history.

Billy Hayes
General Secretary
CWU

LIST OF PLATES

DO – District Organiser

ADO – Assistant District Organiser

*Photographs by John McDonnell

Chapter 1

LONDON POSTAL WORKERS
AND 19TH CENTURY LONDON

In the 19th century the population of London expanded at an extraordinary rate. Between 1801 and 1901 it grew from just over one million to six and a quarter million with half the country's population living in the capital. London was the biggest city in the world and the centre of Government for the worldwide British Empire. It was governed by the Metropolitan Board of Works until the establishment of the London County Council (LCC) formed in 1889 from the cities of London, Southwark, Westminster and parts of Middlesex, Kent and Surrey. This existed until 1963 when London expanded to form the Greater London Council and then the Greater London Authority in 1999. Whilst the population of Metropolitan London was expanding the original 'City' of London was changing with the massive rebuilding programmes of the 1860s and 1870s. At the heart of the 'City' was the Bank of England which was surrounded by a multitude of Credit Houses, Banks and Insurance Companies. The City's human inhabitants disappeared at the same time, pushed aside by the expansion of the City as the financial centre of the world. Its population fell from 128,000 in 1851 to 51,000 in 1881 and to 27,000 in 1901. By 1971 its population had declined to 4,000.

Vast fortunes were being made at home and abroad and the resulting profits were used to finance Britain's imperial expansion. The City of London was the financial powerhouse for those changes as the profits from Banking, Insurance and Shipping became ever larger and more important. Income from these services grew from £24 million in 1851 to £134 million in 1911 and income from overseas dividends grew from £12 million to £152 million during the same period. Whilst the City of London was the Empires financial centre, the City of Westminster housed the countries centres of government, religion, judiciary, treasury and the military.

In stark contrast to the wealth and power of the City there was another side to 19th century London. In the sweltering summer of 1858 the stench from the Thames became so offensive that Parliament had to close for a number of days during what became known as the 'Great Stench'. The prevailing winds ensured that the wealthy tended to live in the West and South West of London and the poor in the East and South East. Mansions and boulevards extended across West London from Bloomsbury to Chelsea where pleasure gardens and tea gardens were established increasing the areas appeal to the rich and powerful. Chelsea and Kensington were considered to be the ideal places for the rich and wealthy to live. Large houses, private schools and Royal hospitals popularised the area and market gardens supplied the City with fruit and vegetables well into the middle of the 19th century.

In East and South East London the magnificent houses and buildings of West London and the City gave way to the vast expanse of riverside warehouses, workshops, docks and factories, railway viaducts, overcrowded housing and courtyards that stretched along the Thames from Vauxhall to Poplar.

In 1800 the world's largest purpose built docks were constructed in the Port of London. Further east in Stratford the Great Eastern Railway had its workshops and engine depots, the largest in Europe. Along the southern bank of the river stood a wall of brick warehouses stretching from Vauxhall to Surrey Docks and beyond. On 3 November 1857 Brunel launched what was then the world's biggest ship from the Napier Shipyard in Millwall. Across the river the East Indian Company had its Headquarters and further along the south side the Royal Navy Dockyards were based at Greenwich. On the North and East rim of the City, areas such as Clerkenwell, Hoxton and Whitechapel, the old 'East End', housed the biggest concentration of slums in Europe. Families with 5-6 children lived in housing of one or two rooms, in tenements and back to back housing with no running water and no toilets. A whole street of families would have to share a single toilet and water pump. The water from the pump was often polluted and sewers ran down the middle of the streets.

Cholera epidemics broke out in 1832, 1848, 1849 and 1854. More than 33,000 people died throughout Britain during an outbreak of cholera in 1849 and of those 13,000 were in London. The average life expectancy of a manual worker in London at this time was half the age of a middle-class Londoner or a manual worker from the rural areas surrounding the capital. Prince Albert, the German born husband of Queen Victoria, died of typhoid in 1861 and it was only when the disease threatened the wealthy that measures were taken to improve sanitation and housing. It is not surprising that many children from poorer families never made it to adulthood. Three out of every ten children died before the age of one, yet *The Times* campaigned against sanitary improvements arguing that 'We prefer to take our chances of cholera and the rest rather than be bullied into health'.

A major cause of disease and pollution was Smithfield Market and its slaughter houses, known as the 'shambles', situated within the City of London. There were many attempts to re-site it to Islington but the toll charged for the sale of livestock, market dues and public house rents was a rich source of revenue for the City Corporation. The waste from the abattoirs was discharged into the River Fleet and the rotting flesh often blocked its flow into the Thames. Each day drovers herded thousands of cattle into the market blocking the surrounding streets and creating unbelievable chaos amongst the dirty streets, lanes and alleys, the haunt of poverty and crime. City merchants fattened up their cattle in the fields of Islington before driving them into the market.

Politics in Victorian Britain

In the early part of the 19th century political power was dominated by two political factions – the 'Whigs' and the 'Tories'. Political power swung between these two parties in a Parliament that was undemocratic and corrupt with the majority of people prohibited from voting. Although a few Independent MPs argued for an extension of the franchise, neither of the parties wanted to risk genuine democracy because they believed it would threaten their power and wealth.

Parliament in 1865 was dominated by a small group of landed families. More than half of all parliamentarians were related in some way and in addition there were 100 MPs sitting in the commons connected with the aristocracy by marriage or descent. These connections allowed the same families to control the country's wealth and military. A few middle-class Radicals advocated Parliamentary reform but when a Whig Government extended the right to vote in 1832 to include the upper- middle-class their passion for democracy was satisfied. The middle-class 'reformers' had used the working class to achieve change for their own benefit and once this was accomplished they turned their backs on the thousands of ordinary people who had made the greatest sacrifices to bring this about. This act of treachery became known amongst the working class as the 'Great Betrayal'.

Two of the organisations important in the struggle for democracy were based in London. The first was the London Working Man's Association (LWMA) formed in 1836 and the second was the East London Democratic Association formed in 1837. Members of these organisations campaigned and organised throughout the early mid-19th century to break the dictatorship of the Whigs and Tories. Many suffered incredible hardship and hundreds were imprisoned or transported to the penal colonies in Australia. Some were killed in clashes with the military and others maimed and injured. Despite this they laid the foundations for many of the changes and improvements of later years.

Although neither of the two political parties believed in democracy, some, with an eye on the upheavals taking place on the continent, talked of the need to reform, believing that only a controlled move towards democracy would avoid bloody revolution. Others argued that parliamentary reform would allow the working class to use the state machinery to threaten their power. Robert Lowe, a leading Whig politician, the Member of Parliament for Calne, a 'Rotten Borough' with a population of only 170, and a close friend of Lord Rothschild was a leader of those Whigs and Tories who opposed the extension of the franchise to working people. In a speech to Parliament he urged his fellow MPs to stand fast in opposing the extension of the vote: 'Nothing is so remarkable among the working classes of England as their intense tendency to associate and organise themselves. It is impossible to believe that the same machinery which is at present brought into play in connection with strikes would not be applied by the working classes to political purposes. You know very well that they will soon possess the secret of their own power, and then what is to prevent them using it'.

London was a major centre of political opposition to the wealthy interests who held political and economic power. For many ordinary Londoners every day was a struggle against poverty and hardship. Working people organised themselves politically and industrially to defend their interests and improve their lives. In the early 1800s there were several large trade unions, and in London trade unionism was strongest amongst the skilled workers and tradesmen. Although most workers were not in trade unions this did not stop the Government becoming alarmed at their growing influence. Many trade unionists around the country were imprisoned and others transported to Australia on the trumped up charge of 'swearing an illegal oath'.

The Tolpuddle Martyrs were perhaps the most famous victims of the Government's repression but by no means the only ones. Many workers recognised that trade union organisation alone was insufficient to bring about lasting economic improvement and working people began to organise to bring about political change. In 1830 only 478,000 people out of a population of 24 million were permitted by law to vote. Even after the 1832 Reform Act, which extended the vote to the upper- middle-class, less than 4% of the population were permitted to take part in elections. There was a strong tradition of rebellion amongst the working people of London and this sometimes involved campaigning and petitioning for democratic change and on occasions a more militant, defiant tactic emerged which manifested itself in street fighting and riots. Between 1816 and 1884 serious civil disturbances erupted in various parts of London on a fairly regular basis. In 1848 a large section of the London democratic movement, frustrated by the lack of progress being achieved by peaceful means, attempted an armed uprising. However, a network of police spies had infiltrated the rebels and the badly armed democrats had little chance against the well-armed police and military. Despite the arrests, imprisonments and deportations, the struggle continued – sometimes peacefully and sometimes violently.

In the second half of the 19th century there was a growth in trade union activity. Initially this was amongst skilled craftsmen, carpenters, printers and engineers but later dockers, gas workers and postal workers began to organise themselves into unions. In July 1888 1,400 mainly young women went on strike at the Bryant and May match factory in Bow, East London. Most of the women were under the age of 15 and worked under appalling conditions. Their success and courage in taking on a powerful employer became an inspiration to other London workers and in August 1889 the Great London Dock Strike brought thousands of previously badly organised dock workers into the trade union movement. This dispute, known as the strike for the 'Dockers Tanner', was a milestone in trade union history and showed once again what determined and well led workers could achieve.

These important steps forward for working people were assisted by political changes that had taken place twenty years earlier. In 1867 many trade unionists had obtained the vote as a result of the 1867 Reform Act which extended the vote to some working class men. In 1871 Gladstone, the Liberal Prime Minister, introduced the Trade Union Act and the Criminal Law Amendment Act which restricted the effectiveness and influence of trade unions. The Conservative Party promised the trade unions that they would introduce legislation to assist the unions and as a consequence many trade unionists used their vote to oust the Liberals. The new Conservative Government introduced legislation that allowed trade unions the right to peaceful picket, vastly improving their effectiveness.

Although some workers experienced an improvement in their standard of living during the second half of the nineteenth century, for most working people, Britain remained the centre of the 'Empire on which the sun never rose'. Many Londoners lived in poverty and some in abject poverty. In the late nineteenth century a report published by the London County Schools Board declared that each day 55,000 children attended school in a state of hunger. In 1902 Jack London, an American journalist and author, observed in his book 'People of the Abyss', that 55% of East End children died before they were five years old. Thousands of abandoned and starving children were only saved from poverty or death by the work of people such as the Irishman Dr. Barnardo who established a network of homes across London where destitute children could find sanctuary.

In 1885 Charles Booth, the son of a Liverpool businessman, head of the Lamport and Holt Steamship Company and a Liberal Party supporter, angry at a claim in the *Pall Mall Gazette* that 25% of the population of London lived in abject poverty, undertook a survey of London in an attempt to discredit the newspaper's claim. He recruited a team of researchers (amongst whom were Sidney and Beatrice Webb who was Booth's cousin) and the results of his investigation, published in 1889, shocked both Booth and many in the Liberal establishment. Booth's research showed that 35% of Londoners rather than the 25% as reported in the Gazette were living in abject poverty. It was against this background that a small group of trade union activists struggled to light the spark of trade unionism amongst London's postal workers.

Chapter 2

ROWLAND HILL
AND THE PENNY POST

Rowland Hill, the man credited with introducing the 'Universal Postal Service' was the third son of Thomas Wright Hill, a failed businessman from Birmingham. Thomas Hill came from a Protestant dissenting background of small traders and had six sons and two daughters. His wife's name was Sarah and it was said that his children inherited an ambition 'to improve their position in the world' from their mother.

Undeterred by his failure in business, Thomas opened a private school which he imaginatively named 'Hill Top'. The school was in Birmingham and it became a family enterprise in which his sons became teachers. The boys transformed the school into an institution dedicated to educating children from the 'middling and higher ranks in the principles of laissez-faire capitalism and the values of political reform'. In 1827 the Hills moved to London and opened a school at Bruce Castle, Tottenham, which then became the family's new home.

Rowland Hill's character was shaped by a number of influences. His family were Unitarians, one of the dissenting Protestant churches that had refused to accept the doctrines of the Church of England principally regarding their rejection of the Trinity. As a consequence they were excluded by law from numerous areas of business activity and advancement, including civil and military service. In the early 19th century they were also prohibited from attending the only two English Universities, Oxford and Cambridge, where students were required to subscribe to the 39 Articles of the Church of England and regularly attend an Anglian service. Collectively the dissenting Churches were known as non-conformists, which included, amongst others, Baptists, Quakers, Congregationalists, Unitarians and Methodists. Their exclusion from the highest levels of society encouraged them to develop their own schools and institutions. These were dedicated to providing an education that would equip them with the skills necessary to succeed in the activities they were not excluded from. Consequently the non-conformists provided a large proportion of the entrepreneurs and industrialists in the 19th century. They also tended to support the Whigs who promised them civil and religious liberty as opposed to the Tories who opposed religious reform.

Amongst the many famous businesses started by non-conformists were Whitbread's Breweries and Truman's Breweries, started by Samuel Whitbread and Benjamin Truman. In banking both Barclays and Lloyds were started by non-conformist Quakers. Their exclusion from mainstream middle-class society encouraged them to support each other in business enterprises and by the mid-19th century they had become very influential and ceased to be a marginalised minority. In 1851 a census revealed that almost 50% of Protestant churchgoers were non-conformists. London attracted many of these businessmen and Clerkenwell and Finsbury were areas where many of them settled because of its closeness to the City where their religious activities were restricted by the City's regulations. They were forced to live outside of its boundaries where evidence of their presence can be found in the non-conformist cemetery in Bunhill Row, situated just off Old Street in EC1, and the non-conformist chapels in the surrounding area.

He was also influenced by the ideas of Jeremy Bentham, the leading exponent of Utilitarianism, an ideology also known as Philosophical Radicalism. Bentham was a leading liberal theoretician whose ideas he claimed were based on the belief that there was no such thing as natural justice or 'natural rights' and that actions were right if they tended to produce the greatest happiness for the greatest number of people. Unfortunately the people that he referred to were the wealthy, and consequently the poor suffered when his ideas were put into practice. Utilitarianism was re-named 'Brutilitarianism' by working people and although he died in 1832 his ideas influenced politics, economics and society for many years to come. Bentham also believed that the principle motivation for human behaviour was the desire for pleasure and the avoidance of pain. When this idea was applied to the problems of poverty and unemployment it resulted in many of the worst excesses of inhumanity and distress associated with the nineteenth century.

In 1834 the 'Poor Law Amendment Act' was introduced. Its application was met with civil disorder and opposition from working people across the country. According to Benthamite principles an applicant for poor relief would have to pass the 'workhouse test'. The unemployed and destitute would have to weigh the 'pleasure' of staying outside of the workhouse with the 'pain' of entering it, and only the truly destitute would accept relief. The fact is that the fear of having to go into the 'workhouse' terrified workers, the elderly and the disabled. It was a cruel threat aimed at controlling workers and their families. Workhouses were worse than prisons where the food was inadequate and many of the inmates were virtually starving. Families, husbands and wives and children were separated and forced to work for no pay. The attitude of many wealthy people was summed up by Patrick Colquhoun, a Provost of Glasgow, who was brought to London to reform the capitals police force: 'Poverty is a most necessary and indispensable ingredient in society. It is the lot of man – it is the source of wealth, since without poverty there would be no labour and without labour there would be no riches, no refinement, no comfort and no benefit to those who may be of wealth'.

The 'Benthamites' gained increased political influence when the Whigs were returned to power in 1830 and King William IV asked Earl Grey to form a Government. Edwin Chadwick, had been Bentham's literary secretary and was the son of a successful Manchester businessman. He became Secretary of the Poor Law Commission and emerged as the driving force behind the introduction of the workhouse as a replacement for unemployment assistance. One of his initiatives for saving money was to prohibit the ringing of church bells at pauper's funerals. 'Benthamites' in the Government also sponsored the 1832 Anatomy Act which allowed the confiscation of paupers' bodies for scientific dissection. In the 30 years that the law remained on the statute books the bodies of 50,000 poor people were confiscated and taken for dissection from London hospitals alone. According to an 1836 Parliamentary Report the measures introduced during this period to control working people had the required effect as the guardians of the Maldon Workhouse in Essex observed: 'The habits of the labouring class are certainly improving. They cannot now compel an overseer to relieve them as they used to do; they are consequently more cautious how they spend their earnings and duly appreciate a good master'.

Despite this, working people continued to campaign and protest about the imposition of these cruel and inhumane policies. Demonstrations were held to oppose Chadwick's policies and the cruel treatment of working people provoked even Tories like Richard Oastler to campaign against these policies. He was so shocked by the cruelty and hypocrisy of some employers, many of whom claimed to be God fearing, Church going Christians, that he urged workers to use strikes and sabotage to improve their conditions. In particular, he was appalled at the treatment of young children who were forced to work long hours in terrible conditions, some of whom were as young as four years of age. He overcame his dislike for democracy and trade unions to lead a campaign to restrict child labour. In 1830 he commented, 'British workers suffered a worse slavery than the hellish system of colonial slavery'. His actions provoked a sharp reaction from his employer, Thomas Thornhill, a North Country Landlord which led to him being imprisoned for debt in 1840. He was held in Fleet Prison for four years until his debt was repaid. On his release he resumed his campaign on behalf of children and working people.

Rowland Hill made his own contribution to the debate on the issue of poverty. In 1832 he published *Home Colonies* in which he recommended that agricultural work camps should be set up where the poor would be required 'to work insulated from vice and when the habit of industry had been learned they would be allowed to re-join society.' The working classes, he concluded 'must be made familiar with the circumstances which regulate the price of their labour'.

In 1837 he turned his attention to the British Postal Service. British commerce and industry required a good transport and communications system. Canals, roads and railways were constructed to transport goods across the country but it also required good communications. The cheap and efficient transportation of letters, parcels and packets was an essential ingredient in the development of British industry and, in particular, the City of London. In 1835 the Government set up a commission to investigate and report on the workings of the Post Office. Prior to the report the Post Office was a department of the Civil Service, responsible for collecting and delivering mail throughout the country. Postal charges varied according to distance and cheap local postal services existed in London and other large cities. The cost of sending a letter in the City before 1840 was two pence and the charge for longer distances was between four pence and a shilling for distances of up to 300 miles. One penny was charged for each additional 100 miles. The charge could either be paid by the sender or the recipient but the vast majority of letters were sent without prepayment.

In the early 19th century employment in the Post Office was based on a system of patronage and recommendations. Employment was obtained through influence and personal connections. Influential people would secure Post Office employment for their loyal servants and their servant's children. However the changes taking place in industry and commerce required a transformation in the way that the Post Office was run. Although Hill believed in so-called free trade and laissez-faire economics, which he argued should be applied where possible to the Post Office, he saw no contradiction between that and his ideas for a state run Post Office. His plan relied on low postage rates, pre-payment to reduce costs and improved distribution methods to attract more traffic. He argued that the increase in the volume of traffic and the lower cost of handling each item could be achieved without increasing staffing levels. Hill was an outside critic of the existing Post Office management but had powerful supporters. His main backers were City of London bankers and merchants. A pressure group called the 'Mercantile Committee' collected petitions and distributed propaganda on his behalf. The Lord Mayor of London and 12,500 City merchants submitted a petition in support of his proposals. The chairman of the 'Mercantile Committee' was Joshua Bates of Baring Brothers the bankers, and the treasurer was George Moffat, a leading tea merchant.

The history of the Post Office during this period is seen almost exclusively through the eyes of Rowland Hill. Hill was a skilful self-publicist who produced numerous articles and papers supporting his ideas. In his view the Post Office employed too many people and paid them too much money. However, he was not without his critics and some of these argued that the move towards a uniform postal rate was developing before Hill's initiative and that his overbearing arrogance made its introduction more difficult. In 1836 the permanent head of the Post Office was Lt. Col. W.L. Maberly who had been appointed following a long and distinguished career in the military and parliament. Maberly considered Hill to be an interfering amateur with no administrative experience and argued that Hill's plan for the postal services were 'a most preposterous plan, utterly unsupported by facts, and resting entirely on assumption'. He argued that from his experience a reduction in rates would not have a significant effect on the levels of traffic. In response to the claim by Hill's supporters that a reduction in the cost of postage would benefit the less well-off members of society and make the service accessible to the working-class one critic commented: 'The benefit which this class derives from cheap postage amounts to nothing, when compared with the benefit derived from it by merchantile firms, the class of bankers, London and provincial and by the rich generally... Indeed, the point is too plain for argument, that the Penny Postage is a boon to the rich instead of to the poor, and is a sacrifice of national revenue to swell the coffers of a class which do not require it'.

In 1893 the Government offered Hill a position at the Treasury with special responsibility for the Post Office but with no direct control. He was initially offered a salary of £500 per year which he considered to be an insult for a man of his standing and following his protests this was increased threefold to £1500. His appointment placed Maberly in an awkward position as he was forced to implement the ideas of Hill against his own better judgement. When, following the introduction of the Penny Post, traffic failed to increase at the rate that Hill had predicted and the costs increased, Maberly believed that his doubts had been vindicated. Revenue fell by £1,132,975 or 69.3% and did not recover to 1839 levels until 1863. Hill argued that the successful implementation of his ideas had been subverted by a conspiracy of his opponents amongst the 'Old Guard' at Post Office Headquarters in St. Martins le Grande but the failure of Hill's predictions to materialise weakened his position in the Treasury. He counter-attacked by claiming that it was the Post Offices failure to control expenditure that had undermined his plan and that the department employed too many people who were paid too much money. He further argued that the cost of transporting mail by railways was too high and that these needed to be driven down. Hill refused to admit that his ideas had failed and announced that he would not accept any criticism of his plan until it was implemented in full. Maberly argued that it was as a direct result of Hill's reforms that the whole system was close to breakdown.

Rowland Hill urged the Government to give him Maberly's position and make him permanent Head of the Post Office. However, it was not until 1846 when the Whigs were returned to power that Hill moved a step closer to his goal when he was appointed Secretary to the Postmaster General. His old enemy Maberly, however, still held the position of Secretary to the Post Office and in the following years Hill used all his energy to remove Maberly and replace him as the senior Post Office Administrator. Using his political and commercial connections he went over the head of the Postmaster General to appeal directly to the Head of the Treasury. In 1851 he secured a job for his brother Frederic as head of the Post Office department responsible for the railways and in 1854 completed his mission when Maberly was finally removed and he became Head of the Post Office.

After fifteen years of scheming Hill finally achieved his ambition and with his adversaries out of the way he imposed an autocratic administration which allowed no dissent or criticism. Costs had to be made to fit the assumptions he had made and he promised to sweep aside any obstacles to his plan and pledged to make the Post Office a servant of laissez-faire economic theory. Hill ordered that each department of the Post Office should be made a stand-alone business unit. Any other policy, he said, would be contrary to the true principles of free trade and the monopoly 'should be removed wherever the service is performed with less than the greatest efficiency and cheapness.'

Hill spent the remaining years of his service arguing with his fellow officials, defending his ideas and complaining about his subordinates. His status in Post Office history is largely as a result of his abilities as a self-publicist. Following the failure with his ideas on poor law reform he decided to turn his attention to the emerging communication industry and postal reform. He was able to secure the support of the most powerful people of the day, the bankers and financiers of the City of London but in the words of Anthony Trollope, the author and fellow Post Office official, Hill was a disastrous administrator about whom he said 'I never came across anyone who so little understood the ways of men – unless it was his brother Frederic.'

Hill spent his last ten years with the Post Office arguing with the next generation of administrators who viewed him in much the same way as he had viewed Maberly. Foremost amongst these were John Tilley and Frank Ives Scudamore who saw their function as improving an important public service. They fell out with Hill over the issue of wages, and Tilley in particular, refused to accept Hill's insistence on low wage rates which he believed were unrealistic and threatened efficiency. Hill's view was that wages should be determined only by the ability of the Post Office to recruit staff. Tilley's view was that this led to poor quality recruits and problems with retaining suitable staff and he argued that wages should be set at a high enough level to recruit and retain efficient and trustworthy workers. Finally, the years of conflict, his bad administration skills and his age took its toll and in 1864 he resigned following the rejection of his ultimatum that he be given more power. He was paid a pension for the rest of his life that was equivalent to his full salary and a massive £20,000 golden handshake. Against the background of the changes taking place in British society, industry and commerce, Rowland Hill's ideas fitted easily into the political and commercial dynamics of the period. Other changes were taking place in reaction to the transformation of the industry and postal workers had begun to organise themselves into trade unions. Rowland Hill's ideas and their effect on postal workers had unintentionally contributed to the development of trade unions and the new political ideas developing amongst working people.

Chapter 3

EARLY POST OFFICE TRADE UNIONISM
AND THE EMERGENCE
OF 'THE PHALANX' 1839-1860

In 1840 Princess Victoria married Prince Albert Saxe-Coburg-Gotha, her German cousin. Work had just begun on building the present House of Commons and in defence of 'free trade' the Opium Wars were being fought with China. In London, postal workers began to organise themselves to improve their pay and conditions. They were frequently dismissed on suspicion of dishonesty and anyone found guilty of stealing from the mail faced a long prison sentence. In 1832 John Barrett, a 23 year old London Postman, was the last man to be executed for stealing from the post. When a Bill went before Parliament to remove the death penalty for Post Office theft it was opposed by the Post Office on the grounds that it would lead to a 'frightful increase in losses'.

Dismissals were frequent and often for trivial offences. The loss of employment could lead to the workhouse, not just for the individual but for the whole family. Consequently, trade union organisation amongst the letter carriers and sorters began in secret and at considerable risk to those involved. The changes that Rowland Hill introduced had resulted in the employment of more sorters and letter carriers but at lower rates of pay. Evidence that postal workers were reacting against this first occurred in 1840. A number of petitions from London postal workers were presented to the Post Office asking for higher pay to compensate them for the extra work they were doing following the introduction of the Penny Post. About this time a London sorter called Jonathan Roberts was suspended for refusing to train newly recruited sorters who had been employed at a lower rate of pay than existing staff. This was the first recorded indication that postal workers were beginning to form what the Post Office described as a 'Confederacy'. The authorities became alarmed when they noted that the wages that Roberts lost during his suspension were made up by a collection amongst his work mates.

The period between 1840 and 1860 was very important for the development of the postal service and the postal trade unions. The service was transformed from a relatively small department of the Civil Service into what was to become a nationwide comprehensive communications service stretching from John O'Groats to Lands' End. Previously, employment in the service was obtained by patronage or family connections. By the end of this period applicants were required to pass an examination to demonstrate their ability to do the job but ironically, although this insured a better educated workforce, they were worse off financially and their conditions declined. The numbers employed in the service increased considerably but they were employed at lower rates of pay. However these changes also resulted in the emergence of the first workers organisations amongst postal workers.

In 1845 a dispute arose between the workers in the General Post Office, St. Martins le Grande and Frederick Kelly, the Chief Inspector of Letter Carriers. Some managers made money by corruptly allocating duties and benefits through a system of 'grace and favour'. Kelly earned a large income from producing a directory of London addresses and he rewarded those 'favoured' letter carriers who assisted him to compile it with the best duties.

A postal worker named Robert Grapes led a protest, of sorters and letter-carriers, not only against the corrupt activities of Kelly, but also against a whole list of other grievances including the imposition of compulsory unpaid overtime, punitive disciplinary penalties and for an improvement in pay. Although the campaign had considerable support amongst the staff and they were also able to gain the support of a number of sympathetic MPs, the Post Office refused to even consider their complaints. On 18 June 1845 they held a meeting at the Owen Glendower Tavern in Aldersgate Street to build support for their claim. The meeting agreed to launch a campaign for an improvement in pay and various other issues, including some related to gratuities (i.e. tips), about which they felt particularly aggrieved. Further meetings were held and on 31 July 1845 they organised a Public Meeting and invited along the London Press. Post Office management refused to discuss or even consider their grievances which they considered to be 'outrageous'. Concerned about the attention they were receiving from the press and a number of MPs who were threatening to raise the issue in Parliament, they announced their intention to initiate an investigation into the 'discontent' and the allegations of corruption against Kelly. However this turned into a 'witch-hunt' against Grapes and those members of staff that were supporting him. Thomas Mitchell, a sorter and one of Grapes' main supporters, was dismissed just before he was due to give evidence to the Inquiry concerning allegations that Kelly was attempting to intimidate witnesses. The so-called investigation was a whitewash and a year later Grapes was also dismissed. Mitchell and Grapes were the first trade union 'Martyrs' in the history of the Post Office but despite this early setback the struggle continued.

Viscount Melbourne, was the Whig Prime Minister from 1835 until 1841. Melbourne supported the ideas of Rowland Hill and as a consequence Hill was able to exert considerable influence over the running of the Post Office despite his on-going problems with Maberly. Sunday working was common in the Post Office outside London, but it had never been introduced into the capital. When management attempted to introduce it the London post workers began a campaign to oppose it and received considerable support from various quarters including the Bishop of London and the Lords Day Observation Society.

They also received support from a number of City merchants who were quite happy to see the mail, which arrived at the London docks from abroad, delayed over the weekend on the basis that it gave them a commercial advantage over their provincial competitors. However Rowland Hill felt that any attempt by post workers to oppose Sunday working was part of a plot to undermine the Penny Post and was a 'symptom of direct insubordination' stirred up by a 'cabal of mutinous spirits'.

Despite this the campaign against Sunday working continued throughout the 1840s and in early October 1849 postal workers held a public meeting in a church chapel in Aldersgate Street. The meeting was well attended and gained considerable public support however, Hill ignored their arguments and pushed ahead with his plans issuing threats against anyone who opposed him.

On 28 October 1849 he gave instructions for his plans to be introduced. In protest some of the workers at the General Post Office placed obstructions in front of mail coaches and a letter carrier named Hewlett was dismissed for distributing leaflets suggesting that Sunday working would ultimately lead to Sunday deliveries. A number of postal guards who refused to load mail bags onto the mail coaches were instantly dismissed but the campaign continued and with the help of the Lords Day Observation Society it began to make progress. Over half a million members of the public signed a petition in support of the complete abolition of Sunday working throughout the Post Office and Lord Ashley MP, a supporter of the postal workers campaign, persuaded the House of Commons to back the abolition by a majority vote of 93 to 69. However a major counter-attack was launched by the owners of the Sunday Newspapers who had come to rely on the Post Office to deliver their publications. With the support of a number of Hill's political allies they were able to organise a campaign to reverse the previous decision and in September 1850 Sunday working was re-introduced. Despite the fears of the letter carriers this did not lead to the introduction of Sunday deliveries which did not occur until 1899 and only then following an agreement with the workforce.

Throughout the 1850s several issues arose that resulted in London postal workers combining together. In 1850 management introduced regulations stopping letter carriers from accepting Christmas Boxes from their customers. Christmas gratuities were an important part of the letter carriers income and following a successful campaign management were forced to abandon their proposals. Postal workers were clearly becoming organised and on 29 May 1853 a meeting of 500 London postal workers elected a committee to represent their grievances to management.

In 1856 the Post Office introduced a re-organisation which led to significant changes in the grading structure, overtime payments and seniority. This led to further industrial relations problems and a number of meetings were held across the capital to oppose the imposition of these changes. Threats were made against the organisers and two of the staff's leaders were suspended. In an attempt to stop the growing discontent a new regulation which forbade post workers from campaigning publicly against management changes was introduced. This new rule also prohibited postal workers from submitting petitions to Parliament without the Post Office being informed beforehand, but this did little to reduce the growing support for workers representation and in the summer of 1858 this was publicly demanded for the first time.

Two secret organisations were formed in London in the 1850s to represent the interests of postal workers. One was called 'The General Commission Agent' and it restricted itself to publishing the various grievances that affected postal workers. The other organisation was called 'The Phallanx' (meaning a group of people united for a common purpose) and in the summer of 1856 a meeting of letter carriers was held in The Hole in the Wall, a public house in central London. It was held in defiance of Post Office regulations, but nevertheless, the meeting elected a Committee to represent them and took a decision to seek a meeting with Lord Colchester the Postmaster General, who, much to their surprise, agreed to meet them on 28 July 1858.

Their representatives were John Carter, who was Secretary of the newly formed Committee, and William Small the Committee's Chairman. They were accompanied by two other representatives, one from the South West District Office and another from the North West District Office.

When they met Colchester they outlined a whole range of grievances that had been raised at the meeting including pay, delivery workloads, covering the sick absence of colleagues for no extra pay, night collections allowances, disciplinary fines, extra deliveries without extra pay and reports of bullying by some supervisors.

On 21 August 1858 a meeting of almost the entire London workforce took place at the Pathenium Hall in St. Martins Lane. The delegation reported that they had received a fair hearing from Colchester and were hopeful it would produce results. However a word of caution was given by a letter carrier called George Padfield who expressed the view that the 'Honourable Lord', based on the delegates report, had not actually promised anything and that they should not raise their expectations too high.

Padfield's comments proved to be true because after several months there had been no progress on any of the issues they had raised with Colchester. It seems likely that Lord Colchester had used the meeting simply to identify the men's leaders and after they held another meeting, this time at the Blue Coat Boy in Victoria Street, Westminster, management went onto the offensive. They began a campaign of intimidation and victimisation against the leaders of the Committee. John Carter, the Committee Secretary, was suspended and then dismissed. John Martin who had chaired the Westminster meeting was also sacked, William James who had played a prominent role in organising the meetings was suspended, and six other men had their pay reduced. The men organised a campaign for their reinstatement but Colchester refused to even reconsider the decision. They organised a collection to support them financially but the dismissals were a bitter blow to the struggle. The Post Office no doubt believed that by sacking the ring leaders this would demoralise and intimidate the rest. In fact it had the opposite effect because it led to calls from some of the men for a Letter Carrier's Union and although this was still some years away the momentum and resolve was growing.

The massive gulf between the lives of ordinary workers and the opulent lifestyles of the plutocrats and aristocrats who ruled the country was demonstrated in a medical report commissioned by Lord Argyll who was Postmaster General between 1855 and 1858 and again in 1860. He commissioned a Medical Officer's Report on the health of the postal workers employed in St. Martins le Grande. It concluded that the shortage of suitable housing and the need for the men to live near to where they worked resulted in them being forced to live in badly ventilated, unsuitable housing, 'totally unfit for human habitation in which smallpox, scarlet fever and similar contagious illnesses were common'.

Argyll commissioned the report because the high levels of sick absence caused severe disruption to the service and had little to do with any concern for the welfare of the workers. A sensible and humane solution to this problem would have been to improve the workers' pay and conditions so that they could afford decent housing, diet and health care. This however, would have increased costs and disrupted the Rowland Hill plan, so instead the report suggested that a type of barracks should be constructed near to the General Post Office in St. Martins le Grande where the letter carriers and their families would be housed. They argued that this would not just produce improvements to the levels of sick absence but it would also enable the staff to be summoned to work by bugle call in the event of delays in mail arriving late from abroad. They also pointed out that this would also enable them to keep an eye on the morals and behaviour of their employees. It was suggested that the cost of building the barracks would be covered by the rents which would be deducted directly from the men's wages. Ultimately the scheme was abandoned as impracticable because the initial cost of building and maintaining the accommodation was considered to be too expensive. However, they did agree to offer staff a death benefit insurance scheme that would provide death benefits and cheap decent funeral arrangements. These were presumably provided on the principle that even if they did not treat them fairly whilst they lived at least they did when they died. It remains a good example of the attitude that the 'nobility' and 'gentlemen' who administrated the Post Office had to ordinary workers. A leaflet secretly distributed amongst the London postal workers at the time, and believed to have been written by one of the sacked workers, shows what they thought of Rowland Hill.

O Rowland Hill! O Rowland Hill!
Thou man of proud imperious will!
Forbear to crush, with iron hand,
The drudges under thy command;
And strive to purify thy frame
From stains that now defile thy name
Has thou all sense of justice lost
Great Monarch of the Penny Post
Thou takest care, O Rowland Hill
Thy own big-bellied purse to fill.
But woe betide the hapless wight
If thou canst nibble at his mite
Is not the service rather dear
At fifteen hundred pounds a year
Thy brother with a thousand too
Methinks is pretty well to do
And then thy son that hopeful strig
Five hundred hath to laugh and jig
So thou hast feathered well thy nest
And now canst giggle with the best
But sometimes Rowland cast a thought
On those by labour overwrought
Nor crimp them at their scanty pay
That thou mayst revel with the gay
Invoke their blessing not their curse
And thou wouldst never fare the worse

Chapter 4

THE 'COMMISSION OF INQUIRY'
AND THE 'COMMITTEE' 1860-1870

In March 1860 an article appeared in *The Times* which thrust the Post Office's industrial relations into the national limelight. It accused the business of being more concerned with profits and revenue than the welfare of its workforce and that as a result postal workers were both 'indifferent to how they carried out their duties' and 'unafraid of dismissal'. Within a few days the Government were forced to establish a Committee of Inquiry to look into the allegations. Rowland Hill, although seriously ill at the time, was determined that the Inquiry would not interfere with his plans for the industry and through his brothers tried to ensure that any recommendation from the Inquiry would require their approval before implementation. This obviously had some effect because the Inquiry was suspended following his intervention and when it was re-activated in May 1860 Hill had succeeded in placing two of his henchmen on the Committee, although it also included Frank Scudamore and Anthony Trollope two of Hill's fiercest critics.

The workforce were urged by management to suspend any campaigning whilst their grievances were examined, but having been tricked in the past they ignored management's demands and all the main London grades produced their own list of grievances and submitted them to the Inquiry. These included allegations of bullying, low pay, unfair promotion procedures and inadequate grievance and disputes procedures. The Inquiry interviewed 116 witnesses, including some of the workers' leaders and in July 1860 they produced their report. To the workers surprise its findings were surprisingly sympathetic to the men's complaints. They suggested that the pay rates and conditions were insufficient to attract and retain staff of the necessary quality.

They also proposed that seniority should be introduced as a fair method for job selection, that some grades should be given a pay increase, a minimum rate of pay for established letter carriers should be introduced and that 'the men were as a rule underpaid'.

Hill believed that its recommendations presented a direct threat to his plan and that because it 'sins against every principle of subordination' should not be published. The workers became aware of Hill's attempts to suppress the report and in September 1860 organised a mass meeting to demand its publication. When Lord Stanley of Alderley, who had been appointed Postmaster General in August 1860, agreed to meet them their hopes were raised. The men had established a 'Committee' and were represented at the meeting by the Chairman John Richmond, Llewellyn Tilley the Secretary, and two other representatives, Henry Hines and Joseph Roseman. When they met with Alderley they urged him to publish the report and implement the Commission's recommendations. Alderley responded by saying that he was unable to do that because the report was still being considered by the Government, although it seems more likely that he was waiting for Rowland Hill to recover from his illness before making a decision.

The Committee continued its campaign throughout the rest of 1860 and into 1861. In January 1861 the 'Committee' held a further meeting with Alderley but once again little progress was made. By the winter of 1861 the campaign had begun to decline but the 'Committee' continued its activities and on 27 March 1862 another mass meeting was held at Exeter Hall in central London. The workers received the support of a Conservative MP called George Bowyer, who had previously assisted them with another issue. He was able to pursue the Commons to debate the issue and on 22 July 1862 Bowyer presented the postal workers case before Parliament, calling for the report to be published and a select committee established to look into the issues it raised. He was opposed by none other than William Gladstone, the future Liberal Prime Minister and at that time Chancellor of the Exchequer. Gladstone's father had been one of the country's biggest slave owners before its abolition and had considerable interests in the West Indies where he had several thousand slaves working on his Demerara Sugar plantation.

Gladstone had used his maiden speech in Parliament to defend slavery. He argued that postal workers were not badly paid compared to other workers and that 'those involved were men of humble station and naturally inclined, like other men, to believe they were underpaid when they were told so'. He went on to argue that they were not dissatisfied because they had genuine grievance but because they had 'found a gentleman of ability and character willing to take up their case'.

Unfortunately Bowyer was no match for Gladstone and he was forced to withdraw his motion through lack of support, but Gladstone underestimated the resolve of the workers and within a week of the debate the Committee called another meeting. The meeting was chaired by George Padfield who, four years earlier at a previous meeting, had pointed out that a previous Postmaster, Lord Colchester, could not be trusted and had been involved in all the main campaigns waged by London postal workers in the 1850s and 1860s. He was more than capable of answering Gladstone's arguments and pointed out that because other workers were badly paid that was no argument for paying postal workers low wages. He argued that 'the great question for us now is better pay, for I believe it is the duty of every man in the world to try and benefit the class to which he belongs'.

Like his predecessors Robert Grapes, Thomas Mitchell, John Carter and William Small, Padfield was fully aware of the likely consequences of his actions. He was willing to risk a great deal on behalf of trade unionism and the inevitable management counter-attack which was already being planned by Lord Stanley and Rowland Hill. Padfield was a marked man and it was only a matter of time before they moved against him.

Management infiltrated the men's meetings and the company's spies monitored the leader's activities. Nevertheless, the Committee continued their campaign and in 1863 they were granted another audience with the Postmaster General but once again he rejected their claims and warned them against further campaigning.

The activities of the Committee declined for the next couple of years although a new front was opened up when the postal clerks began to organise and in 1863 Lord Stanley met a delegation of London Clerks. However they were no more successful than their uniformed colleagues and Alderley rejected their complaints with the same contempt. In the mid-1860s there was a sharp increase in the rate of inflation and although this resulted in wage rises for many groups of workers, postal workers fell behind.

In March 1866 Alderley issued a memorandum prohibiting postal workers from holding public meetings. He believed that by issuing an instruction that was punishable by summary dismissal he would in his own words; stop the 'few turbulent men creating a spirit of discontent amongst the lower body of Post Office servants'. A new Committee was formed and this time it included all the main grades, sorters, stampers and letter carriers and once again their grievances were raised by sympathetic MPs in Parliament and once again Gladstone defeated their supporters on behalf of the Government. Alderley seized the opportunity to attack the Committee and George Padfield, after thirteen years in the service was dismissed.

The Committee's response was to go underground again and this was how they continued for a number of years. However in August 1867 the first issue of *The Postman* began to appear in sorting offices throughout the capital. It was the first newspaper published by postal workers and was produced by the Committee on a small printing press. In its first edition it declared that its aim was to 'win the support of the true hearted and tyrant hating masses of the population', not only in London but across the country. Undeterred by the loss of their Chairman, George Padfield, the campaigning continued, with large meetings being held in September and December and the temperature was raised when senior Post Office officials awarded themselves large pay increases.

In defiance of a ban on public campaigning the 'Committee' issued a statement under the name of James Johnson, the Secretary, condemning management's actions and supporting their own claim for better pay and conditions. Sixty-two different newspapers published their statement and this gave the new Liberal Postmaster General, Lord Hartington an opportunity to sack Johnson who was summarily dismissed on the basis that he had attempted to 'subvert all discipline and authority'. Threats were also issued against the other members of the Committee.

Johnson was unemployed for eight months before he found work and he and his family were only saved from complete destitution by the financial support of his old workmates. However the struggle for basic rights continued and in 1867 it took a political turn. Postal workers, along with other civil servants, were prohibited from voting in General Elections even though in 1867 the franchise was extended to include some working class men. In fact, even high ranking civil servants were debarred from voting. In 1782, Lord North the Prime Minister, had threatened all those senior civil servants who had the vote and lived in marginal constituencies that he would make things difficult for them if they did not vote for the Tory candidates. To make things worse, the Whigs made a similar threat and as a consequence those few high ranking civil servants who had the vote, campaigned to have their right to vote removed and this was agreed by the House of Commons. As a direct result of this, when the vote was extended in later years, to include a larger number of the population, all civil servants were excluded. Many civil servants, including postal workers, joined the campaign to demand the vote. True to form William Gladstone opposed any attempt to extend the vote to Government employees. However, the campaign gained the support of a significant number of MPs and even Frank Scudamore, Assistant Secretary to the Post Office and Anthony Trollope, a senior Postal Administrator and later in life a famous novelist, gave their support.

In 1868 Charles Monk, a Liberal MP, took the first step towards achieving the franchise for civil servants with his Bill to extend the vote to Revenue Officers. Gladstone continued to oppose extending the vote to civil servants and it was only achieved with the support of a new Conservative Government in 1874.

The development of Post Office trade unions in the 1860s had begun in secret and a decade later little had improved. Every attempt to improve wages and working conditions led to further repression and more dismissals. Despite this the early Post Office trade union pioneers continued the struggle and every victimised champion of the movement who was dismissed was replaced by others willing to pick up the baton. The 1870s however, were to produce a change in the fortunes of the movement and Post Office workers found new ways of taking the struggle forward.

Chapter 5

WILLIAM BOOTH AND THE
BENEFIT SOCIETY 1870-1880

If Alderley thought that by refusing them the right to hold public meetings he could gag the spirit of the Post Office trade unionists he was wrong. For a time things did remain quiet, however throughout this period they were organising in secret. William Booth, a dismissed activist named Edward Hawkins and a sorter named Haley, stepped forward to carry the torch into the 1870s. William Booth was a City letter carrier who lived in Brixton, which in 1870 was a suburb of London in the county of Surrey. He first came to the attention of Post Office management as a friend and supporter of George Padfield a few years earlier. Padfield had been dismissed for publicly criticising Post Office management and the Chancellor of the Exchequer, William Gladstone. James Johnson was sacked shortly after this and the remaining activists had to be careful not to leave themselves open to possible dismissal.

For a number of years they operated in secret whilst steadily building a nucleus of activists and carefully building support under the noses of management who were aware that secret meetings were being held but were unable to identify the leaders. When they felt the time was right they began to hold meetings in the letter carriers and sorters kitchens where they prepared their own food. Even today, meetings held in London on Post Office premises during working hours are still referred to as 'Kitchen Meetings'. Sometimes these meetings were held with official permission and sometimes without. Management spies attended the meetings to report any breach of Post Office rules back to the authorities. Booth found a way around Post Office regulations by maintaining that the meetings were in fact lectures, and as a consequence did not contravene the rules. Whilst both on and off duty the activists movements were monitored by management who considered any challenge to their authority as almost an act of treason.

Booth's house was kept under almost constant surveillance and to avoid the authorities following him he often had to skip over his back garden wall, dodging through a neighbour's house and emerging later on in the evening at a meeting. It was by using these methods that the men gradually built their organisation.

In 1870 they held a meeting in a coffee room in Gunpowder Alley, just off Fleet Street, which was the first cross-office conference ever held by postal workers. It involved representatives from all the London postal districts although they hoped to begin a movement that would include postal workers throughout the country. On 17 May 1872 they held another meeting this time in the Congregational Church, Borough Road where the premises were lent to them by the Reverend G.M. Murphy, a long-time supporter of postal workers. This was the inaugural meeting of the Post Office and Telegraph Employees Benefit Society and its aims, agreed at the meeting, were to build a country wide organisation to improve wages, abolish compulsory Sunday working and achieve an honest, open system of promotion for all postal workers.

In the following weeks they recruited new members and made contacts with postal workers in other towns and cities. They also built a network of political contacts from both political parties to support their aims in Parliament. The organisation grew but they faced a new challenge when management introduced a new grade of letter carrier employed on lower wages than the existing staff. They were known as auxiliary or assistant letter carriers. An established letter carrier could earn 30 shillings a week after twenty year's service. An auxiliary was paid as little as 15 shillings and had almost no chance of ever obtaining work at the higher grade. They had no regular hours and had to attend for work whenever the employer required them to. Their wages were less than that of a casual dock labourer and most had other jobs to supplement their low income.

Sometimes management's treatment of staff boiled over into serious confrontations. One evening in March 1873 the London papers carried the headline 'Riot at General Post Office'. Whilst the incident may not have been a riot it was nevertheless a serious confrontation. The Post Office introduced a new service called the Newspaper Rate. It cost the customer half a penny and was designed to attract newspapers and circulars for delivery through the postal system. From managements point of view it was a great success and it resulted in a large increase in the amount of work the sorters and letter carriers were expected to do but although it required them to work beyond their normal finishing time they were not paid any extra for doing this.

On this particular occasion a well-known entrepreneur called Baron Grant took advantage of the new cheaper rate and commissioned the Post Office to deliver a large number of prospectuses for his latest enterprise the 'Emma Gold Mine Company'. This was a very large posting and the postmen knew that it would take them past their normal finishing time. It appears that management had anticipated trouble because extra doorkeepers and supervisors were on duty that morning.

The men began work at 4.30 a.m. and were due to begin their deliveries at 9.00 a.m. At 9.00 a.m. they went as usual to their lockers to collect their coats but when they attempted to leave the building they found their way barred by supervisors and doorkeepers. They were ordered back to their workplaces and informed that they would not be permitted to leave the building until all the extra work had been sorted. The men insisted that unless they were paid overtime they would not clear the work and as other workers arrived from different sections and floors, the crowd grew bigger and angrier. The supervisors tried to force them to return to their workplaces and although at first some did, others, in particular the younger postmen and sorters, pushed forward towards the exits. From the rear, balls of string and sticks of sealing wax were thrown at the supervisors blocking the doors. At the front, punches were exchanged and the supervisors retreated to side rooms allowing the men to leave. The doors burst open and the crowd of postmen spilled out into Aldersgate Street where according to press reports it caused a Hansom Cab to bolt into the early morning traffic. A great cheer went up and the traffic was held up for half an hour. Although the police were called no arrests were made, but in the following few days six of the presumed leaders of the confrontation were suspended and later dismissed.

The 1871 Trade Union Act had made the activities of trade unions legal within certain limits. The time arrived when the London postal workers felt it was the right time to transform their Benefit Society into a proper trade union.

The first step was to present a petition to the London Controller seeking permission to hold meetings in preparation for putting their case to Parliament. In the 19th century petitioning Parliament was one method used by workers and other groups to try and improve their conditions. They were very careful to move forward in an orderly way and not give management an excuse to attack their organisation before it had even got off the ground. To their surprise, permission was granted but with the condition that meetings were held on official premises, no newspaper reporters were allowed to attend and outside supporters would also not be allowed to attend. The men's leaders, for good reason were very suspicious. For they believed this was another attempt by management to identify the leadership in order to dismiss them as had so often happened in the past.

The Benefit Society had an agreed list of objectives, including improved pay and requested a meeting with Lord Emley, the new Postmaster General. The men's claim had the sympathy of the London management because of the recent increases in the cost of living and they recommended to Emley that the men be given a pay rise. Emley agreed and although he made a recommendation for an increase to the Treasury they rejected his proposals. This caused a flood of anger amongst the workforce and this resulted in the Treasury officials demanding that the organisers of the campaign be disciplined.

On 28 June 1873, the Benefit Society decided it was time to take their campaigning to a new level and called a mass meeting at 8 p.m. in the Newspaper Branch on the top floor of the General Post Office in St. Mary-le-Grande. The room was large, capable of holding two thousand people. There was no seating available other than a few bundles of mail bags and upturned baskets. At eight o'clock, following the last dispatch, the organisers waited with anticipation, still not sure how many men would turn up. Their fears were unfounded and at eight o'clock several hundred sorters, letter carriers, coach drivers and clerks swarmed up the stairs from every corner of the building into the meeting. Their numbers were swelled by the arrival of postal workers from other London offices. All the districts were represented and the gas lit room was packed to capacity.

The men were well aware that amongst them were the usual management spies eager to identify the ring leaders and report every word said back to the authorities. Also, amongst the crowds was a reporter from *The Standard*, smuggled in with the district men and who the following day wrote a full report of the proceedings. The men stood on the facing tables and sorting frames and others climbed onto the girders, thirty feet above the floor, to get a glimpse of the platform. The platform was constructed using upturned mail baskets, covered with mail bags. Most of the men had never seen Booth or his fellow activists but were well aware of their efforts to build a union. They were eager to see and hear the men who had withstood all the threats and attacks aimed at strangling their organisation at birth. Over the din of the assembled crowd someone called for order and finally when the noise died down a hush fell over the audience.

William Booth climbed onto the makeshift platform to a tumultuous outbreak of cheers, applause and the banging of fists on the sorting tables which continued for over a minute before Booth was able to address the crowd. It was reported that Booth was not a particularly good speaker but he was able to articulate the feelings and aspirations of the men. He was described as a rather short, sturdy man with a full head of hair and side whiskers. His nickname was 'Bulldog', a reference to his thick set build and his strong determination. He spoke for half an hour and argued that the men needed to build a strong trade union and take their case to Parliament. Others followed him onto the platform and supported the proposal to build the 'Benefit Society' and the Parliamentary petition. A committee was elected to draw up the petition and *The Standard* reported that the meeting ended with thunderous applause and cheering. The committee agreed to ask Parliament to appoint a Select Committee to investigate their claim for better pay and improved conditions and to spread their campaign to postal workers throughout the country. This meeting was the first attempt by British postal workers to build a national organisation.

Meantime, less than a mile away in a Treasury office just off Whitehall, a very different meeting was taking place. A small group of senior Post Office officials had assembled to assess the strength of the fledgling union and its support amongst the workers. Reports of the meeting were arriving in Whitehall even before it had finished. Lord Emley had ordered that a full transcript on the meeting should be on his desk the next morning. The London Controller and his close advisers were preparing the report and, from their point of view, it was not good news. Not only had the meeting attracted the overwhelming support of the London postal workers but it was clear that the organisers were in contact with postal workers across the country.

The men had agreed to introduce a weekly subscription for members and were in contact with several MPs. They were also planning to send thousands of circulars through the postal system to workers in other towns and cities. There was outrage in the Treasury who feared the spread of trade unionism and felt that the actions of the London Controller in allowing the men's meeting to go ahead had given encouragement to the activists and their influence was spreading. The Treasury officials demanded immediate and decisive action from the London Controller and within a few days of the meeting in St. Martins le Grande the Petition Committee was summoned to the Controller's office. The Controller, who refused to accept Booth as part of the delegation, branding him a trouble maker, informed the Committee that their actions had 'exceeded the bounds that management were prepared to tolerate'. The members of the Committee were also informed that their actions were 'Fermenting an agitation throughout the entire service' and unless they immediately disbanded the Committee and stopped their activities then they would be summarily dismissed.

To avoid their immediate dismissal they made a tactical decision to disband the organisation. Almost immediately however, they re-launched it under a different name, the 'United Kingdom General Post Office and Telegraph Service Benefit Society'. It was a grand title but rather misleading because they had no recruits amongst the Telegraphists who were developing their own organisation, the 'Telegraphists Association' under a leadership based in Manchester and Liverpool.

The new Committee decided that attack was the best form of defence and began preparations for a public meeting. They had come to the conclusion that their previous tactics were not working and that more decisive action was needed. They were attracting recruits to the Society but many more were scared of the possible consequences, whilst others joined but kept their membership secret. Booth, in particular, felt that a focal point for the organisation's activities was needed and they set about organising a protest meeting to take place on 5 August 1873 at the Cannon Street Hotel. On 28 July a number of friendly MPs had attempted to raise the postal workers issues in Parliament and this attracted a public attack on the Society by the

Postmaster General and other Government Ministers. By the time of the meeting, Booth had been suspended and the Committee decided that it was now time for resolute action to back up their campaign and to get Booth reinstated. The Committee called on postal workers from across London to assemble in the early evening in Finsbury Square from where they would march to St. Martins le Grande in time to join with the City postmen as they finished work at 8.00 p.m.

A huge crowd of supporters and sightseers followed the procession as it set out towards Cannon Street to the accompaniment of no less than five bands playing an array of popular music hall tunes and military marches. The huge hall was full to capacity and an impressive collection of politicians and supporters sat on the platform. The meeting was chaired by Sir John Bennett, the renowned clock manufacturer who had premises in Cheapside. He was a strong supporter of the postmen and allowed those in uniform to purchase his world famous pocket watches at a 30% discount.

Another guest speaker was Henry Broadhurst, a working stonemason and the representative of his union on the Trades Union Congress (TUC). In the 1880 General Election he was one of the first MPs to be elected to Parliament on a Liberal/Labour platform. Alongside Broadhurst sat George Potter, another leading trade union figure and Editor of *The Beehive*, a working class newspaper that supported the trade union movement. In the 1850s he had been active in a number of disputes in the building industry and was elected as leader of the Carpenters and Joiners Union. In 1871 he had been elected as President of the TUC and was a respected and popular figure amongst rank and file trade unionists. A number of MPs from both parliamentary parties, Tory and Liberal, also attended the meeting. The men made a tactical decision that none of the Committee would speak from the platform because of the threat of dismissal. The aim of this meeting was to assert their right to organise a public meeting and the question of free speech would come later.

The meeting was a great success and the confidence of the members was growing but the Committee were expecting repercussions. When Booth was summoned to the Controller's office the following day they expected the worst. Much to their surprise Booth was, in fact, reinstated. Management were nervous about making Booth a martyr and had decided on another tactic to undermine the Union. In an attempt to divide the men they increased the pay of a minority of the senior City letter carriers. It was an increase of £52 per year but it was to be phased in over fifteen years and as such made little impression on those who were to receive it, but made those that were not even angrier. This intensified when they discovered that the Post Office had awarded the supervisors both bigger pay increases and improvements to their annual increments. This particularly annoyed the men because the supervisors were already fairly well paid and had not supported the campaign being waged by the sorters and letter carriers. With the Society's campaign gaining more support, management decided to revert to their previous tactics and make another move against Booth. The Society had agreed to affiliate to the London Trades Council and this was seen as a particular act of defiance by senior management. The Trades Council was considered to be a hotbed of revolutionaries and their affiliation sent a message to management that the leadership had connections beyond the confines of the industry and were building alliances with other trade unions. Within days, Booth was once again called before the London Controller and suspended from duty.

The Committee had little alternative other than to go on the attack and the next morning leaflets and circulars reporting details of the Cannon Street meeting, the Society's campaign and Booth's subsequent treatment, were being distributed in sorting offices throughout the capital. The following day Booth was reinstated, and although this was seen as a victory for the men, management were building a case for his eventual dismissal.

The Society still had only 700 paid up members and their campaigning had already taken up a great deal of their funds. The authorities were well aware that the Society had influence well beyond their number and that they were building contacts in other parts of the country. Committee members were kept under constant surveillance and the authorities raided and searched Booth's home in Brixton on a number of occasions taking away papers and documents. However, management were interested in more than just sacking him. Their aim was a charge of conspiracy and Booth's arrest and imprisonment. Although the laws governing trade unions changed making it easier for unions to operate, postal workers were still vulnerable to criminal charges because they were Government employees.

In the following weeks the society's activists worked day and night to build support for their campaign. Booth, in particular, put a great deal of effort into building political contacts which included the influential MP for Birmingham Joseph Chamberlain. Management, in an attempt to frustrate Booth's activities, forced him onto an evening delivery, which finished at the Angel Islington, the furthest point of any delivery in the office from his home in Brixton. However, after some time he managed to transfer to the Temple Walk where he built contacts with a number of solicitors and lawyers who had their chambers there.

During this period the Tory Party showed considerable sympathy for the Postmen's campaign. The Liberals were in power and the Tory Party were eager to increase their support amongst postal workers. The 1872 Reform Bill had extended the vote to many more postal employees and meetings held at the House of Commons were attended by MPs from both parties, but in particular the Tories. Postal Workers became active in canvassing for parliamentary candidates who promised to support their campaign for a Select Committee Inquiry into postal workers grievances. They produced a newspaper called *The Postman* and many of the articles were written by a postman called March who had connections with printers in Clerkenwell, and in later life, after he left Post Office employment became a successful publisher.

The Post Office would not allow *The Postman* to be sold openly in sorting offices so it was passed secretly amongst the men. Its circulation quickly grew, although the effort needed to produce it was considerable and as a consequence its production was irregular. They received help from George Potter, who allowed the postmen to use the pages of his journal, *The Beehive,* to advertise their meetings and argue their case. Edward Hawkins, who had previously been dismissed by the Post Office for his union activities, was employed on the paper and he was also Chairman of the Benefit Society. Their campaign was going well and they were steadily building their membership and strength.

The attitude of the postal authorities often helped their cause. One well publicised example of this concerned a meeting between representatives of the Society and the London Controller. He was described in a report as a 'fat, overfed gentleman who enjoyed a salary in excess of £1,200 per year'. When the delegation raised the issue of pay he replied that even he was having to cut down on his luxuries. One of the men replied saying that they could not afford luxuries and needed more money simply to keep themselves and their families in the necessities of life. The Controller replied that this was not his concern as he did not employ their wives and children.

On 18 November 1873 they held another mass meeting, this time at the Exeter Hall in the Strand, and it turned out to be even bigger than the August meeting. They decided that it was time to challenge the Post Office's ban on employees speaking in public about their grievances. Once again they assembled in Finsbury Square and marched behind their banners to the accompaniment of brass bands playing 'The Postman's Knock', 'Work Boys Work and be Contented' and 'Rule Britannia', arriving at the General Post Office at 8.00 p.m. where they were joined by the evening shift of sorters, stampers and coach drivers as they finished work. The procession went along Fleet Street where it brought the evening traffic to a halt. By the time they reached the Exeter Hall they had been joined by hundreds of supporters and fellow trade unionists. The Hall was filled to capacity and an overflow meeting was chaired by Roger Eykyn MP and alongside him sat George Odger, President of the London Trades Council. Numerous MPs from both sides of the House addressed the meeting and pledged their support for the Postmen's campaign, but it was the opposition Tory Party that the men hoped would deliver the changes that they needed.

The meeting was considered to have been an outstanding success. The Committee's strategy was to build enough support amongst the Parliamentarians to force a Select Committee to address their grievances. More and more MPs were pledging their support and the Post Office and Treasury authorities were becoming increasingly concerned at the success that the Society was having. Within a few days several Committee members were summoned by the Postmaster General to disciplinary hearings. Considering that a number of Committee members had violated Post Office regulations by speaking at the meeting, it came as a surprise that they were only awarded reprimands. However, management were preparing plans for what they thought would be a permanent solution to the problem of the growing support that the Society was attracting.

The authorities considered the Societies' activists little better than saboteurs and conspirators. They increased their surveillance and began to build the case against William Booth which they hoped would rid them of him once and for all. His personal correspondence was routinely intercepted and the contents examined. A procedure usually reserved for foreign revolutionaries and criminals was being routinely used against their own employees. Their plan to charge Booth with conspiracy was gathering pace. However, whilst the Post Office had their spies and detectives gathering information on the trade unionists, Post Office officials sympathetic to the men's campaign were passing information to the Society's activists. They were informed that a legal brief containing charges of conspiracy had already been prepared and was due to be issued within the next few days. William Booth was facing a prison sentence of at least two years and his colleagues could look forward to several months each.

A hurried meeting was arranged with a group of sympathetic lawyers. They were told that in order for a charge of conspiracy to succeed, it was necessary for the authorities to prove that more than three individuals were involved in the alleged plot. After some discussion, and with the help of their legal advisors, they devised a scheme to frustrate the authority's plans. The next day an emergency meeting of the Committee was convened and a decision taken to make William Booth the sole individual responsible for organising and representing the Society. Handbills, posters and leaflets were quickly printed and distributed around the London offices advising the membership of the Committee's decisions. It was a brilliant move and within days they received news that the planned prosecutions had been abandoned. For the time being they had survived but it was only a matter of time before the authorities resumed their offensive.

Unable to break the Society by threats and intimidation, the authorities tried another tactic. The eighteenth century was the century of so called free trade and market forces. Unable to break the organisation by the use of the law, they decided to destroy them by the 'indisputable logic of the free market'. Their aim, they said, was to 'test the market' in order to show that the Societies arguments for improvements in pay and conditions were flawed because the workforce could easily be replaced by others willing to work for the current pay and terms and conditions. They advertised for sorters and letter carriers in the London press. Over twelve hundred hopeful candidates applied for the jobs although many of these were excluded because of their bad health and others could not achieve the required literacy standards. At the end of the exercise only a few successful candidates remained and management's attempt to prove that the workforce could easily be replaced was a failure.

The Committee were determined to raise the profile of the Society and contacts had already been made with other postal workers around the country who were keen to build a national organisation. They were in regular contact with postmen in all the major cities but the centre of national trade union activity was the Trades Union Congress (TUC) and they needed the support of the TUC to build a national organisation. The TUC was dominated by several craft unions representing skilled workers, engineers, carpenters, bricklayers and print workers. They were very protective of their craft status and were suspicious of non-craft unions. Postal workers however fell into a strange category because they were neither craftsman in the traditional sense, nor day labourers or unskilled workers. Their status was further complicated by the fact that they were Government employees. However their cause was taken up by George Howell, Secretary of the 'Trades Union Parliamentary Committee' who championed their case and persuaded the TUC to support the postmen's campaign.

In 1874 there was a General Election. William Gladstone was the Prime Minister of a Liberal Government that had shown little sympathy for the London postmen. The Tories were eager to gain the support of the newly enfranchised postal workers and many had pledged their support for the Select Committee Inquiry into their grievances. When the Tories won the election with a majority of forty-eight the expectations of many activists ran high.

Following a meeting at Westminster Palace involving members of the Committee and a number of prominent MPs, it was decided to once again raise their issues in Parliament. William Booth had worked tirelessly to build the union and the pressure had begun to take its toll. He was showing signs of the strain that had been placed on him by years of harassment and victimisation. Several members of the Committee sat in the gallery as John Roebuck, MP for Sheffield, rose to move the proposition calling for the Inquiry. He was a formidable speaker and debater who, as a young man, had supported political reform and the campaign to free the Tolpuddle Martyrs. In 1832 he had been selected by the Whigs to represent Bath but in his later life he became increasingly conservative and in the 1874 election he had stood as an Independent and, with the support of the Tories, won the Sheffield seat.

He had a particular dislike for William Gladstone whom he referred to as the 'Bastard Philanthropist'. Roebuck's proposition was well supported and the activists felt that with their political allies now in power they had reached a turning point in their campaign. However the promises of the Tory Party proved to be as hollow as those of the Liberals a decade earlier. Roebuck was unable to convince the Government to hold an inquiry but in private the Tory MPs assured the men that the new Postmaster General, Lord John Manners, would lend a sympathetic ear to their complaints. Many of the activists felt betrayed and became disheartened but Booth was determined to soldier on. He lobbied MPs, met with officials and campaigned in the press and after a few months Manners agreed to meet representatives of the Society, although he refused to allow Booth to be included in the delegation. The men had mixed feelings about attending the meeting without Booth but agreed that the meeting should go ahead.

It was some time before Manners finally announced his response to the points raised by the delegation and when he did the worst fears of the sceptics were confirmed. The Committee had raised several issues with Manners, including overtime payments and unfair promotion procedures, all of which were rejected and where he recommended pay increases they were minimal and deliberately divisive. The disappointment and demoralisation felt by the sorters and letter carriers threw the organisation into confusion. It was too much for William Booth who, after nearly two decades of struggle was now worn out and unwell and resigned from his position as the Societies leader. He was left with considerable personal debt and although his work colleagues collected money on his behalf, he refused to accept it, following a disagreement with some of his committee colleagues. He spent the next few years struggling to pay off his debts and having done so, with his health failing, he left the Post Office with a small pension. His contribution to the struggle for trade union recognition in the Post Office was unrivalled and it was said that he was one of the most courageous trade union activists of his generation who played an important role in the demise of two Governments. The officials, who for so many years had conspired for his downfall, no doubt felt satisfied that William Booth had gone, but his spirit and courage was remembered and others continued the work he started in the years to come.

Chapter 6

SEVEN YEARS OF STAGNATION
1874-1880

The new Government led by Benjamin Disraeli proved to be no less against the postal workers than the Liberals. Following a re-alignment in British politics, as a consequence of difference that had divided both parties over Irish Home Rule and later free-trade, the modern Liberal and Conservative parties began to evolve.

Lord Jim Manners, the new Postmaster General, was a close friend of Disraeli and as young men they had both belonged to a social conservative political group called 'Young England'. In opposition, Manners had claimed to support the aims of trade unions and encouraged them to campaign for recognition, but in Government he waged a crusade against the trade unions every bit as fierce as his predecessors.

Although there was little progress in building the Union between the early 1870s and 1890, various groups of workers attempted to improve conditions on a sectional basis. In 1870 the Post Office had increased the level of boy sorters employed in the industry. Boy sorters were young lads barely out of school and many were new arrivals from the countryside, forced by circumstances to work away from home. They were expected to do the same work as adults but for a quarter of the pay and tuberculosis and other illnesses connected to poverty were common amongst the youngsters. Living in awful and insanitary lodgings they were subject to many forms of deprivation including child abuse. Child abuse was very common in Victorian London and in 1877 a Parliamentary inquiry identified the extent of this problem amongst the youngsters employed in the Post Office. Measures were taken to improve their conditions and following a campaign led by the young messengers themselves, increases in pay were introduced. However, in 1889 another crisis occurred when it was disclosed that several boy messengers had been procured to work in a male brothel in Cleveland Street, Fitzrovia, West London. The investigation was led by Detective Inspector Fredrick Abbeline, who was also leading the hunt for 'Jack the Ripper'. The brothel owners were apprehended and they named several prominent aristocrats as patrons including Lord Arthur Somerset and Lord Fitzroy, Earl of Euston. Somerset was an equerry to the Prince of Wales, whose son Prince Albert Victor was also implicated in the scandal by a radical weekly journal called *The North London Press*. All three men denied any direct involvement with the scandal but it was widely believed that there had been a Government cover-up. A number of those involved fled abroad including Somerset who never returned to Britain, living in self-imposed exile in Europe for the rest of his life. There is evidence that the Prime Minister, Lord Salisbury intervened to stop extradition proceedings against one of the accused.

Overtime was compulsory for adult and boy sorters and attempts were made by the staff to improve the overtime pay rates. Petitions were drawn up and these were presented to Lord Manners who used every means at his disposal to defeat their arguments, including inflating the average pay of postal workers by including the pay of a new grade of supervisors in the calculations used to compare their pay with other workers. Once he had done this he set about intimidating and victimising all those who had signed the petitions. They were given three days to repudiate their support for the campaign or face dismissal and in an official notice he informed staff that if they did not like their current pay and conditions, then 'they were at liberty to seek other employment'. It was not until 1878 that the men involved in collecting signatures for the petition were allowed to work overtime again.

Even during this period of relative inactivity amongst the London postal workers there were people who were still struggling to build a trade union. Sometimes the struggle was carried out at a very clandestine level and involved little more than the distribution of leaflets. One leaflet that was sold outside the gates of the St. Martins le Grande office to raise money for some recently sacked activists, included some poetic verse that had been penned by one of the dismissed men, Thomas Glamorgan.

To Lord John Manners, Her Majesty's Postmaster General

Democracy will laugh with scorn
And know a noble fool is born
To curse his pedigree
Tis this oppression and this shame
Does beneigh a noble name
Will kill they line for thee

Bright jewels deck thy lady's head
Thy children never want for bread
Born into luxury
They princely mansions so secure
Thy hands nor head could ne'er procure
This gift of destiny

The want and suffering that your hand
Has brought a helpless, martyr's band
Will cry against the deed
The orphans' tears will burn your soul
And curse you till the final goal
Where mercy you will plead

London January 1875

Chapter 7

HENRY FAWCETT – TOM DREDGE
– WILLIAM CLERY 1880-1890

It was some time before the London postal workers recovered from the setbacks and disappointments of the 1870s. Surprisingly this came about as a result of a report commissioned by Henry Fawcett who was appointed Postmaster General in 1880.

Henry Fawcett was the son of a West Country draper who in his early years had been a follower of the philosopher Jeremy Bentham and in 1863 he was appointed professor of political economy at Cambridge University. Fawcett was accidentally blinded by a shot from his father's hunting gun at the age of twenty five and in 1867 was married to Millicent Garrett, a well-known campaigner for women's rights. He differed from many of his liberal contemporaries because he did not support the argument that wages should be set at the 'lowest that would attract any physically capable person of carrying out the job'. He believed, like Frank Scudamore before him, that wages should be set at a level that 'would secure a really efficient service by alleviating discontent'.

Initially it was the telegraphists who began to lobby Fawcett for improvements by organising a campaign of letter writing to the *Civil Service Gazette*. However he also received correspondence from postmen and sorters and it was this that prompted him to turn up unannounced at the General Post Office in St. Martins le Grande. He was shown around the building by a young sorter and spoke to many of the workers, making it known that he would be willing to take a look at their grievances. He also met a delegation of telegraphists and following this produced a report which became known as the 'Fawcett Scheme'. Despite considerable opposition from both the Treasury and his fellow administrators, he recommended a number of improvements to their pay and conditions. Some of his recommendations were implemented but most were not and in later years his report took on an almost mythical status becoming the focus for the aspirations of a new generation of Post Office trade unionists.

Where postal workers saw real improvement to their pay and conditions during Fawcett's administration, these were eroded within a few years as a result of rises in the cost of living.

The spark that led to a new phase of union building was provided by the 1886 Ridley Royal Commission on the Civil Service. The Commission asked postal workers to provide them with details of issues they wished the Commission to consider and grievances they wished to raise. The activists used this as another opportunity to build a trade union but this time the centre of the campaign was not St. Martins le Grande but North West London. The Conservative Party was back in power and the Postmaster General was Henry Cecil Raikes. The Royal Commission had failed to respond to the issued raised by the letter carriers and postal sorters and on 23 July 1887 at the Tolmer Square Institute, Drummond Street near Euston Station and close to the North West District Office a meeting was held.

Twenty three London offices sent delegations, together with a number from provincial offices. The meeting elected a Committee and a young postman named Tom Dredge was elected as the Secretary. He was described as a good speaker with a bluff manner who gave the impression that he would not flinch if it came to a fight. The meeting drew up a list of aims that would be the basis of their campaign which included the following:

- eight hour day
- pay increase
- improved overtime pay
- the provision of boots for all postmen
- lighter clothing for summer wear
- equality for all London postmen
- the resumption of the title 'Letter Carrier' in place of the new title of 'Postman'
- earlier maximum pay
- 18 shillings a week for all second class postmen
- the abolition of the collection and delivery of parcels
- a better pension scheme.

The petition was presented to management but once again ignored and on 13 August 1887 a further meeting was held at the Tolmers Square Institute, this time attended by over one thousand postal workers from across London and the Home Counties. Tom Dredge had made contact with his MP who happened to be H.L.W. Lawson, a Liberal and in later life Lord Burnham, proprietor of *The Daily Telegraph*. Lawson agreed to Chair the meeting and to support the postal workers campaign.

In August 1887 Lawson held a meeting with Raikes to discuss the men's grievances and although he was able to squeeze a few concessions from him the main issues of importance to the men were ignored. However, Raikes had promised to give further consideration to other points they had in their petition and the men felt that they were making some progress, but once again they were mistaken. Within a few days Dredge was summoned before his local Postmaster and charged with a dereliction of duty as a result of his activities on behalf of the Postmen's campaign. As a penalty he was demoted to postman second class, which also involved a loss of pay, and was warned that if he continued with his trade union activities he would be dismissed.

Despite this the Committee decided to push ahead with their campaign. They acquired their own premises and established themselves as the 'London and Provincial Postmen's Mutual Aid Society'. In February 1888 they held another mass meeting and in April that year they changed their name to the 'United Kingdom Postmen's Benefit Society'. Dredge was once again called before the Postmaster and charged with 'persistently endeavouring to stir up agitation' and on the 19 May 1888 he was dismissed from the service. Once again the Post Office and Treasury officials responsible for his dismissal must have congratulated themselves on getting rid of a dangerous agitator. A petition to have him re-instated was organised by some of his colleagues who were themselves then disciplined and demoted. The activities of the Society went into decline and although a 'Grand Smoking Concert' was held to raise money for Dredge, he disappeared from the scene for some time.

In 1886 an East End radical newspaper called *The Toby* began to publish articles attacking the treatment of the sorters working in the St Martins le Grande office and named a number of supervisors who they accused of being 'bullies and tyrants'. J.H. Williams was a middle-aged sorter, teetotaller and practising Quaker employed in the Foreign Branch at the General Post Office.

He began a campaign for the introduction of improvements to the pay and conditions of sorters recommended by Henry Fawcett, which the Post Office had never implemented.

Around the same time a young sorter named William Clery emerged as a potential leader following an incident that occurred on Christmas Day 1886. Postal workers, alongside many other workers, were required to work on Christmas Day. Many of the sorters had been working double shifts on compulsory overtime and they had been told that they would be released from duty at 9.00 a.m. When the time came to leave they found the doors bolted and supervisors blocking the exits from the building. For a while it looked like a repetition of the 'Riot at General Post Office' some years earlier. Tempers were frayed and the men were eager to get home. They hated the compulsory Christmas overtime because they were not paid for the extra work until several months later.

A serious confrontation was avoided by the intervention of the London Controller, a man called Jeffery who was described as a kindly man who had a great deal of sympathy for the London postal workers. He intervened and asked the men why they were refusing to clear the work. Suspicious that this was just another management ploy to identify their ring leaders he was met with a wall of silence. Suddenly the silence was broken by a young sorter called Grove who stepped forward, stuck out his chest and said 'I'll tell you why Mr. Jeffery, it's because we have to wait until the middle of summer before you pay us for the work. If the money was paid quickly most of us would be willing to stop'. It appears that Jeffery was genuinely unaware that this was the normal practice and he immediately assured the men that their money would be paid within a fortnight. The sorters returned to their sorting frames and cleared the work. From that date on Christmas overtime was always paid within two weeks.

This incident led to some of the men, including Clery and Williams, to look into why Fawcett's recommendations had never been implimented. They knew that Fawcett was the first Postmaster General to introduce overtime pay for both Christmas Day and Good Friday. Fawcett's reforms had improved the conditions of postal workers but over a period of time many of these had been eroded. Dissatisfaction was growing and this was particularly so amongst the younger sorters and dispatchers.

In 1886 Lord Randolph Churchill had established a Royal Commission to produce a report on the Civil Service and an invitation was published inviting all Civil Servants to make submissions. Meetings were held amongst the sorters and letter-carriers and petitions were drawn up and submitted to the Commission detailing their grievances. The sorters established a Committee to co-ordinate their submission and J.H. Williams was elected as Chairman and William Clery as Secretary.

Some months later the Commission's report was published but any reference to the Post Office had been left out. However, Clery in particular had developed a taste for campaigning and he established himself as the leader of a group of junior sorters determined to bring about improvements. Their main aim was to change the way that incremental pay increases were given according to the length of service. This meant that sorters could only move up the pay scale if a senior sorter left the industry, retired or died. They argued that pay should automatically be increased after fixed periods of service and in August and September 1887 they held several large meetings to support their campaign for these changes. They drew up a petition and sent it to Henry Raikes the new Conservative Postmaster General, with a request from the junior sorters for him to meet a delegation of their representatives.

After two months of silence from the Post Office Clery organised another meeting in January 1888 to discuss how they could move their claim forward. Once again they wrote to Raikes requesting a face to face meeting and once again he refused to meet them. Clery called another meeting of the junior sorters which turned out to be the biggest meeting of postal workers for fourteen years. Clery and Williams joined forces uniting the junior and senior sorters around a campaign to achieve the full benefits of Henry Fawcett's recommendations. They obtained a copy of Fawcett's report and Williams began to build it into a manifesto of aims for the London sorters. Williams was described by a contemporary as a 'man of grit with indomitable perseverance, combining the qualities of an attorney with the cold blooded zeal of a puritan'.

A meeting was called on 18 April 1889. Postal workers from across London and the Home Counties were invited and the two men laid out their case for the full implementation of Fawcett's recommendations. Williams, the older more cautious senior man, and Clery the younger and spirited junior man, managed to unite practically all the sorters behind their campaign. Williams painstakingly explained every detail of their claim and how the Post Office, following Fawcett's departure, had not only failed to implement his recommendations but had withdrawn some of those that had already been introduced. Clery favoured a more confrontational approach than Williams and proposed that they should go over the head of Raikes and appeal directly to Parliament. He argued that based on past experience, petitions to the Postmaster General were pointless and more decisive action was needed. Williams argued for a more moderate approach and at the end the meeting they agreed with Williams and decided on a petition to the Controller of London. Clery moderated his position for the sake of unity and the London sorters agreed a strategy that united both senior and junior men and established a new organisation for sorters which they called the 'Fawcett Scheme Committee'.

Clery and Williams were elected to the Committee's Executive and the new organisation put together a list of aims based on the research carried out by Williams. Clery meantime, had written and published a pamphlet called 'An Exposition of the Fawcett Scheme'. It was a clever and well written analysis of Fawcett's recommendations. In later life Clery became a famous playwright and actor/manager and in 1930 published his memoirs, but in 1889 he was using his considerable talents to build a trade union. His pamphlet became very popular with the London sorters and Clery was well aware that his publication was a direct challenge to the authorities. Post Office rules still insisted that Post Office employees could not communicate with the press and his pamphlet was being widely quoted in the London newspapers. Many of his colleagues thought his dismissal was inevitable. During the course of the campaign he was suspended from duty 13 times so it was to everyone's surprise when the Postmaster General invited Clery to a meeting to discuss the sorters' grievances. Clery, who had been pressing for a meeting for some time accepted at once. Raikes opened the meeting with the following words 'I have sent for you Mr. Clery, principally because I want to satisfy my curiosity. You have such a bad character that it made me curious to see what you look like'. The meeting lasted for an hour and at the end of it Clery had a better understanding of Raike's character. Clery, the self-educated postman, was not intimidated by Raikes, the university educated ex-public schoolboy and he told the men that despite Raike's friendly disposition, they should expect little sympathy from him.

A tide of trade union activity was sweeping across the country with hardly a single industry being untouched. Post Office and Treasury officials must have been aware that it was unlikely they would escape unaffected. The sorters were determined that their Committee should become the vehicle for building a genuine trade union and a meeting was called at the Foreign Section in St. Martins le Grande on 11 December 1889 at which over two thousand sorters from across London and the Home Counties attended. They debated two motions. The first read 'That the time has arrived for the sorting office staff to combine on trade union principles' and the second read 'To petition the Postmaster General in connection with the unfulfilled condition of the Fawcett Scheme'. They were both carried unanimously. They called their organisation the 'London Sorting Clerks Association' and agreed to launch a campaign in support of their aims.

Raikes meanwhile was aware of the developments and agreed to meet a delegation of the sorters representatives. The delegation, led by Clery and Williams, carefully explained their interpretation of the Fawcett Scheme and how they believed its recommendations had been ignored. Raikes assured the delegation that he wished to settle the matter amicably. 'I will talk it over with the Secretary' he said 'In the meantime, although from your point of view your contention appears a just one, I must say that I do not read this scheme as you do'. The delegation left the meeting disappointed by his response but not demoralised.

Another large meeting, to report back on the meeting with Raikes was held on 16 January 1890 and on 8 February they produced the first edition of their new journal which they called *The Post*. It was a pamphlet sized publication that was sold for one penny and was edited by Clery.

Raikes was keen to avoid a confrontation at this stage and rooms were made available at Mount Pleasant for the Association's offices. He even relaxed the rules on public meetings and on 10 February 1890 an inaugural meeting of the Association was held at the Memorial Hall, Farringdon Street. To give it wider appeal they decided to change its name from the 'London Sorting Clerks Association' to the 'Fawcett Association'. This was the first public meeting held by Civil Servants since 1866 that was not banned by the authorities. Henry Raikes, whilst no friend of trade unions had taken the view that open opposition to the sorters would be counterproductive given the wave of trade union activity sweeping the country. Trade unions throughout the UK were flexing their muscles and both the letter carriers and the telegraphists were organising associations independently of each other. Raikes even agreed to establish a Committee of Inquiry to look at the sorters' grievances and both Clery and Williams were called to give evidence but when the Inquiry published its report in March 1890 it rejected every single point that the Association had raised. Further meetings were held with Raikes and later in the year the Association used *The Post* to publish their list of aims:

- improved holiday facilities
- improved allowances when covering duties of a higher grade
- minimum pay of 24 shillings per week
- better promotion arrangements
- abolition of 'split' duties
- abolition of punitive punishment for alleged misconduct
- no compulsory overtime
- improved sick pay
- better overtime rates
- the facility for sick sorters to transfer to seaside or rural offices to improve their health.

The only issue agreed to by Raikes was the last one, probably because it is the only one that would not cost the Post Office any money. Although he later agreed to improve the sorters sick pay it was thought that this was because problems of a more serious nature were developing amongst the letter carriers and Raikes was trying to avoid the sorters and letter carriers uniting together in a single organisation. The organisation continued to recruit and grow in the following years although it had few members outside the Capital.

Chapter 8

THE POSTMEN'S UNION 1889

In 1890 the industrial spotlight moved away from the sorters and back to the letter carriers. The late 1880s had witnessed a massive increase in political and trade union activity. In February 1887 the Marquis of Salisbury's Conservative Government ordered the police to attack a peaceful but illegal demonstration organised by the 'Social Democratic Federation'. This became known as 'Bloody Sunday' and the following year a group of young women employed at the Bryant and May match factory in East London successfully struck for the re-instatement of several of their colleagues dismissed for complaining about their working conditions. In 1889 Will Thorne, a stoker at the Beckton Gas Works, successfully led a campaign for an eight-hour day and used this to launch the 'National Union of Gas Workers and General Labourers'. In the same year London dock workers came out on strike over what became known as the strike for the 'Dockers Tanner'.

In 1889 a group of postal workers approached an organisation called the 'Labour Union', which had just opened a Branch in Hoxton to seek its help in building a trade union for the letter carriers. A number of London newspapers published articles supporting the letter carriers' struggle to build a union and this led to a meeting on 22 September 1889 at Camberwell Green where about 300 postmen were addressed by John Mahon of the 'Labour Union'. The meeting agreed to establish a union for postal workers but with the clear understanding that the membership details would remain a secret until they had built their strength and influence. As usual, the Post Office had placed spies amongst those attending and the records show that an auxiliary postman from Finsbury Park by the name of E.S. Bull was paid 3 shillings for providing a full report of the meetings to Post Office management.

Another meeting was held on 24 September 1889 at the Central Democratic Club in Grays Inn Road where the formation of the Postmen's Union was officially announced. To avoid victimisation the Executive was entirely made up of non-Post Office employees, although Tom Dredge the postman from North West London who had been sacked the previous year, was included.

They explained to the meeting that the composition of the Executive was a temporary measure until the union was fully established, when they would be replaced by elected working postmen. The Secretary was John Mahon and the Chairman was named Fred Henderson. They called on all postal workers, including the sorters, to join the Postmen's Union and their main demands were based on the dockers' claim for six pence per hour and an extra two and a half pence overtime rate. Speakers at the meeting emphasised the need to keep membership details secret until they were strong enough to withstand the expected attacks by the Post Office. However, within a few weeks a crisis developed when Fred Henderson published a manifesto outlining the Union's aims without consulting Mahon and the rest of the Executive. When Henderson was challenged regarding this he launched an attack on his colleagues, accusing them of being 'self-seeking' and trying to dominate the Union with their own political ideas. He managed to gain the support of a journalist called W.A. Chambers along with Tom Dredge and it looked as though the union was on the verge of tearing itself apart before it had even got off the ground. Mahon and the Executive went onto the attack, expelling Henderson and persuading Dredge to stick with the majority of the Executive.

Differences still existed and a meeting was called in an attempt to reconcile the two sides. John Burns, the prominent dockers leader and Henry Champion, a well-respected journalist, were asked to assist and William Clery, the London sorters leader, also attended. Although the meeting was unable to overcome all the differences, a compromise was reached that resulted in a number of working postmen being brought onto the Executive.

During the next few months the Union's membership grew and Branches were established throughout London and the Home Counties. Contacts were also made with Postmen in Newcastle, Edinburgh, Liverpool and Glasgow and a journal called *The Postmen's Gazette* was also published.

In November 1889 Mahon felt confident enough to write to the Post Office requesting official recognition and although this led to a meeting with management they refused to recognise the Union. However it did lead to management making some small concessions but without giving any credit to the Union. They increased the minimum pay rate. Tom Dredge was given his job back but only after signing a declaration denouncing his previous union activities and in an attempt to cause a division between the letter carriers and the parcel postmen the latter were offered improved sick pay. The Union continued to make progress and by March 1890 the majority of the Union's Executive were working postmen. Further meetings were organised and contacts were made with sympathetic MPs but although the Union was growing stronger many senior men remained wary of joining, mindful of previous attempts at union building.

In May 1890 the London Trades Council held it's first May Day Demonstration and a contingent of 800 postmen marched behind the Postmen's Union banner proclaiming 'Each for All and All for Each'. The Executive was growing in confidence and decided to make a challenge to the ban on letter carriers holding public meetings. The Post Office had organised a celebration to commemorate the introduction of the Penny Post on 15 May 1890. Whilst management were busy congratulating themselves on the success of the Penny Post the Union began preparations for a demonstration to highlight and denounce fifty years of exploitation. They planned a series of marches from different parts of the capital culminating in a mass meeting at Clerkenwell Green. When the Postmaster General became aware of this he was able to get a ban on the processions and the police were ordered to stop the columns of London postmen converging on Clerkenwell Green. About 1,500 postmen managed to make it to Clerkenwell despite considerable police brutality. One of the processions had to reform no less than eight times before they finally made it through the blockade to hear Keir Hardy and Mahon urge the postmen to continue fight the for trade union rights and a fairer share of the Post Office's profits.

Meanwhile management had managed to identify over one hundred of the postmen who had attended the meeting and lost no time in charging them with breaking Post Office regulations. This resulted in thirty one men being suspended without pay and the removal of the good conduct stripes from another eight. This increased the outrage felt by many of the men. Not only had the police brutally attacked their peaceful demonstration, but management had punished their colleagues for simply attending a meeting. There was uproar in a number of offices and a serious threat of a mass walkout when some postmen refused to carry out the work of their suspended colleagues. Mahon managed to calm the situation down when he assured them that the pay lost by those suspended would be made up by the Union and issued a press statement, assuring the public that the Union's aim was to 'peacefully educate public opinion as to their demands'. The tactic appeared to have some effect because over the next few days a number of articles appeared in the London press supporting the Union's claim for recognition. Even the *Civil Service Gazette* ran an article claiming that Raikes, the Postmaster General, was the most unpopular in the history of the Post Office.

The campaign was beginning to show results and before the end of June 1890 Post Office management were forced to meet a union delegation. Following the meeting the rule banning the attendance of letter carriers at outside meetings was withdrawn, although management spies continued to monitor the Union's activities and harass its leading members.

The Union called a meeting in Finsbury Park on 22 June, where management spies took the names of postmen who attended, and thirty postmen were later suspended from duty, despite the change to the Post Office rules on employees attending outside meetings. The industrial relations temperature was rising across London and the situation came to a head a week later when the Union held a meeting in Hyde Park. A number of fights broke out when several management spies were recognised and the police had to escort them from the park for their own safety.

The following week management were preparing another celebrity packed celebration in honour of Rowland Hill and the Penny Post. Telegraphists in every office were ordered to cheer simultaneously in spontaneous celebration of Hill's achievements and when they refused to do so were all threatened with suspensions. Seven union activists were suspended as a result of the Hyde Park disturbances and it was reported that unofficial 'work to rules' and 'go slows' took place in a number of offices. At a meeting held at the St. Martins le Grande office it was reported that the men cheered when a red flag was unfurled and waved above the crowd. The Union's leadership believed that they were not strong enough yet to seriously confront management and were struggling to control the growing anger. This was made more difficult by Raikes' unsuccessful attempt to stop 400 postmen marching in support of a hospital charity. On Monday 7 July 1890 Mahon addressed an evening meeting of 1000 postmen held at Holborn Town Hall where there was a call for industrial action. There was clearly a growing mood of militancy amongst the rank and file and George Shipton of the London Trades Council was brought along to help persuade the men to show restraint and allow the Executive more time to resolve the problems by negotiations. Meanwhile the Post Office was laying plans to attack the Union and this came to a head on Tuesday 8 July 1890.

The 1890 London Postmen's Strike

In the summer of 1890 the Post Office decided that its plans for taking on the Union were ready for implementation. On Tuesday 8 July they ordered all postmen, including part-timers, to report for work early irrespective of their normal shift times and in all the large offices they also brought in a considerable number of casual workers in preparation for carrying out the duties of the Union members in the event of a strike. This caused considerable anger, particularly at St. Martins le Grande and Mount Pleasant where the potential strike breakers were driven from the building by the Union members.

The London Controller, Tombs, tried to persuade the men that it was not their intention to use the casuals to do anyone else's work but nevertheless they were forced to leave the building. On the following day, Wednesday 9 July, there were further disturbances at both Mount Pleasant and St. Martins le Grande but Tombs had decided that he would not provoke a walkout until all their preparations were in place. He had calculated that if he moved against the Union too early this would provoke a London wide strike before the authorities were ready. They had arranged to make their move the following day when they had hoped to have isolated the postmen by making concessions to the sorters and telegraphists. A group of senior postmen also planned to undermine the dispute by refusing to strike following a 'secret meeting'. At Mount Pleasant there were serious disturbances that resulted in fighting and the 'blacklegs' being driven from the building. Tombs called in the police and Mahon tried to calm the situation down in the hope that he could get the Post Office to negotiate.

Having managed to isolate the postmen from both the sorters and the telegraphists Tombs prepared his next move. Henry Raikes offered the sorters several improvements to their pay and conditions, and the sorters who were getting nervous at the growing strength of the Postmen's Union were anxious not to get dragged into a dispute not of their own making.

That evening the Union held a meeting at Clerkenwell Green where the usual confrontation with the Post Office spies occurred. Although some of the members were demanding more decisive action, Mahon was still calling for restraint and the next morning the London papers were carrying conflicting reports about the likelihood of a walkout. Henry Tombs now had his plans in place. The strike-breakers had been recruited and several hundred policemen were on hand to deal with any disturbances. Henry Tombs, Sir Arthur Blackwood, Secretary to the Post Office and Lewin Hill the Principal Clerk, nephew of Rowland Hill had already decided on mass sackings and what they thought would be a fatal blow to the Union. At 4.00 a.m. they appeared on the sorting office floor at Mount Pleasant and announced the dismissal of over 100 union activists. They then left the building and accompanied by nearly 500 policemen, quickly made their way across London to St. Martins le Grande to head off any solidarity action that might occur there.

Postmen arriving for work were telling an army of reporters massed outside the buildings' main entrance that they would not work unless the victimised workers were re-instated. Meanwhile a 'flying picket' was making its way across the City picking up some telegraph messengers on the way. When they arrived they found the building surrounded by a massive army of police including mounted officers, making it impossible for them to reach their City colleagues. Inside the building 200 police officers were patrolling the corridors and with no clear guide from the Union the City postmen were in a state of confusion. Most of the City men were established postmen with pensions and long service. They were severely intimidated by the police swarming all over the building and the presence of several hundred paid strike-breakers waiting to replace them if they refused to take their deliveries out. Managers told the staff that if they refused to take their walks out they would be dismissed on the spot and inevitably the spirit of some of the men began to break.

Some postmen under the watchful eye of the police and supervisors began to drift out onto the streets with their deliveries. The pickets were stunned and offered no resistance whatsoever. Maybe they understood the pressure their City colleagues were being placed under or maybe it was the police presence. They held a quick impromptu meeting and decided to dispatch emissaries to a number of other London offices. This resulted in solidarity action in the Leicester Square, London Bridge, Holloway, Finsbury Park and Whitechapel offices and at Waterloo station a number of sympathetic parcel postmen found themselves locked in the building by management. Strike-breakers were on hand to take the jobs of the Whitechapel strikers but could only do so with military protection because of the hostility from the local population. The Leicester Square postmen who had walked out, most whom were junior and unestablished, were all instantly dismissed.

However most of the London postmen remained at work and John Mahon, desperate to regain the initiative, called a mass meeting for the evening of 10 July at Camberwell Green. He called for an all-out strike and the following morning pickets were dispatched across London handing out leaflets entitled 'Who Would Be a Rat'. Wherever they went they were confronted by the police and in East London several arrests were made.

Meanwhile, the authorities were laying further plans to isolate the strikers. Henry Raikes met with a moderate faction within the Union in order to try and stop the strike spreading. This group included a City postman called Charles Churchfield who had previously written to Raikes stating his opposition to strike action. Raikes offered them concessions on pay and to make sure this received the maximum publicity, supervisors held meetings with groups of postmen across the capital. John Mahon sought the help of John Burns, the dockers leader, but he was busy organising a group of London cabmen. Burns referred him to the London Trades Council but by Thursday evening things were not looking good. Some of the strikers were feeling isolated and began to blame Mahon. That morning *The Times* reported that 'as the day progressed it became more and more evident that the neck of the movement had been broken.'

On Saturday 12 July a meeting of 300 sacked postmen took place in Holborn Town Hall but by now the dispute was effectively over. At a meeting called the following day only 100 men turned up. It seemed that once again the Post Office had defeated the men's attempts to build a union. The Postmen's Union were up against a powerful opposition which included not only the Post Office but the State and all its agencies, including the police, military and judiciary. These massive forces were pitted against a small group of several hundred London postmen with limited resources, facing the prospect of unemployment and poverty if they failed. The authorities had skilfully sown the seed of division amongst the ranks of the postmen but there were several hundred men brave enough to stand up against this oppression and Henry Raikes was forced to make concessions, if not to the strikers then to those that followed them. An internal Committee of Inquiry was established which within a year of the strike was recommending major improvements for postmen not just in London but across the country.

The Postmen's Federation 1891

On 15 August 1891 a meeting was held at St. Martins le Grande to establish a national trade union for postmen and in September a meeting of representatives from 33 London offices and 38 provincial offices met to form the Postmen's Federation. Many of the delegates had been activists in the Postmen's Union. The meeting elected Charles Churchfield, the London postman who, during the strike had held meetings with Henry Raikes, as their General Secretary. A thousand London postmen attended a General Meeting the following year and the Federation produced the first edition of its journal *The Postmen's Gazette*. In the same year representatives of 4,000 postmen nationwide attended the Federation's first Annual Conference and by the end of 1892 all the main grades of postal workers had established unions. For many years divisions remained in London and it took a long time for the resentments built up during the dispute to subside, but in time they did and postal workers began to appreciate the contribution made by the heroes of 1890 to later generations of postal workers. The Postmen's Federation recognised this when their National Chairman opened their 1891 Conference with the following words:

'We cannot proceed without paying a tribute to the Postmen's Union which undoubtedly paved the way for the establishment of our present and constitutional organisation. The pluck and method of organisation displayed by members of the Postmen's Union are ever worthy of a place in our memory' and thirty years later at the inaugural conference of the Union of Post Office Workers (UPW) a speaker recalled in a speech from the platform that, 'We have the men of 1890 to thank for the large measure of freedom and liberty enjoyed by the Post Office employees today.'

After the strike things were never the same again and it was thanks to the sacrifices of the trade unionists in 1890 that not only was trade unionism finally established in the Post Office but that all public employees won the right to be represented by a union. In the fifty years between 1840 and 1890 the Post Office was transformed from a medium-sized Government Department to a nationwide service stretching to every corner of Britain and Ireland. The numbers employed grew from 9,505 in 1835 to 138,738 in 1895. Its income in 1835 was £2,320,000 and in 1895 it was £13,672,000 making an annual profit of £2,928.000.

The 'great' postal reformer, Rowland Hill's reputation as an innovator and pioneer of the Universal Service was overshadowed by his contempt and disregard for the people who provided the service. He cared little for their welfare and saw any attempt by the workforce to improve their conditions as an act of sabotage, and an attack on the 'iron laws of the free market'. The so called golden age of the Victoria period was, in fact, for the majority of working people one of repression, poverty and hardship whilst at the same time the ruling elite enjoyed a level of wealth and power unheard of in previous history.

The scientific and industrial achievements of the era were eclipsed by the dreadful exploitation and inhumanity imposed on millions of ordinary people. Democracy was beginning to emerge after years of repression and working people were at last understanding the benefits that political and social progress could bring them. In 1895 the Marquess of Salisbury was Prime Minister and the Conservatives were back in power. They would remain the governing party until 1905 when Salisbury's successor, Arthur James Balfour, was replaced by the Liberal, Henry Campbell-Bannerman.

Chapter 9

WILLIAM CLERY
AND THE COMMITTEES OF INQUIRY
1891-1900

Henry Cecil Raikes, Postmaster General, died on 24 August 1891. It was said that in the months following the 'Postmen's Strike' he attempted to put right some of the injustices inflicted on the London Postal Workers. The sorters, in particular, appeared to believe this and their Secretary, William Clery, wrote a lengthy tribute to Raikes which appeared in *The Daily Telegraph*. The postmen, meanwhile, were pushing ahead with building the Federation and on 16 September 1891 they agreed a number of policies to take the Union forward. These included a claim for a minimum national wage, yearly increments, three weeks holiday and an eight-hour day. Details of the programme was distributed throughout the network and within the next few months two hundred and fifty separate meetings of postmen in towns and cities across the country had adopted its policies.The sorters, however, were beginning to have second thoughts about Raikes' legacy and once again were feeling let down and betrayed. Clery, in particular, was becoming impatient at the length of time it was taking to implement some of the promised changes.

The new Conservative Postmaster General was Sir James Ferguson and one of his first acts was to prohibit the distribution of the sorters journal on Post Office premises. This was like a red rag to a bull as far as Clery was concerned and against the advice of Williams he launched another campaign for a Committee of Inquiry. When Clery's policies were adopted by a meeting of the Association on 15 June 1892 Williams resigned as Chairman. Clery replaced him as Chairman and a sorter from the Western District Office called Wallace Bligh Cheesman replaced Clery as Secretary. A General Election was looming and Clery saw this as a good opportunity to gain support for the Association's call for an inquiry. As far as Ferguson was concerned, he saw this as a direct challenge to his authority and in July 1892 dismissed both Clery and Cheesman. The two men received some support in the London press when a number of both Liberal and Conservative newspapers condemned the sackings. Two sympathetic members of parliament, Sam Woods and William Cobb, raised the matter in the Commons but Ferguson refused to reconsider the matter.

Meanwhile, the Postmen's Federation, who had never fully supported the sorters call for yet another inquiry, were busy mounting a campaign to get their colleagues, who were dismissed during the 1890 strike, reinstated and with the support of an MP called George Howell, were having some success. Clery, who following his dismissal had plenty of time on his hands, put it to good use by travelling the country whipping up support for the Association's campaign and Cheesman's and his own reinstatement.

The 1892 election put the Liberals back in power and Gladstone appointed Arnold Morley as the Postmaster General. Morley had been a vocal supporter of the sorters' case whilst in opposition, but true to form, once in power he refused to reinstate both Clery and Cheesman. This must have been a big blow to Clery who was an active supporter of the Liberal Party and had worked hard during the General Election to get them elected. A vigorous campaign was launched involving cross party support. Keir Hardy, the new MP for West Ham, played a prominent role and meetings were held up and down the country with the active support of the TUC. In 1895 Clery and Cheesman were being paid as full time officials by the Fawcett Association, Clery receiving £2.50 per week and Cheesman £2. They were still campaigning for an inquiry and their own re-instatement and their cases were still being raised by sympathetic MPs in the commons on a regular basis. They must have felt some satisfaction when on 11 June 1895 Morley appointed Lord Tweedmouth to hold the first of many inquiries into the finances of the Post Office and the men's grievances. The Postmen's Federation was growing in strength and by 1895 had 20,000 or more members spread across the country. The postal clerks were also busy building their own union with Kier Hardy playing a leading role. The Telegraphists Association, which was amongst the most militant of the unions, was also expanding and organisations representing every conceivable grade sprung up eager to present their particular case to the inquiry. Head Postmaster, Sub Postmasters, supervisors, linesmen, tracers and writers; along with porters and doorkeepers all formed organisations in the hope that collectively they might influence the outcome of the Tweedmouth Committee's inquiry.

The Committee was comprised of the heads of a number of Government Departments, Sir A. Godley, Sir F. Mowatt and Mr. Spencer Walpole with Lord Tweedmouth as its President. The more experienced amongst the unions were not convinced that the inquiry would bring them any benefits but, nevertheless, were willing to give it a try on the basis that they had little to lose. Arnold Morley had drawn up the terms of reference for the inquiry and it included the following paragraph: 'The Post Office is a great Revenue Department and that in the words of the Select Committee on Revenue Departments in 1888, said it is more likely to be conducted satisfactorily if it should also continue to be conducted with a view to profit, as one of the revenue yielding Departments of the State.'

Clery had encouraged the sorters to remain involved with the inquiry in the hope that his own and Cheesman's case might be reviewed. In the event, the Committee not only refused to discuss the issue but also refused to allow him to personally present his union's case to the inquiry on the basis that he was 'no longer a servant of the Post Office'. The Committee held its first meeting on Monday 24 June 1895 in Committee Room B at the House of Lords. The sorter's evidence was taken first and in the absence of Clery, H. Groves, the Treasurer, presented their case. Another witness, a sorter called E.J. Neville, made a noble attempt to raise the issue of his two sacked colleagues but was ruled out of order by Tweedmouth. Throughout the proceedings witnesses were openly intimidated by senior Post Office personnel seated inside the room where the inquiry was being held. This resulted in the men having to get a personal assurance from Tweedmouth that they would not be punished for giving evidence to the Committee. Spencer Walpole, Permanent Secretary to the Post Office, was particularly aggressive and it was said that he held a perpetual sneer on his face throughout the proceedings. Each organisation in turn sent its spokesmen forward to present their case to the inquiry and each one was met with the same hostility. Lewin Hill, nephew of Rowland and Assistant Secretary to Walpole, had inherited his uncle's contempt for postal workers and was particulary hostile to the postmen's representatives.

The Committee had begun its work in June 1895 but the postal workers had to wait until March 1897 before its findings were published. When it was it was met with widespread anger and disappointment once its contents became known to the unions. The provisional sorting clerks said they were 'bitterly disappointed'; the Postmen's Federation said they were 'dumbfounded' and the Telegraphists were 'overwhelmed with consternation'. Only the London sorters could claim any satisfaction from the contents of the report. Their maximum pay was being raised to £160 per year but this only gave an immediate pay increase to the senior men with nothing for the junior sorters. Even they commented that they were 'by no means satisfied' and whilst the Telegraphists began talking about industrial action, the sorters considered legal action. The findings of the inquiry were met with almost total opposition from the trade unions and it set a precedent for the numerous other inquiries established between 1904 and 1914. These included the 'Bradford Inquiry' in 1904, the 'Hodhouse Inquiry' in 1906, the 'Holt Select Committee' in 1912 and the 'Gibb Committee' in 1914. Postal workers received very little from any of these inquiries and when they did they recommend small improvements and invariably they were undermined by either the Post Office or the Treasury. However the unions continued to consolidate their positions and build their membership.

Clery who was now a paid official of the Fawcett Association was still campaigning for re-instatement eight years after his dismissal and friendly MPs were still raising his case in the House of Commons. As a result of the union's outrage at the outcome of the Tweedmouth Report, a supplementary inquiry called the 'Norfolk-Handbury Conference' took another look at the postal workers grievances but it proved to be no less helpful than its predecessor and the industrial relations problems in the industry continued.

Postal workers, however, were making some headway in building unity in the wider world of public sector trade unions. Clery and the Association were big supporters of the 'Government Workers Federation', an organisation aimed at uniting Government workers across the various sections of the Civil Service. The postal unions were building closer links with the TUC and were growing in both membership and influence. In 1898 an attempt was made to unite all the postal grades in an umbrella organisation called the Postal Federation. The disappointment created by Tweedmouth and subsequently Norfolk-Hanbury Conference was an incentive to build closer co-operation between the unions and the Federation held its first Congress in September 1899 in Derby. London activists played a full part in the campaigns to unite postal workers into a single trade union organisation although it would be another twenty years before this became a reality and a further sixty before the process of uniting rank and file postal workers was completed.

Political Change and the Postal Trade Unions

On 13 January 1893 one hundred and twenty delegates met at the Bradford Labour Institute to launch the Independent Labour Party (ILP). Most of the older craft unions continued to support the Liberals and some trade unionists, including Clery, had stood as Liberal/Labour candidates in elections. The more militant political activists like Tom Mann, Henry Champion and Kier Hardy, supported the ILP and in London the Social Democratic Federation remained a strong force amongst politically active workers.

In the 1890s a concerted attempt by employers to reverse the gains of the previous decade forced many activists to reconsider their tactics. British employers complained that competition from America and Germany was hitting profits and the trade union's opposition to wage cuts was making them uncompetitive in world markets. They formed the Employers' Associations and the Employers Federation Parliamentary Committee to pressurise the Government into introducing legislation to restrict the power of the unions. Even the older unions, those closest to the Liberal Party, were becoming concerned at the turn of events. In 1899 when the Appeal Court passed a judgement that restricted the right of workers to picket peacefully, they became increasingly disillusioned with the Liberal Party who had amongst their membership some of the country's most powerful employers. The political landscape was beginning to change.

In 1898 West Ham became the first local authority to have a Labour majority. This was achieved with the support of local socialists, mainly the Social Democratic Federation. In 1899 the TUC agreed a resolution calling for an increase in the number of Labour members in Parliament and in 1900 Keir Hardie, an old friend of the Postmen's Union, was elected as MP for Merthyr Tydfill. On 27 February 1900 at a meeting held in the Memorial Hall in

Farringdon, delegates from across the country met to discuss the problem of how to increase labour and workers representation in Parliament. This has been widely recognised as the foundation meeting of the Labour Party and in the next few years most of the existing workers' parties would unite to build a 'United Labour Party'. This was given more momentum by a House of Lords ruling in July 1901 in favour of the Taff Vale Railway Company in South Wales and against a group of striking railway workers, members of the Amalgamated Society of Railway Servants. The financial implication of the judgement convinced most of the waverers that a party representing the interests of organised labour was an 'immediate necessity'.

A split with the Liberals was now becoming inevitable and the Liberals, in a belated effort to keep the Liberal/Labour pact together, agreed to support a number of Labour Representation Committee (LRC) candidates in the 1906 General Election. The Liberals won the election and thirty successful LRC candidates declared themselves the Labour Party and took up their seats on the opposition benches in the Commons. This had an immediate effect on the Liberal Government who was eager to maintain the support it had from working class voters. Sydney Buxton, the newly appointed Postmaster General, issued a statement giving the Postmen's' Federation official recognition.

Between 1900 and the First World War the Fawcett Association continued to grow in influence within the Trade Union Movement. From their Headquarters at 55 Doughty Street, London WC1 they continued to be led by William Clery and Wallace Cheesman. Whilst remaining a committed supporter of the Liberal Party, Cheesman also supported the formation of an independent Labour Party. The Association remained London based with most of its members coming from the St. Martins le Grande office with a smaller but significant number working in the District Offices, the Parcels Section and the Travelling Post Office (TPO) At the peak of their strength and just before the amalgamation in 1919, they had 6,422 members which was almost 95% of those working in the areas where they organised. The Association and its members had earned a reputation for being elitist and sectarian in their relationship with the other postal unions. This was not without some justification and their attempts in 1901 to ensure that promotion to the supervisory grades would be restricted to those from their own grade led to a serious rift with the Postmen's Federation. In 1903 Clery was removed from office because of political differences with the Association's executive and alleged financial irregularities, whilst Cheesman remained in office, as General Secretary until 1919 and the amalgamation.

Meanwhile the Postmen's Federation was going from strength to strength increasing its membership from 3,721 in 1892 to 61,910 in 1919. Its first General Secretary Charles Churchfield was a postman from the Eastern Central District Office (ECDO). However, the majority of its Executive came from outside of London. During this period differences between London postal workers and those in the rest of the country began to emerge. There was a view nationally that the Tweedmouth Report had a 'London bias' and in London memories of the 1890 Postmen's Union strike were still strong and in some areas membership of the Federation remained fairly low. The Postmen's Union was nominally still in existence until almost the end of the century. In 1906 one of several breakaway unions emerged. This was called the 'Central London Postmen's Association' (CLPA) and they claimed to be the genuine successors of the Postman Union. The CLPA considered themselves to be the true inheritors of the traditions of the Postmen's Union. They boasted that their roots were the oldest and that they represented the most dedicated and loyal trade unionists in the Post Office. They accused the Postmen's Federation of being little more than a 'Mutual Benefit Society' whilst claiming they were a proper trade union who had once 'set the pace in postal agitation' and although they never had more than a thousand members, they played an important and active role in the development of the London trade union and labour movement. The relationship between the Federation's leadership and the London membership came under strain in 1911 when a mass meeting in London was called to put pressure on the Government over the outcome of the Holt Report and the leadership accused the leaders of the campaign of disloyalty.

Another significant organisation was the London Postal Porters Association. They were not a breakaway organisation but were forced to form their own union because neither the Fawcett Association nor the Federation would accept them as members. Formed in 1895 their first General Secretary was Tommy Sanders, a London porter, and when he retired he was replaced by a porter from the Inland Section (IS) called W.H. Manning. In 1907 they had a membership of 500. Even by the standards of the time, porters were very poorly paid. However, they built a strong organisation with a Mutual Benefit Scheme and a monthly journal called the 'Postal Porter', which later changed its name to the 'Postal Advocate'. A large proportion of their members was ex-servicemen and like the CLPA and the Fawcett Association organised the union through an Annual General Meeting (AGM) which elected its Executive Council.

Considerable inter-union rivalry existed between two other London based organisations – one called The Tracers Association and another called The Sort/Tracers Association. The former were employed full time to trace record and find telegrams whilst members of the Sort/Tracers Association spent half the day sorting and the rest working as tracers. The hostility between these two organisations continued right up until the amalgamation in 1920. In 1910 some of these smaller unions came together to form the Post Office Servants Federation (POSF). These included the Central London Postmen's Association, the Sort/Tracers Association, the Adult Messengers and a number of auxiliary postmen working in the capital. The Women Sorters Association (WSA) representing women doing specialist work in smaller Sorting Offices was another London based union. Their General Secretary was an outstanding and brilliant organiser called Rose Smith-Rose who led the organisation from 1904 until 1933 when they amalgamated with the Civil Service Clerical Association. The National Union of Auxiliary Postmen (NUAP) was set up in 1910 by a Croydon auxiliary postman called Thomas Easthope. Its main aim was to organise the auxiliary postmen who felt they could not get proper representation from any of the other established unions. They had about 500 members mainly in the southern Home Counties.

There were two other small unions in London. These were the Tube Staff Association (TSA), formed in 1903 with about 120 members working as tube attendants and night collectors at the Central Telegraph Office and the Post Office Writers Association (POWA) representing book room staff with 107 members and established in 1903. All of these organisations, other than the Women's Sorters Association, joined together to form the UPW in 1919.

Chapter 10

LONDON POSTAL WORKERS
AND THE GREAT WAR 1914-1918

At the outbreak of the First World War the postal unions in London and throughout the country were in a healthy position. Every major grade had an organisation to represent them and the membership was growing. A nucleus of activists was helping to develop the organisations both industrially and politically and this allowed them to influence their working conditions and pay in a way that became an example to other public servants. With the outbreak of war, thousands of postal workers volunteered to fight in the trenches. In 1908 the 24th Middlesex Rifle Volunteers, whose roots went back to 1868, became the 8th Battalion City of London Regiment (the author's grandfather was the colour sergeant of the 8th Battalion). So many London postal workers enrolled that by September 1914 a second regiment was formed and in 1915 a third was formed and together they became known as the 'Post Office Rifles'. By the end of the war over 1800 members of the regiment had been killed, 4500 wounded and the Regiment had earned 27 battle honours. Across the country over 70,000 postal workers had joined the forces and George Stuart, General Secretary of the Postmen's Federation appeared on platforms alongside senior Post Office officials urging 'every young man who is physically fit and capable of bearing arms to rise to the occasion'. The vacancies produced by the departing volunteers were filled by 'temporaries' many of whom were women. For the first time a significant number of women were carrying out jobs previously performed by men. The Post Office Rifles had fought with bravery and distinction in all the major battles of the war. At the Battle of Wurst Farm Ridge in September 1917 the two battalions of Post Office Rifles lost over half their fighting strength, dead or wounded. They were awarded a total of 40 individual commendations for bravery including Sergeant A.J. Knight who was awarded the Victoria Cross.

Union membership fell during the war because so many of its members had joined the forces. The Federation began to recruit the 'temporaries' and equal pay for women became an aim of the Union. The Liberal Party was in power and Herbert Asquith, 1st Earl of Oxford and Prime Minister, had appointed C.E.H. Hobhouse as Postmaster General. Arnold Bennett, Author and Director of Propaganda at the War Ministry had described Hobhouse as 'hopelessly prejudiced, stupid and ill-informed and responsible for a great deal of the class friction that had recently been developing'. When a delegation from the Postmen's Federation met with Hobhouse on the issue of equal pay for women, he rejected their claim out of hand arguing that women only earned 'found money'. Amongst other things, this led to an increase in militancy amongst postal workers who saw their standards of living falling whilst those of others improved because of the labour shortages. Branches began campaigning for wage increases to compensate for their falling living standards and as usual the Treasury refused even to consider this. However, as a result of rising working class militancy and growing trade union influence, an inquiry headed by Sir James Woodhouse awarded them a small cost of living increase. This was something of a turning point in the campaign for improved pay and despite the Treasurer's attempts to block the award, pressure was put on the Government by Arthur Henderson, leader of the Labour Party and other Labour members of the War Cabinet and in September 1915 the increase was paid in full and backdated to 1 March 1915.

As the war dragged on prices continued to rise and whilst many other workers received compensation, postal workers saw their pay fall behind again. The postal unions had established a National Joint Committee (NJC) and this met with the Postmaster General on a number of occasions to press their claim. In London and throughout the country Branches held mass meetings to build their support for improved pay. Other sections of the Civil Service were also feeling the effects of war time inflation and this brought about the introduction in November 1916 of the Conciliation and Arbitration Board for Government Employees who were given the responsibility of looking into the question of civil servants pay.

In March 1916 the NJC presented its first claim to the Board. Once again postal workers placed themselves at the forefront of the struggle for equal pay for women when the NJC included it in their 1916 wage claim and although this was rejected and the Board's overall pay award fell far short of the NJC claim, it began a new phase in the development of Post Office trade unions. The experience of the unions co-operating and working together increased the demands for amalgamation. Further pay increases were agreed in December 1917 and in March 1918 the Federation once again put in a claim for equal pay for temporary and women workers.

The Arbitration Board proved to be popular not only with the postal unions but right across the public sector. The arbitration awards became the reference point for pay negotiations until well after the war ended. The first pay award made to postal workers by the Board exceeded all the increases from the previous enquiries added together. It was the postal union's first step towards collective bargaining, allowing the unions to present their case to the Board with reference back to previous settlements. The interference from the Treasury was removed and if Post Office management attempted to delay or veto improvements the unions could refer disagreements back to the Board. By the end of the war the unions were stronger and more united with the foundations for amalgamations firmly laid. The idea that trade unions would have an opportunity to present their case to an Independent Arbitration Board and that the Board could override the Treasury was considered almost revolutionary in some quarters. Radical ideas were developing amongst ordinary people and as one of the Civil Service journals noted at the time: 'There are Bolsheviks abroad and mild mannered and moderate men are gradually being converted to their views, something more far reaching than mere recognition will be demanded.'

These changes led to another significant development in industrial relations when against the background of the increase in industrial militancy throughout British industry; the Government introduced the 'Committee for Industrial Unrest' chaired by the Liberal MP, John Henry Whitley. Initially, the Committee were asked to concentrate their efforts on the considerable industrial relations problems in the private sector. The unions in the public sector saw here an opportunity to improve their negotiating position and foremost amongst those was George Stuart, General Secretary of the Postmen's Federation. He made a direct approach to J.H. Whitley and convinced him to include civil servants in his second report published in 1917. By the end of the year, both the Treasury and the Ministry of Labour had accepted the idea and the Post Office was required to apply Whitley's principles to Industrial Relations throughout the industry. In 1918 the Postmen's Federation endorsed the proposal and a campaign was undertaken to promote the idea amongst the general membership. In July 1918 the War Cabinet gave the go ahead for the idea and Sir Thomas Heath, Parliamentary Secretary to the Treasury, was appointed by the Government to oversee its implementation. He immediately set about trying to limit the influence of the unions but Stuart and the Federation forged a powerful coalition of public sector unions and on 28 May 1919, the Government conceded all the main points demanded by the Unions.

The first meeting of the National Whitley Council was held on 23 July 1919 and sometime after a network of departmental committees were established throughout the Civil Service. This was an important watershed in public sector industrial relations. For the first time and after more than 75 years of campaigning, workers, not only in the Post Office but across the public sector, established machinery for resolving grievances and disputes. More importantly, 'the assumption that wages of Post Office servants are settled by bargain or agreement' was firmly established.

Amalgamation and the Inter-War Years 1913

Postal workers had been talking about 'One Big Union' since the late 19th century. Differences between grades and different parts of the country had always made this difficult. It was the effect of the war years on industrial relations, the formation of the National Joint Committee (NJC) and the establishment of the Whitley Councils that created the conditions that finally brought this about. George Stuart was a great advocate of amalgamation and as early as 1913 the Postmen's Federation had held a meeting at London's Caxton Hall to discuss the issue. Fourteen other unions attended and they went as far as electing a steering committee and agreed a name, 'The Postal Workers Association'. Unfortunately the idea was scuppered from within the Postmen's Federation when their Executive Council rejected the idea.

In June 1914 the Postal Telegraph Clerks Association (PTCA) begun talks on amalgamation with the Fawcett Association but these were hampered by the Fawcett Association's insistence on separate negotiating machinery for

London. However the effects of the war had driven the unions closer together and by May 1917 the main unions had arranged further discussions but on this occasion it was the PTCA that were unable to agree. On 11 August 1917 the Federation made another attempt to bring the two unions together. Significant progress was made and on 13 September 1917 agreement between the two unions was reached. At the insistence of the Fawcett Association it was agreed that they would have a separate London District Council for sorters and two reserved seats on the Executive.

Several of the smaller unions, including the Central London Postmen's Association, the London Postal Porters and the Sorting Assistants, showed interest in joining the new organisation. The Fawcett Association's Executive held a meeting in January 1918 and an overwhelming vote of their member's supported the idea of amalgamation. However Stewart, who had played such a leading role in encouraging the amalgamation of the postal unions, decided to resign as both Secretaries of the Postmen's Federations and the National Joint Committee following a disagreement with the new unions' Executive. Consequently, he chose not to put his name forward as General Secretary of the new Union of Post Office Workers (UPW) and ended his involvement with the Post Office as Secretary of the Sub-Postmaster's Association.

In the following years the Union of Post Office Workers (UPW) went from strength to strength but its growth was not without its difficulties. Whilst many of the smaller organisations joined the UPW, other groups of workers split away and the majority of these were in London. In 1921 a group of West Central sorters led by Joseph Shesgreen formed the Guild of Postal Sorters. It managed to survive independently until 1948 and was able to claim a membership of 3,407 in 1925 declining to 2,443 in 1946. It managed to establish negotiating rights at an office level and was one of the main reasons why separate grade Branches persisted in the London UPW until the 1992 re-organisation. The Guild always remained outside of the Trade Union Congress (TUC) and on occasions associated itself with the Conservative Party. Another London based breakaway organisation was the National Federation of Postal and Telegraph Clerks (NFPTC). It was established in 1921, at a time when the wages of many postal workers was falling behind, as a result of a decline in the cost of living index to which their wages were linked. In 1921 the UPW introduced a strike levy of six pence (6d) per week, which was quite a significant amount at the time. The Union was also taking a strong political stand over a number of high profile international issues. These included support for a national strike to oppose British military intervention against the newly established Soviet Union and a boycott of Hungarian mail in protest against the overthrow of a trade union backed Government by reactionary and conservative forces. The strike levy had been endorsed by the Unions Annual Conference and was supported in a ballot of the members. Some of the Union's Executive warned against introducing the levy at such an inappropriate time but others argued that if it resulted in a smaller membership, then at least they would all be conscious of the Union's policies and prepared to back them. However, it did present those who opposed the Union policies with an opportunity to instigate a split. They aimed their attack, not against the strike policy but the increase in union subscriptions that had recently been introduced.

In January 1921 they held a meeting of 806 sorters in a West End Theatre with delegates from the Eastern District Office (EDO), Western Parcels Office (WPO) and the South West District Offices (SWDO) attending. The London leadership of the Union informed the national Union that in their opinion they would lose up to 40% of their members unless the policy was changed and urged the Executive Council to reverse the policy. On 21 September 1921 the Executive agreed by a narrow majority to suspend the levy. The breakaway group, encouraged by the support that they had received from as far away as Sunderland, Wrexham and Scunthorpe, issued the following statement: 'The Union is the laughing stock of Great Britain. All those who were tired of Communist clowning and Bolshevik buffoonery should come and join us'.

The majority of London postmen remained loyal to the UPW and when it dissolved in 1948 most of the NFPTCs members returned to the UPW. Nevertheless, it existed for almost 30 years and highlighted significant political and industrial differences between the London sorters and the London postmen. These differences emerged again in 1930 when another breakaway group emerged in London. The London postmen were reacting against what they believed was the privileged position of the sorters within the London network. It was called the London Postmen's Association and claimed a membership of 3,354. Its Headquarters was located at 9, Highbury Terrace, Islington and in 1933 it changed its name to the National Association of

Postmen. The Association was openly hostile to the sorters and its journal *The Postmen's Alarm* spent much of its time expressing this view: 'Today the work of the postman and sorter is so interwoven that it is impossible to discern a dividing line, especially in London' they said in the first edition of *The Alarm* in 1930 but by 1940 they had begun to lose members to the UPW and in May 1944 it was wound up.

The amalgamation of unions to form the UPW brought with it a strange and unique political development. Guild Socialism was a largely academic, middle-class theory that developed in the early part of the 20th century as an alternative to state socialism. The idea was originated by Arthur J. Plenty in his book 'Restoration of the Guild System' and the National Guild's League was established in 1915 with the aim of bringing about, 'The abolition of the wage system and the establishment of self-government in industry through a system of National Guilds working in conjunction with the state.' A number of leading members of the Postal and Telegraph Clerks Association (PTCA) came under the influence of an Oxford academic and Guild Socialist called George Douglas Howard Cole. In 1917 he wrote 'Self-Government in Industry' and John Newlove, who was Secretary of the London and Home Counties District of the PTCS, and George Middleton who was the first Editor of *The Post* became strong supporters of his ideas. This tradition was continued by Francis Andrews, Editor of *The Post* in 1931 and Jim Chalmers, who became Editor in 1945. John Newlove was the General Secretary of the PTCS between 1914 and 1917 and during this time other enthusiasts for Guild Socialism joined its Executive. When the UPW was formed some of their ideas were incorporated into the Union's new Rule Book and at the 1921 Annual Conference the Union agreed a proposition that called for 'The organisation of Post Office Workers into a comprehensive industrial union with a view to the service being conducted and managed as a national guild'. They also argued for the election of managers and supervisors, and the Union's Rule Book called for the joint management of the Post Office in conjunction with representatives of the state. Although these ideas did have a number of strong advocates amongst sections of the Union's leadership right up until the 1960s it never gained any noticeable support amongst the Unions rank and file, and despite its advocates controlling the Union's journal for a number of years they failed to convince the membership to support the Guild Socialists ideas. In fact many of the

Union's activists were openly hostile to the ideas of Guild Socialism which they considered were very close to the ideas of fascism. George Lascelles, the first General Secretary of the Postal Clerks Association (UKPCA) remarked in 1943 that: 'It smells too much like the corporate state of Mussolini' and there was some justification for this because closer to home, Sir Oswald Mosley's British Union of Fascists was promoting similar ideas. George Williams, Secretary of the Manchester Branch, remarked during one debate that 'It seems fairly obvious that no capitalist Government would agree to workers control'. But despite this, the argument continued throughout the inter-war years.

The membership must have looked on in bewilderment as the Union debated Guild Socialism whilst unemployment grew, wages fell and war loomed in Europe. Yet the Union continued to argue for these ideas, both within the TUC and the Labour Party, throughout the 1950s and 1960s. It was probably only the termination of the 1970s Post Office experiment in industrial democracy introduced by a Labour Government and ended by the Conservatives that brought the debate to an end. Although it should be noted that the ideas behind the Post Office experiment with Industrial Democracy had little to do with Guild Socialism.

1 Postmen's Federation Christmas Card 1895

2 Postmen's Union membership form

3 William Booth (1840–1907) London
letter carriers leader 1866–1874

4 William Clery (1861–1931) London
sorters leader 1886–1903

5 William Bligh Cheesman (1865–1947)
Fawcett Association leader, Assistant
Secretary UPW

6 George Harold Stuart (Bunning)
(1880–1947) General Secretary
Postmen's Federation

THE OFFICES OF THE UNION OCCUPY THE SUITE OF ROOMS
ON THE SECOND FLOOR

7 Postmen's Union HQ, 2nd Floor, Swinton House, Grays Inn Road WC1

8 Post Office association leaders 1913

9 South East District Office UPW members 1971 strike

10 Tom Jackson UPW General Secretary, Hyde Park UPW rally 1971

11 Dickie Lawlor (1915–1974) London Postmen's Leader and UPW National Officer 1969–1971

12 Front Row (L to R) Dave Percival and Don Fails (ADO) Croydon Branch and London District Council

13 (L ro R) Frank Osie-Tutu, John Taylor, Tom Jackson, Bill Willoughby

14 Speaking Mike Hogan London DO 1983–1990, National Officer 1990–2001

15 Speaking George Durrack Secretary NWDO No. 1 Branch, LDC '3' Committee

16 Speaking Derek Walsh London DO and National Treasurer and (left) Eric Lovett, East London Counters Branch and National Officer

17 Speaking Lionel Sampson Dartford Amal, London DO 1990–1992 and Hughie Bowles (left), Fred Jepson (right)

Chapter 11

THE GENERAL STRIKE 1926

In 1919 the UPW was confronted with the first of a series of events that would seriously test the new union and its leadership. The first of these was a national rail strike called by the National Union of Rail Workers (NUR). The close connection between the rail transport system and the postal service ensured that the Union was very quickly drawn into the dispute. One indication of the political and social tension at the time is illustrated by a statement made by John Bowen, the Union's General Secretary: 'It is quite easy to say that the position as we find it today is one that may easily turn to revolution, but that is beside the point. What we ourselves are particularly concerned with at the moment is how far we can stave off revolution in order to have a more suitable opportunity to fight the workers' cause.'

Bowen was involved in the TUC and Government negotiations to resolve the dispute and had also obtained an assurance from the Post Office that UPW members would not be asked to handle diverted rail traffic. In the event, the dispute was quickly settled; however, it was not long before the Union was facing another serious challenge. In 1921 a dispute between the miners and the coalmine owners led to a lockout. This took place on 15 March 1921 and became known throughout the Labour Movement as 'Black Friday'. The miners were threatened with wage cuts and their opposition to this had led to the employers locking them out. The miners had joined with the Rail and Transport Unions to form the Triple Alliance in 1914. This was an agreement to support each other in the event of an attack by the employers on any one of the unions – however when tested, the other two unions, the National Transport Workers Federation (NTWF) and the National Union of Railwaymen (NUR) felt they were unable to deliver their members. Again the UPW sought and obtained an assurance from the Post Office that they would not be forced to do other workers' jobs and they also collected almost £9,000 from amongst the rank and file postal workers to assist the locked out miners.

The next challenge came in May 1926 when the miners once again found themselves bearing the brunt of the post war economic crisis. This led to the General Strike and although Government workers, including those in the Post Office, were not called upon by the TUC to take industrial action, they provided considerable support to those who were on strike. An Emergency Committee was established and £25,000 collected to support those on strike and another £5,800 was donated from the Unions' central funds. After nine days the TUC called off the strike but the miners, once again faced with wage cuts, continued to fight on for several months.

In the North West London District Office blackleg drivers were ejected from the canteen and a blackleg's vehicle was sabotaged outside the South East London District Office. The North London Branch introduced a 2 shillings per week levy per member to support the miners, although the National Executive had decided against introducing this nationally. The Union experienced a small loss of membership during this period but the vast majority of members supported the mineworkers. At the 1926 Annual Conference a motion attacking the TUC for its 'ignominious surrenders' was moved by the South West London postmen but failed to get a majority.

In the wake of the miners defeat the Union's enemies went on the attack. Some of the management grades used the UPWs support for the miners as an excuse to withdraw from the Whitley Councils. A press campaign, led by *The Daily Telegraph*, a newspaper which fifty years earlier had supported the formation of the Postmen's Federation, sought to prohibit Government workers from affiliation to the TUC and the Labour Party.

In August 1926 Winston Churchill, on behalf of the Conservative Government, announced the Trades Disputes Act. This not only restricted the right of Government workers to strike but also prohibited trade unions from affiliating to any organisation that 'was not confined to persons employed by or under the Government or any federation comprising such organisations' and also prohibited them from affiliating to any organisations that were not confined to other Government workers. This led to a meeting on 1 April 1927 between the UPW General Secretary, John Bowen, and Winston Churchill but following the collapse of the General Strike the meeting had little chance of success and later in the year the Union was forced to disaffiliate from both the TUC and the Labour Party. This had an unusual effect on the Union's relationship with the Labour Party. Rather than end the Union's association, a number of the Union's national figures stood for Parliament and were elected as MPs.

The Union already had a number of full-time officials who were also Members of Parliament.

In 1922 Charles Ammon, the Union's Organising Secretary, had been elected in a by-election as the Member of Parliament for North Camberwell and the Union's Assistant Secretary, Walter Baker, was elected to represent East Bristol in the same year. The Editor of *The Post* George Middleton, was also elected to Parliament in 1922.

However, the big breakthrough in terms of the Union's influence in Parliament came after the forced disaffiliation. The 1929 General Election resulted in a hung Parliament. In fact, the Labour Party had lost the popular vote but gained more seats than the Conservatives and McDonald became Prime Minister for the second time. Amongst the new intake of MPs ranks there were no less than seven MPs, who were either senior officials of the UPW or closely associated with it. These were:

John Bowen – General Secretary

Walter Baker – Assistant Secretary

George Middleton – Editor *The Post*

Charles Ammon – Organising Secretary

Harry Wallace – Outdoor Secretary

Fred Riley – Indoor Secretary

Dr. H.B. Morgan – UPW Medical Advisor

The pioneers of the Post Office trade unions had hoped that an effective block of postal MPs would deliver benefits for the Union and its members. However, there was an alternative view amongst some activists that 'expectations of Labour Party loyalty took precedence over Union loyalty.' This view gained support when the General Secretary, John Bowen, led the Union's MPs into supporting the establishment of the 'May Committee'. When the economic situation deteriorated Philip Snowden, Chancellor of the Exchequer, appointed a committee headed by Sir George May to review the state of public finances. The 'May Committee' produced its report in July 1931 and its recommendations included public sector wage cuts, large cuts in public spending (notably in unemployment benefits) and as a consequence a split in the ranks of the Labour Party developed. The TUC refused to support McDonald and he was defeated in the Cabinet over its implementation and defected to form a coalition 'National Government' with the Conservatives and the Liberals. At the 1931 Annual Conference, the Unions MPs came in for considerable criticism which went as far as one delegate commenting: 'What they had was machinery, a bureaucracy of trade union officials with vested interests and the machine had got them, and the rank and file had to fight for their own salvation'.

In 1932 following the experiences of the previous years, the Union introduced a new rule prohibiting officers from standing for Parliament without the agreement of the Executive.

Bowen was the Unions General Secretary from 1919 to 1936 and interestingly, according to Dr. Andrew Prescott (Centre for Research into Freemasonry at the University of Sheffield) and John Hamill (United Grand Lodge of England) in Labour History Review Vol 71 No 1 April 2006), was a founder member of the New Welcome Lodge and an active Freemason before he entered Parliament. The New Welcome Lodge was created in 1929 at the suggestion of the Prince of Wales (afterwards King Edward VIII) who was concerned at the antagonism between Freemasonry and the Labour Party. It was claimed by some of Herbert Morrison's supporters that the Lodge had considerable influence within the Labour Party during the 1930s and 40s and played a significant role in helping Clement Attlee defeat Herbert Morrison in the battle for the Labour Party leadership.

Since 1915 the wages of all civil servants were linked to what were originally war-time bonus claims and later cost of living claims. These ran alongside normal pay negotiations and were negotiated jointly by the Civil Service unions. Bowen was a staunch defender of this arrangement and even when both management and some of the other unions were arguing for consolidation Bowen opposed this saying that 'He had no hesitation in saying that the Civil Service Cost of Living Bonus Scheme was easily the best in the country and they should, therefore, consider only the possible conditions and consequences of any alteration'. As the financial crisis deepened, inflation turned to deflation and the effect of this was to reduce the pay of civil servants as the price of goods fell. A deal on consolidation was finally agreed in 1932 following negotiations between the heads of the Civil Service and staff side leaders of the National Whitley Council. This was far lower than what had been on offer earlier but given the political and economic crisis it is hardly surprising that when the Union's branches were consulted they reluctantly accepted the deal by 311 votes to 14.

Britain and the world was in the grip of an economic slump but despite this the Post Office accounts showed that profits continued to rise. Wages however, declined for the next three years, both in real terms and as a percentage of Post Office income. Between 1927 and 1937 falling prices resulted in Civil Service cost of living bonuses adversely effecting postal workers pay. Further record profits were reported between 1935 and 1938 but once again this was accompanied by a further decline in pay as a percentage of profit. However in the period between the wars the Union established itself as a national union able to represent and negotiate on behalf of its members at the highest levels. A job as a letter carrier or sorter was relatively well paid and attracted fringe benefits such as pensions and sick pay unavailable to most occupations. In 1939 Europe was once again at war and the large scale of evacuation of children from London was being prepared. The Second World War would result in other landmarks in Post Office history which would have lasting effects on the lives of workers in the industry.

The Second World War and its After Effects 1939-1945

Following the outbreak of the Second World War on 3 September 1939 once again many postal workers joined the forces and a large number of older workers joined the Home Guard. The October 1939 edition of *The London Post* reported the death of the Union National Chairman and Chairman of the London District Council, Jim Halsey, a postman from Streatham. It also reported the efforts of the Union to encourage members of the break-away 'Night Telephonists Guild' to return to the union fold. The looming war dominated the October *Post* and articles by several leading officials, including Fred Woods, the Council Secretary, lamented the political decisions that had devastated the German economy following the Treaty of Versaille leading to the rise of the Nazis and the claims by the national politicians that it had been 'a war to end all wars'. Although supportive of the war effort they were critical of the 'statesmen' who had created the pre-war situation and warned of the need to remain vigilant against attempts by the Government to 'shackle' the trade union movement. They also wrote of their determination to create a fairer, more democratic country once the war was over.

In 1940 the German air force launched the London Blitz and large areas of the capital were laid waste. The Battersea Delivery Office took a direct hit in June 1940 but local deliveries still took place the next day. Mount Pleasant and the City Office were both badly damaged in the same year during a German bombing raid. Staff were trained to take on extra duties connected to the war effort and the auxiliary bomb disposal unit set up at Mount Pleasant earned a commendation from the commanding officer of the Royal Engineers for their efforts during the war. On 16 October 1940 a high-explosive bomb fell on Farringdon Road causing the road to collapse and leaving the parcel block yard impassable. As the war progressed the debates in *The Post* on how post-war Britain should be governed intensified. Letters from serving soldiers were published which showed the changes in ideas that were taking place amongst the soldiers. A postman from ECDO serving with the British Expeditionary Force wrote in the March 1940 edition of *The Post*: 'Where I am at present we have made real pals out of a few French 'solders'. I often wonder whilst we are laughing and joking together, trying to air our (somewhat limited) knowledge of the opposite languages, how is it that the ordinary people of the world, of all nations, are ever downright mugs as to want to be at each other's throats every few years. I believe the common people of this world of ours can and must prevent this sort of thing'.

The paper also reported that one regiment had so many UPW members that they had formed a Branch and their Secretary had made written representation to their Commanding Officer on behalf of the Union members. Other articles on 'The Ultimate Goal – Trade Unions in War Time' written by Ron Smith and 'The Job Ahead' by Ron Wood who was elected National Chairman in 1940 covered similar themes. The paper also reported that a resolution to suspend the Unions Annual Conferences for the duration of the war failed to get a seconder at the 1940 Annual Conference in Blackpool. In 1941/2 the District Council elected Dorothy Pearce as their 'Madam Chairman', G.A. Stevenson as Secretary, and Ron Smith as the Editor of *The Post*. As the war progressed articles appeared supporting equal pay for women, opposing the introduction of 'Scientific Management Techniques' and expressing concern at the rising level of part-time staff. On 18 June 1943 the Parcel Section building was completely destroyed by a single bomb which caused a fierce fire setting the whole building ablaze. The fire raged for four hours and two members of staff were killed and another 34 injured. Almost the entire building was gutted and 77,000 parcels destroyed.

Winston Churchill brought Trade Union and Labour Party leaders into his War Cabinet in May 1940. Once again the industry increased the number of women and temporaries employed because of the effects of conscription into the Armed Forces. Bargaining continued to be conducted through the Whitley Councils and all Government workers secured pay increases from the re-introduction of 'Wartime Bonuses'. The changes taking place amongst the membership began to have an effect on the Union's policies and at the 1942 wartime Annual Conference a resolution was passed, against the recommendation of the Executive, which called for equal pay for women and full adult pay rate at the age of twenty one.

In 1944/45 the Post Office's combined profits reached a record of almost £40 million and the Union's 1944 Conference proposed a substantial pay claim for both established staff and the war time temporaries.

Throughout the inter-war years the Union had achieved improvements in pay and conditions through the National Whitley Council and the Government established Arbitration Boards. Since the First World War pay and conditions in the Post Office were negotiated either through some kind of arbitration with reference and comparisons to 'outside' industries or the Whitley Councils. In the 1930s the 'Tomlin Formula' was the method used to establish comparisons and in the 1950s it was the 'Priestly Formula'. Priestly was the Head of a Royal Commission on Civil Service Pay. The 'Formula' was based on a comparison between Government workers pay and the pay of broadly comparable workers in the private sector. Inevitably, this led to disagreements, with the employer choosing the lower end of the labour market and the unions going for the pay of more skilled workers.

Following the Second World War the industry moved away from arbitration, Royal Commissions and Whitley Council towards more traditional wage bargaining. This was an inevitable consequence of the change in the Post Office's role from a cash generating department of the Civil Service to a state owned limited company and like the changes introduced a hundred years earlier it would have an effect on industrial relations. The UPW would be forced by the changing circumstances to flex its industrial muscles rather than relying on political lobbying, influencing commissions of enquiry and arbitration panels to achieve its objectives. In 1949 and 1951 postal workers' pay was still settled by arbitration and in 1952 the National Whitley Council was the vehicle used to resolve the pay negotiations, but in 1954/55 straightforward pay negotiations were used for the first time. Since the middle of the 19th century the Post Office had been a source of revenue for successive Governments, pumping millions of pounds into the Treasury, effectively subsidising taxation, and at the same time providing a world class, comprehensive communications service nationwide. In 1957 the Post Office was only able to pay £5 million into the Treasury. In September of the same year a major international financial crisis resulted in a reduction in Post Office income and the business produced its first loss for thirty five years. In 1962 a new period of industrial relations began that forced the UPW to adopt a more confrontational industrial stance in its dealings with the employer.

Post War Britain and the London Postal Workers 1945-1960

The post war changes caused considerable difficulties for the Post Office. British industry began to transfer production back to peace time needs and the demand for labour grew at the same time. This resulted in significant recruitment problems, particularly in the London area. At the same time Post Office profits declined, postal traffic increased from 7,600 million items in 1947/8 to 9,000 million in 1957/8, and wages as a percentage of revenue increased. In the pre-war years the Post Office had relied heavily on part-time workers but in the post war period they were proving difficult to recruit and retain because of full employment. The situation was made more difficult as a result of the increase to the school leaving age and other educational reforms. Before the war the Post Office had the pick of those working class 14 year old school leavers looking for a secure, reasonably well paid job with sickness and holiday benefits. In the post war years the terms and conditions of workers across British industry improved, making employment in the Post Office less attractive. Furthermore, many pupils stayed on longer at school and for the first time an increasing number of working class youngsters had the opportunity to go to university. A job in the Post Office was a less attractive job than it had been in the pre-war years.

In the 1920s and 1930s Post Office management had deliberately encouraged the break-away unions but this changed after the war. The post war ethos supported by the Labour Party encouraged the recognition of trade unions. The Post Office began to accept that the continuation of fragmented and separate unions led to confusing and difficult negotiations. In 1945 when the Labour Party won a landslide victory over Winston Churchill's Conservative Party, Clement Atlee became the first Labour Prime Minister to have a working majority and enjoyed a great deal of sympathy amongst trade unionists.

Charles Geddes replaced Thomas Hodgson in 1944 to become the Union's third General Secretary. Throughout his term in office he was an uncompromising anti-communist at a time when communists were very influential in certain sections of the Labour Movement. Geddes was born in 1897 in Deptford, South London, had left school at 13, was the son of a postman and joined the Post Office as a boy messenger in 1911. He later went on to become a telegraphist and an activist in the UPW. In 1946 he joined the TUC General Council.

In 1949 a financial crisis resulted in Sir Stafford Cripps devaluing the pound and when Cripps managed to persuade the TUC to accept the policy, Geddes, who was a loyal supporter of the Labour Party, convinced the Union to go along with a period of pay restraint. This did not last for long and by the 1950 Conference the Union's mood had begun to change. In December 1950 the Union lodged a claim which included a substantial pay increase for all UPW represented grades. Three months later the Post Office made their first pay offer which fell well short of the Union's expectations. When the offer was put to members it was rejected by Branches representing 91,000 members and accepted by Branches representing only 7,000 members. Although it included a larger increase for London than for the rest of the country, the first sign of organised opposition against the pay offer came from the capital. On 17 April 1951 an unofficial work to rule began at both the West Central and Eastern District offices. In an attempt to defuse the growing unrest the Executive referred the claim to arbitration but the London District Council (LDC) had already made a decision to spread the action across the district and on 25 April Mount Pleasant walked out on unofficial strike. Although the LDC was willing to reconsider their decision, other London offices also walked out and the dispute spread to Leeds where there was also a walk out. Although the Council made attempts to call off the action, a mass meeting at Mount Pleasant on 2 May voted to continue the strike. In an attempt to get the situation under control the Executive called a mass meeting on 3 May at Central Hall Westminster which was attended by over 8,000 London UPW members.

Geddes efforts to convince the strikers to return to work was greeted by such a barrage of booing and shouting that he was unable to get himself heard for twenty minutes. Les Morgan, who was the LDC Secretary between 1955 and 1965, tried to calm the situation down but he was also unable to make himself heard. The unofficial action had an almost immediate impact on the negotiations with Geddes using all his influence to speed up the arbitration process and within two weeks the Court had met to consider the claim and after five days published their findings. They proposed an increase considerably more than the management's offer. For the majority of staff it amounted to a 6.8% increase and it also went some way to meeting the Union's claim in other areas including improvements to pay differentials based on age. The award was backdated to January 1951 and in general it was considered a good deal by the members.

In October 1951 a Conservative Government won the General Election and Winston Churchill became Prime Minister again. The post war Labour Party had to deal with the difficult task of reconstruction and although they gained more votes than the Conservatives, they ended up with less MPs. Labour had adopted a 'hands on' approach to the economy and the Conservatives promised to adopt a different approach, with tax cuts, less Government expenditure and less interference in public sector pay negotiations. Although industrial relations over the next few years remained relatively calm, by the time of the Union's 1953 Conference the picture was beginning to change.

A new generation of Union activists was emerging; many of whom were fresh from service in the Armed Forces and this was beginning to have an effect on the Union. Prominent amongst these was London postman, Jeremiah Richard (Dickie) Lawlor.

Lawlor was born in 1915 and was brought up in the Elephant and Castle area of South London. He was the son of a postman who had worked at the

South West London District Office for forty years and who had also been an active member of the Postmen's Federation before the formation of the UPW. Lawlor's father was a veteran of the First World War, and Dickie Lawlor had been a front-line soldier during the Second World War who had seen military action in many countries across Europe. He had begun work as a boy messenger in 1930 and returned to work at the London West Central Office when he was demobbed from the Army. Like many of his contemporaries he was determined to improve the lives of working people and almost immediately became a UPW activist. He became Branch Secretary of the WCDO No. 1 Branch in 1947 and in 1951 he was elected to the London District Council. Later in the year he became Assistant District Officer (ADO) LDC 3 Council and played a leading role in the 1951 pay dispute which brought him to the attention of the UPW General Secretary, Charles Geddes. Lawlor was a member of the Communist Party and Geddes accused him of putting his political views above those of the UPW membership but despite the attacks he remained a popular figure and withstood all the attempts by the union's leadership to have him removed from office.

In the period between 1951 and 1955 pay remained at the top of the UPWs agenda. The 1953 Conference held a long debate on pay but finally they agreed to refer the issue to arbitration. However the tribunal's award was not as well accepted as in previous years and the LDC called for a 'work to rule'. In 1954 a new claim was submitted and although there were some calls for strike action the Union's Bournemouth Conference voted to accept the offer. Some progress on pay was made in 1956 but the view was growing that postal workers pay was falling behind workers in other industries and the discontent was growing.

In May 1955 the Conservatives were returned to power with an increased majority. Earl de la Warr, who had been a Minister in the first Labour Government and had been appointed Postmaster General by Churchill in 1951 was replaced by Charles Hill in April 1955. Inflation was increasing and the Government commissioned Sir Raymond Priestley to produce a report on the future of the Civil Service, which was published in 1955. This marked the first step towards a new business model when the Post Office was removed from the direct financial control of the Treasury and long term financial targets for the industry established. The Geddes era was coming to an end. He was finding it increasingly difficult to deal with the changes taking place in the industry and at the 1956 Conference he was replaced by Ron Smith. In 1957 Geddes received a knighthood and at the age of 60 took up a number of posts including membership of the Governments Economic Planning Board, the London Transport Board and the Atomic Energy Authority and in 1958 he was elevated to a life peerage in the House of Lords where he remained until his death in 1983.

A new generation of Union activists were emerging who were prepared to confront the challenges of the post war period. Ron Smith rode to power on the back of this discontent. Smith was a Londoner born in 1915 and had followed his father into Post Office employment. He was Chairman of the Travelling Post Office Branch (TPO) and rose to prominence through the London District Council where he served as Assistant Secretary and Editor of *The London Post*.

After the war the Post Office wanted to change the grading system which was a particular problem in London where it had not changed since the Tweedmouth Inquiry in 1897. Their plan included the elimination of all the London specialist grades and the introduction of the new Postman Higher Grade (PHG). Ron Smith, on behalf of the London District Council, argued at the 1945 Annual Conference that the Union should not agree to any changes whilst many of those most affected were still serving in the forces. Smith was elected to the Union's Executive in 1945 and the grading changes, which included considerable improvements to pay, were introduced in 1946. He became General Treasurer in 1953 and replaced Geddes as General Secretary in 1956.

Smith, like Geddes, was an enthusiastic opponent of communism and the Communist's influence in the UPW. Nevertheless, Lawlor and others continued to have a significant effect on the Union's policies.

The Priestley Report was published in November 1955 and almost immediately the UPW's Executive had to deal with the consequences of the reports' recommendations. Although the report was aimed at the Civil Service overall, it dealt with a number of issues specific to the Post Office. In particular pay, working hours, holidays and pensions were affected. The Union had made its own detailed submissions on these issues, but when the report appeared it was a disappointment to the Union. The Government and the employers' side of the Whitley Council moved quickly to accept the recommendations and they referred the outstanding pay issues to the newly established Civil Service Pay Research Unit with the condition that the package could only be accepted or rejected as a whole. The report recommended a reduction in the working week and working hours but little else and although a great deal of dissatisfaction remained, that year's Annual Conference in Margate cautiously accepted Priestley's recommendations. Priestley's report recommended the replacement of arbitration with the introduction of traditional wage bargaining and although negotiations continued to be conducted through the Whitley Council, it represented a significant shift in industrial relations. Negotiations continued throughout the year and by the 1957 Annual Conference a package on pay and working hours had been agreed. This deal represented the most significant improvement to pay and conditions since the 1946 Re-Allocation Agreement. It also achieved the first reduction in hours since the beginning of the century and Smith was brought to his feet by the applause of the Conference delegates.

The euphoria did not last for long and when the agreement was implemented a number of problems arose, particularly in London. In many offices there were long standing local agreements which provided extra 'unofficial' tea breaks and when management used the 1957 Agreement as a pretext to remove these, UPW members in West Central, East Central and Mount Pleasant took industrial action that disrupted the mail for several days. This resulted in the tea breaks being restored but it also drew the accusation from the Executive Council that London was breaching the Unions national policy. The increase in unofficial industrial action in the London area during the early 1950s made it clear that LDC 3 was beginning to challenge the strategy that the national Union was following. In past conflicts between London and the national Union this had led to divisions and break-away organisations but the post war generation of activists were not interested in that kind of action and were very careful to conduct their activities within the rules and structures of the Union.

The 1958 Conference agreed to submit a further claim for a shorter working week. The Post Office responded by arguing that this had been dealt with in 1957 and although a joint Post Office/UPW Joint Working Group was set up to look at the issue, little progress was made. This resulted in growing frustration amongst London activists and an LDC meeting made a decision to launch a campaign to build support for industrial action. This took place on 25 November 1958 at Central Hall, Westminster and although Ron Smith was invited to address the meeting, on the instruction of the Executive, he did not attend. Dickie Lawlor addressed the 2,700 strong meeting and announced that a demonstration and march to the Union's Headquarters in Clapham would take place on 26 November. Over a thousand, mainly London members, marched through Clapham to hand in a petition to the General Secretary. This increased the tension and resulted in a predictably hostile response from the national Union. Norman Stagg, Editor of *The Post*, wrote an article condemning the 'Wreckers and Communists' behind the demonstration and in response *The Post* was inundated with letters to the Editor opposing Stagg's views. One 'Conservative trade unionist' commented that he expected the leadership 'to be more enlightened than to resort to digging up the Communist skeleton' in order to attack their opponents.

The internal debates and disagreements on how best to achieve the Union's objectives continued throughout the late 1950s and in 1960 the Unions Annual Conference agreed a proposition instructing the Executive to submit a claim 'for an increase in wages'. Following protracted negotiations that took place throughout the following year, a package covering pay and conditions was put to the Union's 1961 Conference which against all predictions was rejected by the delegates. The Conference also agreed a proposition that gave the Executive the authority to call a strike, should this be necessary, and following the Conference the Union submitted a new pay claim. However, the timing could not have been worse because only two days earlier the Conservative Government had announced a pay freeze for all Government workers, placing the UPW at the forefront of a trade union confrontation with the Conservatives. In October 1961 the Post Office announced their rejection of the Union's claim and for the first time in many years rejected the Union's offer of arbitration on the basis that they could not infringe the Government's pay freeze. In response the Union announced a programme of industrial action which involved a 'work to rule and the withdrawal of good will'. Once the action began delayed mail started to build up in sorting offices throughout the country and a Gallup Poll conducted by a national newspaper showed considerable support for the Union amongst the public even though there was considerable disruption and delay to deliveries.

In an attempt to break the deadlock the Union proposed arbitration and Reginald Bevins, the Postmaster General, responded by accepting the offer, but on the basis that any resulting deal would not be backdated. In talks with the Union Bevins indicated that the pay freeze would be over by the following March and it was on this basis that Smith managed by a majority of 15 to 12 to convince the Executive to call off the action. Although the decision was accepted by the majority of Branches, an unofficial stoppage took place at the Western District Office in protest at the Executives decision.

Negotiations began on 8 February 1962 and in April management offered an increase of 2 per cent. This was rejected and on the casting vote of the Chairman the Executive agreed to refer the claim to arbitration. The Union's case was based on the argument that since 1956 their member's pay had fallen behind the general pay increases in the country as a whole. Management responded by arguing that the Union's claim would increase the general rate of inflation and as such they could not improve the offer. However in June the Tribunal made an award of 4% which was closer to the Union's claim than the Post Office offer. The increase was accepted and the view was that under difficult circumstances the Union had conducted a good campaign that represented a significant breach of the Governments attempts to hold down wages. It was generally felt that the campaign had been a success despite the fact that it was less than that achieved by other groups of workers and was below the cost of living increases.

Although the Conservatives had promised before the election that they would intervene less in the economy, in practice this was not the case and their policies damaged the industry in a number of ways. In 1956 the Post Office was committed to providing the Treasury with a fixed amount of revenue each year but this changed in 1961 when they were required to increase this to a fixed percentage of their total assets. In 1961 the Post Office introduced a pay freeze which not only eroded the position of postal workers in the earnings tables but also damaged the industry's ability to attract and retain staff. Whilst the Government was able to have some control over public sector pay, in the private sector this was more difficult. Recruiting staff became more difficult because of relatively low basic pay and this was often overcome by a heavy reliance on overtime. Attempts to increase part time and casual labour attracted considerable opposition, particularly in London.

During the same period the Post Office went from making a profit to making a loss and at the same time productivity fell and postal workers experienced a relative fall in their pay and conditions. After many years of almost uninterrupted profit and investment, the Post Office entered a period of financial loss and lower productivity. The failed policies of the Conservative Government had long term consequences for the Post Office and also for industrial relations in the industry.

Chapter 12

THE 1964 STRIKE
– DICKIE LAWLOR AND RON SMITH

The Post Office continued to suffer from the failed policies that had troubled it since the end of the war as both Conservative and Labour Governments attempted to regulate the economy through prices and incomes policies which in the Post Office's case resulted in under-investment, recruitment and retention difficulties and low productivity. Postal worker's pay declined in comparison to workers in similar occupations and this came to a head in June 1963 when the Union presented its pay claim for postmen and PHGs. The Post Office referred the claim to the Arbitration Court which, much to the disappointment of the Union, recommended an increase of 2%.

Throughout the Trade Union Movement the tide was turning against prices and incomes policies and Ron Smith, who was an advocate of economic planning and had even served on the Government's National Economic Development Council, found himself coming under increasing pressure. On 23 December 1963 the Union lodged another pay claim. Negotiations began in January 1964 and although the Post Office made an improved offer, this was on condition that the Union accepted a four year pay package. A Special Wages Conference in February 1964 rejected this which resulted in the Post Office making a slightly improved deal, which was also rejected. With the pressure mounting for industrial action and the Government keen to avoid a dispute, Bevins agreed to another meeting with the Union which was also attended by Reginald Maudling, the Chancellor of the Exchequer but despite this no progress was made. The Union's Executive Council responded by calling, for the first time in its history, an official strike of its postal members on 16 April 1964.

Further negotiations took place but once again the talks broke down. The Union argued that a fair pay comparison for postmen and PHGs was with skilled manual workers, but the Post Office insisted that the comparison should be with workers further down the national pay scale and it looked as if a strike was inevitable. However with only three days to go Maudling contacted the Union with an offer to establish a Special Committee to look at the comparability issue and produce a report to resolve the dispute. At a mass meeting held at the Albert Hall, 7,000 UPW members were informed by the leadership that they had achieved an historic victory and the industry action was called off.

The Special Committee was chaired by Arthur Llewellyn Armitage, President of Queen's College Cambridge and included amongst its members Vic Feather, Assistant Secretary of the Trades Union Congress. The Government asked the Committee to provide an interpretation of a particular section of the 1955 Priestley Report which dealt with the issue of 'pay comparability'. However whilst the Committee was sitting the Government imposed a 4% ceiling on pay increases. When the report was published on 11 June, although its recommendation on 'pay comparability' was closer to the Union's than the Post Office's, its outcome was undermined by the Government's pay policy.

Union members across the country felt let down by the outcome and having been promised an historic victory at the Albert Hall meeting, Branches called on the Executive to implement the strike decision. Meetings in London and elsewhere were called and an unofficial walk-out occurred in West London at the Paddington and Hammersmith offices. On Friday 10 July when a meeting was due to take place between the Union and management at Post Office Headquarters, over 2,000 UPW members walked out at Mount Pleasant and, following in the footsteps of their predecessors, marched along the Farringdon Road to St. Martins le Grande. A large, noisy and angry crowd had assembled outside the building and the police, fearing that the situation might get out of control, asked Ron Smith to address the crowd in an attempt to calm the situation down. In fact, it had the opposite effect and Ron Smith was unable to make himself heard. The several thousand postal workers were in no mood to listen and confronted with a wall of booing and shouting, the General Secretary was forced to retreat into the building with the assistance of half a dozen City of London police officers.

That evening several other offices across the country staged unofficial strikes when UPW members in Birmingham, Crawley, St. Helens and Wolverhampton ignored the advice of the national leadership and walked out. Following a mass meeting and a unanimous vote for action, the night shift at London's East Central District Office (ECDO) walked and by Monday morning most of London's postmen and PHGs were involved in some kind of unofficial industrial action. Hardly a city in the country was still working by Tuesday 14 July. Management decided to take a hard line and issued a notice at the Mount Pleasant office threatening the strikers with discipline, loss of overtime and the possibility of prosecution for 'those officers who deserted their posts'. This had the opposite effect to that intended and by the end of the day the remaining shifts had joined the dispute. The Executive were becoming increasingly concerned that they were losing control of the situation and called a one day official strike for 16 July. They also sent two Executive council members, Tom Jackson and Ray Dobson, to address a mass meeting at Mount Pleasant in an attempt to convince the strikers to go back to work. They were unsuccessful and despite Jackson warning the meeting that they were 'degenerating into a rabble' they refused to return to work until after the official stoppage on 16 July.

On 15 July Maudling made a last ditch attempt to avert the official dispute set for the next day. He contacted Smith and offered to resolve the dispute by referring the issue back to the Armitage Committee. This was rejected by the Executive Council, who even if they had wanted to accept the offer, probably calculated that with the momentum built up by the unofficial action there was little chance of avoiding the official strike at that late stage. It is also likely that they saw the official strike as an opportunity for the national leadership to regain the initiative from the District and Branch leaderships that had already spread the dispute around the country. The strike on 16 July was well supported with only a small minority turning up for work. The London District Council organised a rally on the day of the strike and the London evening papers reported that 20,000 postal workers from all over the capital marched in the blazing heat to hear their London leadership address the Hyde Park meeting. The following day there was an orderly and disciplined return to work with Smith and the Executive placing themselves back in control of the dispute.

Support for the striker was strong not only amongst other trade unionists but the general public as well. Within a few days over £300,000 pounds had been pledged by other Unions to support the dispute. George Woodcock, General Secretary of the TUC, offered his services as a conciliator and Ron Smith complained in the national press that his position as a moderate trade union leader was being undermined by the intransigent attitude of Post Office management and the Government. On 17 July the Guardian reported him saying 'We have seen the gradual destruction of a moderate, sensible trade union leadership. That is what Mr. Bevins (Postmaster General) does not understand he has done over the last 18 months.' The following day the same newspaper reported Smith commenting, 'If some people think I am 'Jack Easy' and can be kicked around, then I will have to change my approach'. A large section of the membership began calling for further industrial action and at the next meeting of the Executive Smith decided to go onto the offensive. He proposed that the Union call 'an indefinite strike from midnight on 25 July 1964' and the Executive, although surprised at his move, gave him their unanimous support. It was clearly designed to not only put the Post Office and the Government under increased pressure, but also his own critics within the Union. This move produced a significant turning point in the dispute and within hours of its announcement the Government was preparing to make concessions. An improved offer, above the 4% pay limit, was put on the table and in discussions involving representatives of the TUC and the Government, an increase of somewhere between 5% and 7% began to emerge. The offer was conditional on the indefinite strike being called off and this was agreed by the Executive Council.

When the offer finally emerged it was a 6.5% increase which represented a major breakthrough, not just for the UPW, but for the entire trade union movements campaign against pay restraint and pay limits. It also made a significant contribution to the defeat, some months later, of the Conservative Government and the election of Harold Wilson's first Labour Government.

The Conservative Party had held power for 13 years since 1951. They had used wage freezes and pay restraint as an important part of their post-war economic strategy. Labour was elected with an overall majority of just four and under the slogan of building 'The New Britain' – mobilising the resources of technology under a national plan, harnessing our national wealth of brains and our genius for scientific invention and medical discovery'. Significantly they were not committed to pay restraint as a part of their proposed economic strategy and this assisted with the on-going pay negotiations that were taking place with the UPW. The Union was still looking for a substantial improvement in pay and they had added to this a two hour reduction in the working week. The pay research survey, which had been part of the earlier negotiations, was recommending that both sides should agree a three or four year deal. These were becoming increasingly common in other parts of the public sector and this brought the Union for the first time into face to face talks with the new Postmaster General Tony Benn. The discussions resulted in a three year deal, which incorporated the 6.5% already agreed, a further 4% in January 1965 and 3.5% in January 1966. It also included restrictions on the employment of part-time workers and changes to the household delivery arrangements. The deal was accepted by the Union's 1965 Conference, although some branches including some from London voted to reject it.

The recruitment problems in London that had existed since the 1950s continued into the 1960s and the 1964 pay package did little to relieve the difficulties in the capital. Unofficial industrial action became more common during this period and the rift between the London District Council and the national leadership became more pronounced. Since the 1950s the District Council had been challenging the direction in which the leadership was taking the Union and Dickie Lawlor, Secretary of LDC 3, even went as far as to challenge, in a pamphlet entitled 'Reform or Surgery', whether the principle of amalgamation established in 1919' had been a success. Lawlor had been the subject of a number of verbal attacks from both Ron Smith and his predecessor, Charles Geddes both as the leader of the London membership and because of his membership of the Communist Party. The Communist Party of Great Britain was a well organised and active political force in the 1950s and 1960s which had members who were key activists in many trade unions, particularly amongst manual workers in mining, manufacturing and transport. Their main support was not at national level, but at the intermediate level, amongst shop stewards, local representatives and branch officers and committees.

In London dockworkers, engineers, print workers, power workers and the building trade all had a strong Communist Party influence. Although relatively small numerically, they were capable of challenging both the leadership of the unions and the employers in most industries. Lawlor came from that tradition and he had a significant number of political allies in the UPW at all levels. However, it would be wrong to believe that he could influence the London postal workers unless genuine grievances and problems really existed. Lawlor was able to articulate their complaints and gain their support for the policies agreed by the London District Council and it is clear that the unrest in London had more complex causes than the politics of a few of its leaders.

On Sunday 24 November 1963 during the build-up to the 1964 dispute the London District Council had called a mass meeting in Trafalgar Square. The officers of the Council addressed over 4,000 postal workers from London and elsewhere. Although they were very careful not to attack the Union's national leadership, the following day an article appeared in the Guardian, attributed to an unnamed senior national union official criticising London's decision to organise the rally. This raised the temperature considerably and it took a face to face meeting between the London officials and national officials to calm the situation down.

Discontent over pay, household delivery arrangements and the level of part-time workers continued to cause unrest and during the following few months unofficial industrial action affected several areas of the capital. The London officials felt they had worked hard to resolve these problems but their views were often ignored because of the political tensions between Lawlor and Smith. This came to a head in August 1964 when management informed the Union that they intended to introduce part-time labour into the London offices despite the understanding reached in 1962 that they would not do so. The failure of previous pay deals to resolve the issue of the higher cost of living in the capital and the long-term effects of wage freezes and pay restraint had resulted in a situation where the London postmen had become reliant on a very high level of overtime. Opposition to part-time workers was strong because they felt this restricted their access to the overtime that was necessary to supplement their relatively low basic pay and they also argued, with some justification, that many of the part-time workers had jobs elsewhere.

Following a meeting of the LDC 3 Committee on 15 September, and the later endorsement of the full Council 3, Lawlor advised the London branches not to co-operate with the introduction of further part-timers and introduced a district wide ban on overtime. A conflict with the national leadership became inevitable when the General Secretary, Ron Smith, told LDC 3 that they should agree the part-timers and that the overtime ban was against the rules of the Union, because only the Executive Council had the right to call industrial action.

The London officials believed that if management accepted their alternative proposals to allow Post Office counter clerks and administration clerks to work overtime in the sorting offices and also to plan diversions of work between offices, then the dispute could be averted and they refused to call off the overtime ban. Ron Smith saw this as a direct challenge to the authority of the Executive Council and at a meeting held on 24 September 1964 he proposed to the Executive that the leaders of LDC 3 be expelled from the Union. This was agreed with only three members opposing the proposition including Willie Failes who asked for his dissent to be recorded and Maurice Styles, who was a member of the Executive and Assistant Secretary of LDC3, who took no part in the discussions, both were members of the Communist Party. Those expelled were LDC3 Chairman Harry Jones, Secretary Dickie Lawlor, Assistant Secretary Maurice Styles and three Committee members, J.R. Cooper, C. Kirk and J.P. Regan. These events took place in the three weeks preceding the 1964 General Election. Smith felt he was in a strong position following the success of the pay campaign earlier that year and as a Labour Party loyalist may have felt that a dispute, so close to the election, would damage Labour chances.

The Executive took over the responsibilities of the London District Council and negotiated an agreement to introduce a limited level of part-timer duties. These would be used to handle the extra election traffic and, in return, the household delivery service would be suspended. Support for the expelled London officials was strong in the capital and this was re-enforced when Tony Clarke and Harry Klein, the only two members of the Committee not to be expelled, issued a statement supporting their colleagues. Branches passed resolutions calling for the reinstatement of the six London leaders. A delegation of London Branch officials met with Ron Smith in an effort to resolve the dispute, whilst five of the six who had been expelled were preparing a High Court challenge to the Executive's decision. Harry Jones preferred to take his appeal direct to the Executive Council rather than take the case to the High Court.

On 20 October Bernard Caulfield QC, presented the case on behalf of the five London officials at the High Court in the Strand. Caulfield argued his case before Justice Ungoed Thomas claiming that the five had been denied natural justice because they had not been given an opportunity to defend themselves. After deliberating for several days Justice Thomas issued a writ on 29 October ordering the Union to not only reinstate their membership but to also reinstate their credentials as officers of the Union. The five were only able to bring the case to court with the financial support of the London membership who had held collections to raise the cost of the legal representation. The court case however did not resolve the rift between London and the national union which continued into the next year. Ron Smith and the Executive continued to insist that under the rules of the Union only they had a right to initiate industrial action and the threat of further disciplinary action against the London officials still remained a possibility. Their support in London continued and this was demonstrated when Maurice Styles beat LDC Chairman, Denis Douglas in an election in March 1965. Douglas had not involved himself in the dispute and this contributed to his removal as Chairman.

Both sides recognised that a lengthy and legal battle was not in anyone's interest. Intermediaries worked in the background to bring the two sides together and a Special Branch Circular was despatched in March 1965 informing Branches that the Union did not intend to take any further action. However, it went on to say that the Executive would be submitting a lengthy report to a Special Conference in May seeking endorsement of their position. At the Conference Ron Smith launched a scathing attack on the London leadership accusing them of acting like 'Sawdust Caesars ranting through UPW House followed by their minions trying to intimidate people who had been entrusted by this Conference with carrying out a task on their behalf.' He referred to 'Lynch Parties' and following a lengthy and heated debate the Conference overwhelmingly supported the Executive Council's proposition.

These events had a lasting effect on the Union and although they lost the debate, a number of London officials went on to be elected to senior positions in the Union in the following years. Ron Smith retired in 1966 and was replaced by Tom Jackson. Dickie Lawlor was elected Assistant Secretary in 1969 and in 1972 Maurice Styles became Outdoor Assistant Secretary. In 1980 Harry Jones was elected to the position of Assistant Secretary and in 1982 Tony

Clarke became Deputy General Secretary. Many of those considered to be dissidents and political outsiders in the 1950s and 60s became leaders of the Union including Willie Failes, a Communist and close ally of Dickie Lawlor who became Outdoor Assistant Secretary in 1967. These changes represented a significant change in the political and industrial outlook of the Union.

Changes in the status of the Post Office also occurred during this period. Investment levels in the industry increased between 1964 and 1971, from £187 million to £460 million. More flexibility in pricing was also allowed and this resulted in a three year period of profit between 1964 and 1967. Two significant reports were commissioned during this period. These were the Fulton Committee Report and the McKinsey Report. Some observers believe that it was the McKinsey Report, which was never actually published, that paved the way for the separation of the industry into three separate businesses, postal, telecoms and counters. The instrument used to remove the Post Office from the Civil Service was the 1966 Select Committee on Nationalised Industries. The report was commissioned by the Wilson Government in 1966 and published in 1967.

That year the Government published a White Paper which proposed dividing the industry into three separate business centres. It also proposed that the organisation would cease to be a department of the Civil Service and become a public corporation. At the time there was little opposition to this move from the Union. Although the Union's leadership were fully committed to supporting the Wilson Government, which held power between 1964 and 1970, this did not stop several official and unofficial disputes taking place during this period. These disputes did not involve the uniformed postal grades but the postal and telegraph officers in 1968 and the overseas telegraphists in 1969. However, the Union's relationship with the Labour Party did come under increased pressure over the issues of incomes policy and trade union legislation when Barbara Castle published her White Paper 'In Place of Strife' in 1969.

Chapter 13

THE 1969 POST OFFICE ACT
AND THE 1971 DISPUTE

The 1969 Post Office Act had far reaching consequences for the industry and its workers' pensions entitlements. Since the 19th century postal workers had been conscious of the need for decent pensions. When the Post Office ceased to be part of the Civil Service the Post Office Staff Superannuation Scheme (POSS) was established. Previously the pensions of Post Office staff were funded from the Exchequer. As far back as 1913 the department's accounts were required to reflect a 'notional' pension's provision at the same cost that was required to support a funded scheme. Full valuations took place every so often, apart from the period of the Second World War.

In 1956 there was a change in the relationship between the Post Office and the Treasury. Prior to 1956 the Post Office was expected to provide an income for the Government. After 1956 they were expected to produce only the income needed to cover their own expenditure plus £5 million in lieu of taxation. In 1961 as a result of the Post Office Act the accounts of the Post Office were separated from those of the Treasury. At the same time the Post Office was required to move from a 'notional' pension's contribution to a real contribution. In December 1962 the Government's Actuary reported £165 million in the hypothetical fund. Following this the business was required to make an additional payment of £12 million for sixteen years over and above the normal contribution.

In 1966 discussions began between the Government and the Post Office on the future of the pension scheme and in 1967 discussions between the Post Office and the UPW on the future of their member's pensions began. These were led for the Union by Norman Stagg, Deputy General Secretary, and Billy Marshall, the Union's Legal and Medical Assistant Secretary. There were a number of similarities between what the Union was trying to achieve in its negotiations with the Post Office and what the Post Office was trying to achieve in theirs with the Government.

The Union wanted a scheme that would be managed by a board of independent trustees, of which 50% would be nominated by the Trade Unions. They also argued for improved family and widows benefits and cost of living increases linked to the Retail Price Index (RPI). There were significant differences on the issue of the retirement age with management arguing that male members of the Scheme should retire at 65 not the existing age of 60. This was opposed not just by the UPW but by all the unions in the industry. The Unions jointly mounted a very effective political campaign with their sponsored MPs raising the issue in Parliament. Finally, Edward Short the Postmaster General, conceded the point and the retirement age remained at 60 for both men and women.

The discussions between the Post Office and the Treasury were concluded with the passing of the Post Office Act 1969. The Post Office was finally launched as a public corporation with the business reluctantly having to accept responsibility for the pre-corporation deficiency. Consequently, the Post Office Superannuation Scheme (POSS) began life with a deficit that the actuaries reported as £604 million. The Union had made good progress with its pensions negotiations when, in 1970, Ted Heath won a surprise victory for the Conservatives and Christopher Chataway replaced John Stonehouse as Postmaster General. Chataway objected to a number of points already agreed with the previous administration. These included the right to an annual pensions review, the right of 60 year old employees to draw their pensions whilst continuing to work and the provision of family and widows benefits.

The Union mounted a vigorous campaign to convince the Conservatives to honour the points previously agreed by Labour. On occasions they stood alone amongst the other unions in their determination to force the Government to stand by the agreement and finally Chataway agreed to settle and the Union achieved an outstanding success against the difficult background of incomes restraint and an unsympathetic Conservative Government.

1971 Pay Dispute
The 1971 strike took place against a background of growing militancy amongst both members of the UPW and the wider trade union movement. Negotiations

on the national pay claim had begun in early November 1970 and management initially referred the issue to the Post Office arbitration machinery. The Union's faith in the arbitration process had served them well in the years between the wars. However, this had been dented by the Conservative Government's hostility towards arbitration following several high profile awards to public sector workers in the previous months.

In late November Christopher Chataway took steps to remove Lord Hall from his position as Chairman of the Post Office Corporation. The two men had disagreed over both investment and the Corporation's pay policy. Hall had developed a close working relationship with the Union's leadership and in particular he was critical of the Government's approach to wage bargaining. His virtual dismissal led to an unusual response from postal workers. They took unofficial industrial action and within days walkouts had occurred in London, Manchester, York and Aberdeen. It took the intervention of Tom Jackson and Lord Hall himself to bring the dispute to an end when they both issued statements urging staff to return to work.

On 8 January 1971 the Post Office made a pay offer of 7% and this was almost immediately rejected by the Executive. This was followed by an improved offer of 8% which the Executive also rejected. It was becoming increasingly obvious that the industry was heading towards a dispute and the following week the Executive decided to announce a national strike commencing on 20 January. Support for the strike was confirmed at mass meetings across the country despite the announcement by the Union that they were unable to provide strike pay. The following Tuesday Robert Carr, Secretary of State for Employment, convened a meeting of both sides where the Acting Chairman of the Corporation, William Ryland, made it abundantly clear that he was not about to compromise.

On the first day of the strike there was overwhelming support for the Union and five arrests were made outside the Faraday Telephone Exchange in London when a small number of strike-breakers crossed the picket line. On the same day 20,000 postal and telecoms workers marched from Lincolns Inn Fields to Hyde Park where Jack London, Chairman of LDC, and Mary Spurr of the Telephonists, addressed the crowd. In Crown Offices across the country volunteers attended work without pay to ensure that pensioners were able to draw their benefits from local Post Offices. There was little contact between the two sides over the next couple of weeks. Although there was no strike pay, hardship payments were being provided to those with serious financial difficulties, but the cost of running the strike and maintaining hardship payments were beginning to affect the Union's finances. A number of Unions offered assistance including the NUM, AUEW and ASTMS. Vic Feather of the TUC, and Robert Carr for the Government, made several unsuccessful attempts to mediate, whilst sections of the media, in particular *The Daily Mail*, were running a particularly vicious campaign against the Union and the strikers. However despite their best efforts, the public remained surprisingly sympathetic to the strikers throughout the dispute.

Whilst the strike was still holding firm across the country, secret discussions were arranged with both sides indicating they were prepared to moderate their position. *The Sun* ran an article entitled 'The Man Behind the Man Behind the Strike' which was a savage political attack on Maurice Styles, the Union's Chairman. Norman Stagg who, only a few years earlier, had himself criticised Styles and other Communist Party members over their activities in the Union, mounted a powerful defence of the National Chairman.

The financial situation was getting worse. Most of the money coming from other unions came as loans rather than donations, with rather severe terms being applied. The Co-operative Bank went as far as to demand the deeds of the Union's Clapham Headquarters as security against any further advances. The TUC sent out an appeal for workplace collections but the amount raised was limited and it was becoming clear that the financial drain on the Union and the lack of solid financial support from the rest of the movement was becoming a significant factor in the dispute. Tom Jackson began to prepare the ground for an orderly retreat when he announced to the press that if the Union was forced to end the strike it would not be as a result of a lack of support from its members but the growing financial crisis and the Union's inability to maintain its hardship fund.

On 1 March 1971 Jackson convened a meeting of the Executive and outlined his strategy for ending the strike. The Union's bank overdraft had grown to £340,000 and on 2 March the Executive took a decision to end the dispute. The following morning some newspapers were already speculating that the Union was about to call the strike off and later that day Jackson explained the Executive's decision to a hostile and angry crowd at a mass meeting in Hyde Park. Jackson struggled to be heard and following the meeting he told a pack of waiting journalists that he fully understood the feelings of those opposed to the Executive's decision but that the Union had no alternative. Several Branches, including South East London, Liverpool and Edinburgh, attempted to continue the dispute. However, when the recommendation to end the strike was put to a ballot the Executives decision was overwhelmingly supported.

The return to work agreement included the establishment of a Committee of Inquiry to look into the issues that had led to the strike. The Committee was chaired by Sir Henry Hardman and included Thomas Carlile, Managing Director of Badcock and Wilson who was nominated by the Post Office and John Hughes, the Vice Principal of Ruskin College, who was nominated by the Union. The Inquiry was in the grand tradition of the numerous Post Office inquiries that had taken place over the previous hundred years with each side presenting its case in a similar way as to Arbitration Court.

The Union was represented by General Secretary, Tom Jackson, and the Post Office by Dorothy Fothergill, Director of Personnel. Contemporary reports compared Jackson's performance to Perry Mason, the American TV lawyer, and the Union's case was based on the argument that their members' pay had declined relatively to their last pay award and other workers over the same period. Whilst the Post Office argued that they could simply not afford an increase of more than eight per cent. The Union called a number of Postmen and Postmen Higher Grade as witnesses along with the previous Labour Government's last Postmaster General, Edward Short, as its main witnesses. When the report was finally published in May 1971, it was a massive disappointment for the Union. The three Committee members were unable to agree on the outcome with Hardman and Carlile producing a 'Majority Report' and Hughes, the Union's nomination, producing a 'Minority Report'. The 'Majority Report' recommended a 9% increase, arguing that the overriding consideration was the national interest and the need to restrict wage rises. John Hughes meanwhile, made the point that not only was the award of 9% unfair, but he also correctly predicted that a 9% increase would be insufficient to enable the Post Office to recruit and retain suitable staff.

Staff retention, recruitment and productivity would haunt the industry throughout the seventies and this problem was particularly acute in London.

At the end of the strike many members marched back to work behind their Branch banners in a show of defiance and solidarity. However, the Union would not call another National Strike over pay for 36 years although the Union emerged from the strike numerically strong and organisationally sound. Tom Jackson continued to lead the Union until 1982 and he remained a popular General Secretary with the Union's activists but was less popular with the Union's rank and file. Throughout the 1970s he was a prominent and respected trade union leader, often appearing on television representing the views of the TUC and the Labour Movement.

Chapter 14

THE GRUNWICK DISPUTE 1976

The 1970s began with the Labour Party in power and ended with the Conservatives in power. John Stonehouse had been the last Postmaster General before the title of Political Head of the Post Office was changed in 1969 to Minister of Posts and Telecommunication.

At the end of the decade Stonehouse was serving a seven year jail sentence for fraud following his faked suicide when he left a pile of clothes on a Miami Beach before being discovered some years later alive and well in Australia. This was the same John Stonehouse who, in 1968, had told the Union, in response to the UPWs call for workers representatives on the Post Office Board, that 'management was a specialist, technical function in which ordinary workers could not take part'.

In 1976 James Callaghan replaced Harold Wilson to become Britain's fourth Labour Party Prime Minister and in the summer of 1976, at a film processing company in North West London, 137 workers walked out on strike in a dispute over pay and conditions. It would have been difficult to predict at the time that this dispute would become an historic landmark in the developing struggle between organised labour and big business.

The Grunwick film processing laboratories were owned by George Ward, the Anglo-Indian employer of a predominantly female and Asian workforce. It was suggested that Ward's attitude towards his employees was heavily influenced by the communal strife that took place after India gained its independence when many Anglo-Indians were forced to flee to Britain and many families lost both status and wealth in the upheaval that took place.

Once the strike began to have an effect Ward approached his local Conservative MP, John Gorst for assistance. Gorst happened to be an influential supporter of the National Association for Freedom (NAFF). NAFF was a shadowy anti-trade union organisation with connections to the security services and was formed by, amongst others, Norris and Ross McWhirter, owners of the Guinness Book of Records. In the previous year Ross McWhirter had been assassinated by the Provisional Irish Republican Army (PIRA). NAFF was little more than a well-financed front organisation for an influential group of anti-trade union employers and their political supporters.

The striking workers had joined the trade union APEX and with the assistance of the local trades council sought support from the wider trade union movement. As is usual in these circumstances, UPW members from the local Cricklewood delivery office had refused to cross the APEX picket-line. The Branch Secretary was Archie Sinclair and the Chairman was Colin Maloney. A member of the Branch Committee was Fred Housego who in later life achieved fame as the winner of the TV show 'Mastermind'.

The Branch did not have a particular reputation for militancy, although its leadership were popular with the membership and was well rooted in the local community. The Branch also played an active role in the London District Council 3 which at the time had two formidable District Organisers (DOs), John Taylor and Derek Walsh. Taylor was a postman from the Eastern District Office (EDO) and Walsh was a postman higher grade from the South East London PHG Branch.

In October 1976 Roy Grantham, General Secretary of APEX asked Tom Jackson for help. Although the Cricklewood Branch had been refusing to cross the picket-line since the strike began, the mail was being collected from the office by non-striking Grunwick employees. Grantham wanted wider support. The laboratories relied completely on the postal service for the collection and distribution of its product. In response to the approach from APEX, the UPW Executive voted on 1 November 1976 to instruct its members not to handle Grunwick's mail. This was a decisive move in the dispute and George Ward described the UPWs boycott as a 'threat to our jugular'.

Meanwhile NAFF were active in the background, threatening legal action against the union and encouraging senior Conservative MPs to raise the issue in the Commons. Political pressure from the Labour Government was also being put on the Union who were nervous about the legal and political situation.

On 2 November Ward agreed to meet with the Advisory, Conciliation and Arbitration Service (ACAS), offering to negotiate if the 'blacking' of his mail was lifted. NAFF meanwhile, were threatening legal action against the UPW who they claimed were in breach of the 1953 Post Office Act. Ward, at the same time, began proceedings against the Post Office for the release of his companies' mail which was being held in various sorting offices throughout the country. The Union's solicitors advised the Executive to end the blacking or face the threat of huge fines and legal costs. It was a combination of this, and the political pressure from the Government, that caused the Executive to lift the boycott of Grunwick's mail and allow the Employment Secretary Albert Booth to announce to the Commons that the Union had signed an affidavit lifting the obstruction of Grunwick's mail on the basis of Ward's Agreement to meet ACAS.

Ward had no intention of co-operating with ACAS to resolve the dispute. In fact when ACAS advised the company to recognise and negotiate with APEX he responded by suing ACAS on the basis that when they consulted the workforce on their views they had not spoken to those still working. Employment Secretary Booth established a Court of Inquiry into the dispute and when it published its recommendation in August 1977 Ward dismissed it with the same contempt that he had dismissed and ignored ACAS. Ward now had the support of the Conservative front bench and the majority of the national press.

In May 1977 a number of Government Ministers visited the picket-line to show their support for the strikers, these included Shirley Williams and Bill William who in March 1981 left the Labour Party to help form the Social Democratic Party. At the 1977 Annual Conference there was an unsuccessful attempt to persuade the Union to re-introduce the sanctions when Ron Hale of the Milton Keynes Branch moved an amendment seconded by Frank Osie-Tutu urging the Executive Council to reconsider its decision. In June and July television broadcasts showed bloody scenes of fighting between the police and supporters of the strikers and on 22 June miners from Kent, Yorkshire and South Wales joined the mass picket and Arthur Scargill was famously arrested.

Despite the National Executive's decision the Cricklewood Branch were still refusing to handle the Grunwick mail and in the middle of June 1977 Jack Dromey, Secretary of the Brent Trades Council, who had played a leading role in organising support for the strikers, made an approach, through the Cricklewood Branch to the London District Committee. Within a few days a meeting took place involving the Cricklewood Branch officials, John Taylor and Derek Walsh on behalf of the LDC, Jack Dromey and the Grunwick strike committee. Dromey explained that he was concerned that the dispute was running out of steam. He felt that without the help of the UPW the strike was lost and asked the Divisional Officers to consider re-imposing the boycott of Grunwick mail as the only hope for the strikes success. At the end of the meeting Jayaben Desai, the leader of the 137 original strikers, handed Taylor and Walsh a moving letter from the striking workers. The letter dated 14 June 1977 read: 'As you are aware we have been on strike for ten months to win union recognition. This week we are carrying out a mass picket which has resulted in police brutality against men and women pickets.

People have been kicked and beaten including Len Gristey our organiser and myself. Over one hundred people have been arrested, we have persuaded over 20 people not to go to work and half have joined the picket line. In spite of this production is still continuing and Ward is boasting openly that he will smash the strike and the trade union movement. The company is using coaches and vans to drive workers and materials through the picket lines with police assistance.

They arrest anyone who tries to stop them. We appeal to every UPW worker to black all Grunwick mail because we feel that unless this is done immediately Mr. Ward and his cronies will triumph over the whole of the trade union movement'.

We beg for your support.

Secretary Grunwick Strike Committee

Walsh and Taylor promised the strike committee that they would do whatever they could to help. Following the meeting Derek Walsh and John Taylor returned to the District Offices in Farringdon Road and began phoning the London Branches to build support for a resumption of the Grunwick boycott. A circular was dispatched throughout the District asking Branches not to handle Grunwick's mail. At a meeting of the District Council on 28 June, which Jack Dromey attended, the Officers' recommendation was endorsed. That decision was implemented in every London office other than Dickie Lawlor's old office, the West Central District Office (WCDO). It is not clear why the West Central Branch did not support their London colleagues. John Taylor asked for the opportunity to address the WCDO membership but George Roberts, the Branch Secretary, would not agree to this. Taylor was convinced that given the opportunity he could persuade the West Central members to support the London District Council's decision. There was speculation that it was George Robert's close relationship with Tom Jackson that had led to the Branch taking this decision. Nevertheless the boycott held solidly in the rest of London and Grunwick's mail began to accumulate throughout the district.

In September 1977 an article titled 'Lunatics Anonymous', and written by Harry Burnett, Editor of *The Post* (1967-1980), appeared on the front page of the Union's newspaper. The article was an attack on a clandestine group called the 'Committee of Hundred and Ninety Five' which had been circulating material in support of the Grunwick workers. In the article, Burnett described them as 'evil people, intent upon destroying the Union of Post Office Workers as a force for democracy'. Their name he said 'cloaks the activities of dangerous people' and accused them of running 'an underground campaign aimed at the incitement of Union members, particularly in London, to ignore the constitutional instructions of the Executive Council, and to break the Annual Conference decision'. London offices had been circulated with leaflets attacking the decision of the West Central Branch to handle the Cricklewood work and a letter claiming to have been sent by K.S. Noble, Deputy Director Resources and addressed to Fred Gaunt the WCDO District Postmaster, praising the actions of the local Branch Officials, in particular George Roberts the Branch Secretary was also circulated. A further letter, allegedly from the 'National Front Directorate', was also circulated which according to Burnett was another attempt by the Committee of One Hundred and Ninety Five to 'denigrate the West Central Branch Officials by identifying the decision of the West Central members, to stay with Conference decisions, with the policies of the National Front'. A further circular from the 'Committee' appeared attacking Norman Stagg accusing him of intimidating the Cricklewood members and forcing them back to work. The authors of the 'Committees' circulars were never identified despite the best efforts of the Post Office's Investigation Department to track down the alleged forgers.

Taylor, who had just recently been elected to the Union's Executive, Walsh and the other members of the Committee were summoned by the Executive to meet with Tom Jackson at the Union's Headquarters in Clapham. Ward and his supporters from NAFF meanwhile were threatening the UPW members at Cricklewood with legal action and a Government Cabinet Committee were also urging the Union to bring the unofficial boycott to an end. It was clear that the decision of the LDC not to process Grunwick's work was the most effective tactic that the trade union movement could deploy in support of the Grunwick workers. The mass pickets, despite the best intentions of those participating, were having little effect. George Ward recognised the effectiveness of the boycott when he was reported in the press saying, 'if a long time went by without our being able to get mail out of the company, Grunwick would be slowly bled dry'.

The London District Committee was summoned to meet with Jackson in the 'Boardroom' at the Union HQ in Crescent Lane. A grim faced and angry Tom Jackson asked them to lift the boycott and went on to point out that if they continued to defy the Union's rules they could be disciplined. He argued that the UPW had already done more than any other Union in the country when they blacked Grunwick's mail in November 1976, that no other union had been dragged through the courts and this was at a time when the union had not yet, financially recovered from the 1971 dispute. If the Union failed to maintain the undertaking it had made to the courts they could face both a massive fine and a claim for unlimited damages from George Ward for the losses his company had suffered. Jackson told the delegation that he had approached the TUC to ask for their support in the event of the Union's funds being sequestrated and it was made clear that they could not guarantee this. He went on to say that if this happened, because of the unofficial action in London, then the Union's members would hold the London District Council responsible. Jackson argued that other unions should show more support and that the UPW had already taken official solidarity action and he asked why the electricity and gas workers had not done the same. Jackson's view was that it should be left to ACAS and the Scarman Report to resolve the dispute. He finished by asking the Council to withdraw its circular calling for the boycott and to get the London members back to working normally.

Derek Walsh had been chosen to present London's position and he began by explaining that the Committee had thought long and hard about their decision and that there was no question of the District Council withdrawing their circular. The policy had been agreed by a meeting of the District Council who fully supported the position taken by the Committee. It was the Committee's view that only the UPW could bring the dispute to an end and they had no intention of changing that policy. Walsh went on to say that the London District Council believed that they could not leave the Grunwick workers to fight such an important battle by themselves. Jackson also made his position clear; he was not prepared to have a long debate with the delegation as it was obvious that they had made their minds up. As they left the room, Jackson, in a loud voice asked them "Who do you think you are the conscience of the Union?".

The unofficial boycott of Grunwick's mail lasted from 15 June to 4 July and it had been a great success. On 4 July Tom Jackson, on behalf of the Executive called a special meeting of London District Council 3. He attended the meeting with Norman Stagg, Deputy General Secretary and he ran through the same arguments he had used at the earlier meeting with the Committee. Taylor was in a particularly awkward position because of his dual role as both London District Organiser and Executive Council member. Jackson was a forceful and effective speaker and he told the meeting that if they continued with their action the National Union would be unable to protect individual Branch officials and District officers who he claimed were in breach of the law and were committing a criminal offence by wilfully delaying the mail and persuading others to delay the mail. Their actions, he argued, would prejudice the outcome of the ACAS enquiry and also the Scarman Report.

When the vote was taken Jackson had managed to convince a majority to lift the boycott and reluctantly the District Committee agreed to release the Grunwick mail. The Cricklewood officials Colin Maloney, David Dodd and Archie Sinclair were stunned by the decision but were determined to continue their support for the strikers. When they returned to the Cricklewood office their members agreed to continue the boycott. Later that day the local manager suspended 26 postmen and ordered them to leave the office. The next day a further 87 were suspended and although they attempted to continue working and delivering other, non-Grunwick mail using their own transport, on Thursday 7 July they were locked out by management and the office was closed.

On 10 July the Post Office allowed NAFF to enter the Cricklewood office at 2.00 a.m. in the morning and remove the trapped Grunwick mail. NAFF arranged for 250 supporters to distribute this mail throughout the postal system in unsuspecting areas of the country in an operation NAFF code-named 'Operation Pony Express'. Tom Jackson instructed branches not to handle this mail until the Executive had an opportunity to discuss the matter at a meeting which was due to take place on 12 July. At the meeting Jackson attempted to convince the Executive to make the Cricklewood dispute official again but he was narrowly defeated. A motion instructing all UPW members to handle the work was proposed and agreed by the Executive who also agreed a proposal to pay the Cricklewood strikers hardship pay. They received their first payment the next day and the unofficial boycotts of Grunwick's mail continued to take place in several London offices including ECDO, WDO and the Foreign Section in King Edward Building. Further unsuccessful efforts were made to get the Cricklewood branch back to work and on Friday 22 July a chain of events began that resulted in the Cricklewood Branch being landed a crippling body-blow that would shatter the most resolute trade unionists.

Norman Stagg, Deputy General Secretary was now acting General Secretary whilst Jackson was taking his annual holidays. The Union was informed that the Post Office intended to allow Grunwick to remove 63 bags of inward mail from the sorting office. The Union responded by saying that they had no objection to this and that furthermore BBC radio reported that Stagg supported a Post Office communication urging the Cricklewood workers to return to work. On Sunday 24 July the branch held a meeting where they rejected Stagg's request to address the Cricklewood members and voted to return to work but not to handle Grunwick's mail. There were a number of angry phone calls exchanged between the Branch and Norman Stagg with Colin Maloney accusing the leadership of 'acting behind the member's backs and without consultation'. When they showed up for work on Monday 25 July they were once again locked out. Stagg turned up the heat and on the same day dispatched a Special Branch Circular accusing the Cricklewood Branch of exposing the whole of the Union's funds to the danger of sequestration. The following Monday Stagg persuaded a meeting of LDC 3 to accept this argument and on Wednesday 27 July the Executive Council voted to suspend the hardship payments to Cricklewood members. They were instructed to attend a meeting at Conway Hall, Red Lion Square, where Stagg landed his killer blow. He informed the men that they had not only lost their hardship pay, but they would also be expelled from the Union, sacked by the Post Office and would lose their pension rights if the unofficial dispute continued. Reluctantly they voted by 49 votes to 46 to return to work.

In the aftermath of the Cricklewood dispute George Ward, supported by most of the Fleet Street press, NAFF and the Conservative Party, ignored both the ACAS recommendations and the proposals of the Scarman Report. APEX, the Grunwick strikers union, withdrew its support for mass picketing and as a consequence solidarity support for the dispute began to crumble. However the strike continued for a further year but with the loss of support from APEX and with little support from the TUC it was called off in July 1978. Following the return to work at Cricklewood the war of words between the Branch and the Union's leadership continued. The Union's Discipline Committee fined John Taylor and Derek Walsh, £500 and £300 respectively and Committee members Eddie Lee, Joe Nalty, Ernie Cattermole, Derek Saunders and Dougie Taylor were each fined £100. Financial donations came in from individual members and branches throughout the country and Jack Dromey made an appeal to the wider trade union movement which was so well supported that within a few days the fund was over subscribed and money was returned to the donators. When the issue was discussed at the 1978 UPW conference Derek Walsh, on behalf of LDC, moved an Amendment condemning the Executive Council for their handling of the Grunwick dispute issues. Walsh put up a vigorous defence of the District Council's position and their reasons for unilaterally re-imposing the boycott. The District Council, he said, had decided that, 'it had either to put up or shut up and that someone had to try to help the Grunwick strikers'. He went on to argue that: 'If any Branch Secretary or District Organiser in this hall had been confronted with the same situation as LDC 3, tell me would you have walked by on the other side' and he spoke for many in the Union when he argued that the Executive Council's actions had been 'morally wrong'.

John Taylor took the unusual step for an Executive Council member of speaking in support of the Council's Amendment and in opposition to the Executive. He said that it was with regret that had to express a view that was totally opposed to the actions of the Executive and that he believed that loyalty to the trade union movement, and any committee they sat on was paramount, however there were times when decisions of a corporate body was out of line with the conscience of an individual. He went on to say 'Now I don't believe that this wonderful organisation should adopt such an attitude when they've got the army of the working class behind them. I believe with strong leadership the members of the UPW are one of the most loyal groups in the Labour Movement. The problem with the EC was that instead of grasping the nettle and making sure this liar and cheat at Grunwick was destroyed they adopted an alternative policy of trying to bring the LDC 3 membership and the Cricklewood members into line. I don't believe that's the attitude that should be adopted by anybody within the TUC'.

Colin Maloney from Cricklewood also spoke in support of the Amendment and argued passionately for the position that his Branch had taken. 'To some people on the platform', he said 'small offices such as mine were insignificant. Well I can tell you this much, you're not insignificant if you do what you believe is right. In Cricklewood we did what we believed were right and no one can take that away from us. It's no good going back to our Branches and saying Cricklewood was wrong, they were against the rules. There were no rules for George Ward. He made his own rules and NAFF financed them. Had you been in the same situation as Cricklewood, passing the Grunwick people on the picket-line every day, seeing them standing there and looking for support, you would have done the same as we did'. Several other delegates from London and around the country spoke in support of the London Amendment. However, when the vote was taken the Amendment was narrowly defeated by 9033 votes to 9694.

The outcome of the Grunwick dispute proved to be a massive blow for the trade union movement and it paved the way for the vicious attacks by the Thatcher Government in the late 1970s and early 1980s. The courage of the Cricklewood UPW members and the support they received from London and other parts of the country during the dispute stand in stark contrast to the duplicity and greed of George Ward and his powerful backers. The last stand made by the Grunwick Strike Committee was to go on hunger strike outside TUC HQ where they protested at the lack of support they had received from the trade union movement. On 14 July 1978 a very tired and disillusioned Grunwick Strike Committee announced the end of the strike.

Many union members involved in the Grunwick dispute were disappointed at the way they felt the Grunwick Strikers had been let down by people in positions of authority in the Labour Government and the TUC. They were also disillusioned at the way the industrial and criminal laws of the land had been used to the detriment of the strikers and were used instead as a force to help George Ward and the National Association for Freedom defeat the Grunwick Workers. As far as the police were concerned, especially the Special Patrol Group, many union members thought that the police attitude towards the mass picket was such that it could have been mistaken for George Ward's own private army. In hindsight many observers in later years have commented that it is hard to see how the strikers ever really stood a chance of winning, with the balance of forces so heavily stacked against them.

Peter Hain in his book Political Strikes commented: 'The power of capital, the police and the judges were ultimately more decisive than the formal arbitration procedures that rested on the willingness of employer and employees to arrive at a consensus.'

In 2012, at the Union's Annual Conference, Derek Walsh and Colin Maloney accepted National Honorary Membership, on behalf of all those disciplined by the Union over thirty years earlier, from the CWU General Secretary, Billy Hayes, in recognition of the outstanding contribution they made to trade unionism.

Chapter 15

CIVIL WAR AND IMPROVED
WORKING METHODS (IWM) 1980-1985

As Callaghan's Government limped towards the 1980s the problems that had dogged the postal industry since the end of the Second World War continued. The Union continued to be a strong supporter of incomes policies despite the fact that it was clear to everyone they did not work. The 'Social Contract', a pact between the TUC and the Labour Government, continued to dominate wage bargaining. The aim of the agreement was for the unions to self-regulate and restrict wage claims in exchange for various social and industrial reforms which the Government would introduce.

As part of the Social Contract, in 1975 the Labour Government established the Bullock Committee, to produce a report on introducing industrial democracy into British industry. It was also in response to the European Commission's Draft Fifth Company Law Directive which was established to 'harmonise worker participation in management of companies across Europe'. The Committee, which included representatives of both management and the trade unions, was chaired by Alan Bullock. In 1977 they produced their report and proposed a major role for trade unions in the management of British companies but its recommendations never saw the light of day. The Committee members nominated by the Confederation of British Industry (CBI), who produced a Minority Report, opposed its recommendations. In the Trades Union Congress it was championed by Jack Jones of the TGWU and Clive Jenkins the General Secretary of ASTMS, but opposed by Frank Chapple, EEPTU, Hugh Scanlon President of the AUEW and Arthur Scargill, NUM. In the end it was buried by Margaret Thatcher and the City of London, along with the Post Office's own experiment in industrial democracy.

It was far easier for private sector employers to find ways around the pay ceilings than it was for those in the public sector and as a consequence the wages of postal workers continued to lag behind the rate of inflation. In London the recruitment and retention of staff became increasingly difficult although unemployment levels were beginning to rise. Vacancy levels grew and both management and the Union agreed to provide overtime at a level that would compensate the workforce for the low basic pay. The Post Office found it impossible to retain staff without high levels of overtime and the workers relied on it to maintain their living standards.

In 1978 the pact between the Labour Government and the unions was beginning to fall apart when James Callaghan imposed a 5% pay limit which was well below the rate of inflation and the TUC were unable to accept it. Pressure from the rank and file led to an upsurge in industrial action, particularly in the public sector. This began what became known as the 'Winter of Discontent' as many low paid workers in the public sector, struggling under the weight of increasing prices, took industrial action and in 1979 Margaret Thatcher was elected as the Head of a Conservative Government. She was elected on 3 May 1979 with an overall majority of 43. Although the Labour Party's vote increased by several thousand, the Conservative's vote increased by over 3 million and Thatcher replaced Callaghan as Prime Minister.

In their Election Manifesto the Conservative Party promised to reverse the countries decline, make industry more competitive and above all curb the powers of the trade unions.

Trade union reform, as they termed it, would 'restore the health of our economic and social life, by controlling inflation and striking a fair balance between the rights and duties of the trade union movement'. This, they said, would involve new legislation to restrict picketing, changes to the legislation covering the closed shop, the wider use of secret ballots for trade union elections and secret ballots of the membership before industrial action could take place.

It was against this background that the Union faced the 1980s. Pressure to accept an increase in the number of part-time and casual workers employed in the industry was increasing and in March 1979 LDC 3 met to discuss a number of issues, including an approach by management to increase the level of part-timers and casual workers employed in the capital.

Since the days of Dickie Lawlor, London had maintained its opposition to the use of casuals outside of the Christmas pressure period and summer leave period. The Divisional Officers reported to the meeting that the Executive Council were due to discuss a document that would allow management to increase the use of both casual workers and part-timer labour in sorting offices throughout the country. The meeting agreed to organize an unofficial strike and a lobby of the Union's Headquarters with the aim of persuading the Executive to reject the idea. On 29 March at 10.00 a.m. several thousand London UPW members walked out on unofficial strike and made their way to a rally outside the Union's Headquarters in Crescent Lane, Clapham. This was a repeat of a tactic employed in battles between the District Council and Ron Smith a decade earlier.

The call for action received widespread support and a large crowd assembled outside the entrance to the Union's offices blocking much of Crescent Lane. The crowd began chanting slogans attacking the Union's leadership and some ventured into the grounds and forecourt at the front of the building. As the noise grew louder and the crowd encroached closer towards the entrance to the building the concerned faces of Headquarters staff appeared at the windows. The Executive Council were meeting in the 'boardroom' that was situated on the left side of the building on the first floor and a number of Executive Council members appeared at the windows. This provoked some of the crowd to dislodge clods of earth from the lawn and throw them towards the faces looking out from the 'boardroom'. John Taylor, London District Officer, Executive Council member and the principle organizer of the demonstration, became concerned that things were getting out of hand and appeared at the window in an attempt to calm the situation down. The majority of the crowd had no idea of Taylor's role in organizing the demonstration and before he could get a word out a number of clods of turf were thrown at him. Taylor retreated back into the boardroom and some of the more senior union reps, realizing things were getting out of hand convinced the more volatile sections of the crowd that they had made their point and it was now time to disperse, which they did without any further difficulties.

Pressure was being placed on the industry as a result of reports commissioned by the Government to look into both productivity and the financial performance of the Post Office. The first of these was the Carter

Report established by the Callaghan Government which published its findings in July 1977. The Secretary of State for Industry had asked Charles Carter, Vice-Chancellor of Lancaster University, to produce a report that would 'examine the performance and main features of the organization of the Post Office and the use of its resources and assets'. The report is chiefly remembered for its recommendation to divide the Post Office into three parts, postal, telecommunications and counters. However of equal importance were the recommendations the report made regarding industrial relations, productivity and prices. It concludes that although industrial relations were generally good, it questioned whether this was because management were unwilling to seriously challenge the Union on the issue of productivity. Furthermore the report recommended that 'when pay policy permitted, genuine productivity bargaining, payments negotiated locally and related to local performance within a framework of nationally agreed guidelines' should be introduced.

In September 1979 this process was taken a step further when the new Conservative Government asked Godfray Le Quesne QC, Chairman of the Monopolies and Mergers Commission to 'Investigate and report on the question of whether a monopoly situation exists in relation to the numbered London Postal Districts of the Post Office'.

In its report the Commission made a number of observations before coming to its conclusions. Firstly they claimed that there had been a marked deterioration in the quality of service of both the London Letter Service and the Overseas Mail Service in 1979 and secondly that bad industrial relations was a major cause of this deterioration. They also pointed out that the London Postal Districts employed 16,077 postmen and 5,921 PHGs in 1979 and that the level of female recruits remained low despite the restrictions placed on their recruitment having being lifted. They noted that the basic pay of an Inner London postman was £83.40 and £90.08 for a PHG and as a consequence the Post Office was unable to compete effectively in the London labour market. They also noted that in September 1979 there were 1,927 postman vacancies and 1,355 PHG vacancies and that the Post Office had a policy of maintaining a proportion of duties for overtime in order to meet the expectations of their staff. Staff turnover rates in London were very high and varied between 12% and 17%, however in central London this increased to between 20% and 28%. The industries inability to recruit staff in London was demonstrated by the fact that in the period between April and September 1979 out of 14,500 job applications received only 1,600 new recruits were employed and in the period between 1968 and 1979 productivity in Inner London had declined by up to 25%.

The Commission's response to these facts was fairly predictable. Politically unable to identify low pay as a major contributor to the problems in London they made a number of recommendations that avoided this conclusion. These included changes to the method of measuring the 'quality of service', improving central control of the London van fleet, accelerating the introduction of new technology and improving recruitment methods.

However the most radical recommendation was that for the first time postal worker's pay should be linked to productivity. Recommendation 22 read: 'Pay of postal operatives should be linked to productivity. The Post Offices previous attempts to introduce productivity schemes have been unsuccessful because the work related element of pay was too small, payable retrospectively and did not reflect the extra effort of small groups of individual workers'.

The report completely ignored the failure of the Post Office to recruit and retain suitable full-time staff and instead identified excessive overtime and LDC's opposition to part-time and casual labour as a major cause of London's problems.

In the mid-1970s the Union had agreed a national bonus scheme, that provided an annual bonus payment for all employees in the postal business, called the Mails Operating Savings Scheme (MOSS). It had little effect on overall productivity and provided very little in terms of reward for postal workers. In anticipation of the Commissions criticism of the Union and the possible threat to the letter monopoly, the London leadership began discussions with the London Postal Region on a bonus incentive scheme. The District Organisers, John Taylor and Derek Walsh together with Derek Saunders, Assistant District Organiser, had taken the view that it was better to voluntarily negotiate a productivity scheme than have an unagreed one imposed on them. However, when news of the discussions was reported to the District Council there was considerable disquiet. Even some members of the committee argued that they had been kept in the dark and were unaware that the discussions had been taking place. Tom Jackson had previously written to the Post Office Chairman suggesting that 'the only way forward was a new productivity scheme that would provide a real incentive for UPW members to accept change' opening the door for the London discussions. This had resulted in the London Postal Region contacting the London District Council with an offer to jointly develop a bonus scheme based on hours saved and traffic levels.

In May 1979 Margaret Thatcher appointed Sir Keith Joseph as Secretary of State for Industry with political responsibility for the Post Office. Keith Joseph was a close ally of Thatcher and has been credited with encouraging her hostility to trade unions and the public sector. Pay negotiations had begun in the early part of 1979 and on 23 March the Post Office made the union's negotiators a final offer of 8%. The rate of inflation was running at 13.4% which meant that the offer amounted to a pay cut. The Executive decided to put the offer to a Branch ballot with a recommendation to accept the offer; however the offer was rejected by a margin of 6 to 1. Later in the year the Executive Council called a 24 hour strike in support of the Union's claim to have 27 December classified as a non-working day. This was the first official industrial action called by the Union since the 1971 national dispute and was well supported in London although some Branches argued that the dispute was a distraction from the far bigger issue of job cuts that were looming on the horizon. In 1980 the Union changed its name to the Union of Communication Workers to reflect the changes that were taking place in the industry.

The Union's national rules allowed the District Council to negotiate with the Postal Region on matters directly affecting the London membership. The Executive Council gave them the authority to start discussions on a productivity deal and before the end of the year an agreement had been negotiated for use by those London Branches that wished to do so on a voluntary basis. Prior to these negotiations taking place Tom Jackson called the two London Organisers John Taylor and Derek Walsh to UCW HQ at Clapham and told them that if an agreement could not be reached and if the LDC 3 insisted on keeping the Spanish customs that had built up over the years in London offices then the Chairman of the Post Office Board had warned him that the Post Office intended to have a blitz on the vacant duties held by sub and Head District offices in London for overtime purposes. (The Post Office intended to start by cutting 100 vacant duties in London's Western Parcel Office). Tom Jackson said if this led to a London dispute then don't expect the Provinces to support

London. The Provinces had taken cuts in duties and overtime over the years and there was very little left on the bone and to expect the provincial Office to support London who had all the benefits would be unrealistic. He said the LDC 3 either reached a productivity agreement or they would be on their own without assistance from the rest of the Union.

The agreement that was reached was named Improved Working Methods (IWM) and it resulted in two opposing camps developing within the Council. On one side there were those Branches and individuals who supported the agreement and on the other side a group completely opposed to the idea of locally based bonus schemes. The main opposition came from the Western District Office Amalgamated Branch, Croydon Amalgamated Branch, Richmond/Twickenham and District Branch, Harrow and District Branch and the London North West No. 1 Branch. The arguments for and against the scheme began to dominate the monthly London District Council 3 meetings which were held in one of the two large staff meeting halls located in King Edward Building and Mount Pleasant. Several hundred delegates attended the meetings which were conducted very formerly and acted as a monthly forum where branches debated and agreed policy on all the main issues affecting the London membership.

Dave Percival and Don Failes of the Croydon Branch, Frank Osie-Tutu and Bill Willoughby of the Western District Office, Sid DeJong of the Richmond/Twickenham Branch, Hughie Lenaghan of the Harrow Branch and George Durrack from the North West London Branch formed the leadership of the opposition within the District Council. Support for the scheme came from the East London No. 1 Branch, ECDO No. 1 Branch, London Stations Branch, the North London Branch and various Parcels Branches. The smaller Branches were fairly evenly divided, for and against the scheme, and in many Branches deep internal divisions developed amongst the membership and between officials. Taylor, Walsh and the District Committee obviously argued strongly for the scheme with noticeable support from Hughie Bowles and Peter Dooley of the Stations Branch, Alex Thompson and Fred Baldwin from ECDO and Aubrey Beyer from the East London Branch. Taylor and Walsh, who had led the London membership during the Grunwick dispute and had given strong leadership to the District Council over a number of years, were very popular amongst the London activists and many of their strongest supporters found themselves reluctantly opposing Taylor and Walsh at the monthly meetings of the District Council.

Percival and Failes were supporters of a rank and file organisation which produced a newspaper called *The Post Office Worker*. The paper was edited by Dave Percival, Chairman of the Croydon Branch and to avoid the threat of victimisation he used the nom de plume 'Tom Dredge', the 19th century pioneer of Post Office trade unionism. The General Secretary, Tom Jackson instructed the Union's research department to search through the membership records to identify the culprit, only to be told by an amused research officer who the real Tom Dredge was. *The Post Office Worker* group held meetings at various venues around the capital to build opposition to the scheme and they never missed an opportunity to raise the issue at District Council meetings. The opposition were a fairly loose coalition without any single group dominating, but they successfully built a solid block of branches and individuals opposed to and working against the introduction of the scheme. Taylor and Walsh also had a significant number of Branch officials supporting them and from their dominant position as the leadership of the District Council they were able to convince an equally determined number of activists to support the scheme.

The battle between the two groups continued throughout the year but by early 1980 about 40% of the London memberships were in Branches that had opted to join the scheme. Post Office management were obviously keen to encourage offices to sign-up for the scheme and exerted a great deal of pressure on Branches by reducing overtime opportunities, clamping down on local agreements such as 'clear up and go' agreements and attacking various other local concessions and agreements that members enjoyed. The Post Office claimed that by the end of 1980 offices representing 70% of the London membership had 'joined up'. However the battle then moved to another level when the Executive Council agreed to recommend that the bonus scheme be made available to Branches throughout the country and called a two day Special Conference at the Winter Gardens in Bournemouth on 3 and 4 April 1981 to decide the issue. On 23 February a special issue of *The Post* was published containing a report of the negotiations, a copy of the proposed agreement and a recommendation from the Executive Council that read: 'That Conference accepts that the IWM scheme be endorsed for future use by the Union's membership on a voluntary basis'.

It soon became apparent that the Union was as split nationally over the issue as it was within the District Council and the scene was set for a major debate on the future direction of the Union. The report attracted over 140 amendments and the first was moved by L. Allen from the Aberdeen Branch and was seconded by J. Saul of the Acton Branch and it called for the outright rejection of the deal. It was defeated by 5,812 votes to 5,957 votes, a margin of only 145 votes and there had been 22 speakers in support of the amendment and 23 to oppose it. A second more subtle approach was attempted by the Twickenham Branch when Sid DeJong moved and Fred St Paul of the Western District Amalgamated Branch seconded the following motion: 'Delete all after Conference and insert: rejects the IWM scheme on the basis that it is not in the best interest of the membership, and the EC is instructed to pursue a productivity scheme that will ensure a payment of £10 per week consolidated for full co-operation from all Branches for 18 months to assist the Post Office in the present financial crisis'.

The amendment was not carried by a show of hands. The debate had begun at 9.00 a.m. and finished at 3.55 p.m. during which one delegate had suffered a heart attack. Further amendments were discussed until 12.30 on the second day of the Conference when Arthur Fulbrook from the London Parcels PHG Branch proposed 'that the question now be put' and the National Executive's recommendation to accept IWM on a voluntary basis was carried by a show of hands. At the end of the Conference Tom Jackson in his closing speech congratulated all concerned on what he described as one of the finest debates he had ever taken part in at a Union Conference. In recognition of the differences of opinion that had divided the Conference he expressed his hope that they would be quickly healed but the legacy of IWM would dominate the internal politics of the Union for years to come. This happened in a number of ways. The opposition believed that the deal had only gone through because the majority of London Branches had been pushed into accepting the deal. The supporters argued that it was the correct and pragmatic response to an undefendable attack by management backed up by the Government. The alliances built during this period both within London and across the Union nationally would endure for many years.

Don Failes was elected and held the position of ADO London from 1982 to 1987 and Aubrey Beyer was elected as ADO (PHG) in 1984 and then DO

(Postman) in 1985. In 1983 John Taylor replaced Maurice Styles as the Union's Outdoor Assistant Secretary when Styles retired. Frank Osie-Tutu was elected to the National Executive in 1982 and Bill Willoughby was elected to the London District Council 3 in the same year. Peter Dooley and Hughie Lenaghan both served as London Regional Secretaries. Derek Walsh became National Chairman in 1987 and was elected General Treasurer in 1988.

Post Office management intensified the pressure on Branches to join the scheme and some branches reluctantly joined on the basis of offering the least amount of savings possible. Others adopted a policy of complete opposition which resulted in management attempting to impose unagreed changes and removed locally agreed earnings packages in an attempt to force them in. Those refusing to join the scheme could expect little support from the National Union or District Officers other than the advice that they should do a deal and join the scheme. Management claimed that within two and a half years 83% of London staff had done so although Croydon and WDO, which were large Branches, both remained outside until it became compulsory in 1985. The National Union frequently criticised these branches for not capturing the savings from management imposed cuts in the bonus scheme but even so a sizeable minority chose to either reject IWM or keep their involvement to a minimum.

In the 1980s the Post Office measured productivity in terms of items handled per staff hour. The Monopoly and Mergers Commission had set the Post Office a target of improving productivity by 15% before the end of 1983. Within a short period it was on its way to meeting that target. In his book, 'Royal Mail the Post Office since 1840' Martin Daunton identified the introduction of IWM as a turning point in the fortunes of the Post Office. In 1985 he wrote: 'Since 1980 productivity nationwide has increased by about 12%. In consequence prices have been held below the movement of the Retail Price Index (RPI) whilst still maintaining profits, funding the whole of its large capital investment programme and making a contribution to other public sector investment'.

Supporters of the decision to accept IWM have argued that because of the Post Office's financial situation, the threat from the Monopoly and Mergers Commission and the hostile political climate it was the right decision. Job losses were inevitable and the decision brought financial benefits for the membership. In 1980 average pay stood at £105.50 per week, increasing to £119.70 in 1981 and £133.10 in 1982. The opponents argued that the scheme was divisive and unfair and that the deal amounted to the Union selling jobs for bonus payments and that the Union should have fought and united the membership around a struggle for better basic pay. They believed that it was possible for London to successfully defend jobs and there was no need for a deal. They questioned why management needed to negotiate with the Union if they could impose something without agreement and achieve the productivity savings for nothing. They argued that if London had given a lead they would not have been isolated and that the provinces, who were becoming more militant, would support London. The Union they believed was in a strong position and the Government were in no position to take the Union on. These differences continued within the District Council and the Union for many years after the issue was settled and very few of the main participants ever changed their views on the merits of the scheme. Old alliances were lost and new ones forged. Branches and activists from different regions of the country suddenly found themselves on the same side of the argument and these new alliances endured for years to come. 1981 saw the emergence of the 'UCW Broad Left' and a 'Conference Bulletin' produced by *The Post Office Worker* not only welcomed its creation but criticised the Deputy General Secretary (DGS), Alan Tuffin for urging delegates not to attend 'fringe meetings'. In fact three hundred delegates ignored the DGS and attended the meeting to hear Tony Benn seeking support for his campaign to become Deputy Leader of the Labour Party and although the Union swung behind Denis Healey, the incumbent, he won by less than 1% of the votes.

The Independent Advisory Review Body and Bill Willoughby
In 1980 the Union had changed its name to the Union of Communication Workers to reflect the fact that its members worked in both the Post Office and British Telecoms. The 1980s saw the beginning of economic liberalization. Manufacturing industries began their migration to the Far East and financial de-regulation marked the rise of financial capitalism, as vast areas of the country were de-industrialized.

Unemployment in Britain topped 3 million for the first time since the 1930s. Despite this the Post Office still found it difficult to recruit and retain staff in

London and other areas of the country. The Western District Office in Rathbone Place W1 employed about 1,320 postmen and women but since the mid-seventies had carried a high level of vacancies. It was not unusual for postal workers in central London to work double shifts stretching from 6.00 a.m. to 10.00 p.m. The labour force was drawn from a wide geographical area with only eight of those employed in the office living in the W1 area. Seventy per cent of these lived outside the Inner London area and many travelled extremely long distances to work.

In the period between 1977 and 1981 there were ten disputes in the office which usually took the form of unauthorized Union meetings held during working hours. The Branch had a strong leadership and the membership had a great deal of loyalty to their local officials. Levels of earnings were high due to the amount of overtime available and the tough negotiating stance taken by the local Branch. Working conditions were good, with breaks and concessions well above the national standards and the Union provided a high level of support for members who found themselves subject to the discipline or attendance procedures. The Branch were early opponents of the IWM Bonus Scheme and Branch Chairman Bill Willoughby and Frank Osie-Tutu Branch Secretary, had both been at the forefront of opposition to the scheme in London and later, throughout the country.

On 11 March 1981 an incident occurred involving Bill Willoughby and a WDO staff restaurant manager called Griffiths. Willoughby had approached the manager regarding the issuing of an 'official notice' under the Food Hygiene Regulations which highlighted the individual legal liability of kitchen staff. This had occurred without prior consultation with the Union and during the course of the meeting Griffiths alleged that Willoughby had banged a table with his fist and sworn at him. As a consequence Willoughby was disciplined, which resulted in him receiving a notification of dismissal on 14 September 1981. This incident occurred a month before the Union's Special Conference in Bournemouth to discuss IWM and supporters of Willoughby argued that the decision to dismiss him was a result of his opposition to IWM. There was also a strongly held view that there was a campaign, backed by Thatcher's Government, to victimise and sack leading trade unionists who opposed the direction that British industry relations was taking.

In 1977 Eric Varley, Secretary of State for Industry, appointed Sir Michael

Edwards to run the state owned British Leyland. Derek Robinson, labelled 'Red Robbo' by the tabloid press was the high profile Union Convener at the companies Birmingham car plant. Following a campaign by the Unions in 1979 to oppose Edwards's rationalisation plans, Robinson was sacked. He received little support from his national trade union and even less from the workers in the Birmingham factory. The charges against Willoughby were seen by many as another example of the attacks being waged against trade unionists and encouraged by a hostile Government. An unofficial meeting of activists and Branch officials was arranged to rally support for Willoughby. Representatives attended from North West London, Harrow, Croydon and the West Central Office where the pro-IWM leadership had been replaced by a leadership opposed to the IWM scheme in a recent election. They decided to send a delegation to the Union's Headquarters to put pressure on the Executive to support Willoughby. On arriving unannounced at the Union's Clapham office they asked to see the General Secretary and when they were asked if they had an appointment, George Durak, Branch Secretary of the North West London branch, replied: 'We don't need an appointment – we own the building'. Willoughby had strong support in his own office where he had been a senior representative for eight years and had recently been re-elected unopposed as the Branch Chairman.

On 13 October Tom Jackson, accompanied by the National Chairman and several other National Officers, met with senior Post Office management to discuss Willoughby's case. Jackson argued that prior to the incident on 11 March Willoughby had a clear conduct record. He also argued that the incident on 11 March was a 'storm in a teacup' that under normal circumstances would have only attracted a moderate penalty. Jackson reminded management that there had been occasions in the past when both he and senior management had used similar language during the course of heated debates. Management responded by saying that although he had a clear record this was only because a number of charges against him, between October 1977 and August 1979, had been dropped following assurances on his future conduct from Jackson. On 20 October 1981 the Post Office sent Jackson a long letter detailing the outcome of the appeal. In the document they set out their decision to uphold the appeal and reduce the penalty to a compulsory transfer to another office located in the Inner London Area. The decision was conveyed to the Executive

Council who agreed to challenge the penalty on the basis that not only was the award excessive but it represented a threat to all the Union's senior representatives. They also decided that unless management had a change of heart an Industrial Action Sub-committee would draw up a program of strike action to challenge the decision. Jackson was instructed by the Executive to convey this message to the newly appointed Chairman of the Post Office, Ron Dearing and although Dearing agreed to a meeting, Jackson was unable to persuade him to change the decision. Jackson called a meeting of the main London Branches at the Union's Clapham Headquarters to gauge the support for industrial action and although the majority of Branches responded positively, a minority raised doubts about the level of support for Willoughby and it was clear that the differences over IWM had affected the views of some Branches. The Executive Council then took a decision to bring the London offices out on strike on Monday 2 November 1981. This would allow a few days for Jackson to try a last ditch attempt to convince the Post Office to review their position before the industrial action took place.

On 29 October a deputation consisting of the General Secretary, the National Chairman and several other National Officers met with Ron Dearing and senior Board members to discuss the issue but were unable to agree a solution. The following day Tom Jackson and Maurice Styles, flanked by the LDC Officers and Committee, addressed a meeting of LDC that had been convened at the Friends Meeting House in Euston Road, NW1 where they both urged the meeting to support the strike action. However it was a speech by Maurice Styles that convinced any waverers. Styles told the meeting that a senior Post Office manager had questioned the ability of the Union to deliver the London membership in support of Willoughby. The manager had argued that he believed the majority of the Union's London membership were unlikely to lose money in support of someone who many of them opposed because of his position regarding IWM. Styles told the manager that he was wrong and he told the meeting that this was because they did not understand working class solidarity. They did not understand why workers were prepared to make sacrifices when they would not personally gain from doing so. They did not understand this because they were motivated by a different set of standards and values. Workers believe in solidarity because they recognise that whatever differences they might have amongst themselves, when it comes to an attack on the Union by the employer, trade unionists would always defend their Union. Delegates from across the District, both Inner and Outer London went to the rostrum to pledge their Branches support for the strike and by the end of the meeting it was quite clear that the capital would be out on Monday morning. When the vote was taken only two Branches voted against the strike decision.

Later that afternoon the Post Office contacted the Union and requested urgent talks to discuss the situation, and a delegation led by Maurice Styles and including the main London District Officers, met management at Postal Headquarters. These discussions continued into the following day but little progress was made. On Sunday the negotiations were joined by Tom Jackson and senior Post Office management and by the end of the day they had managed to hammer out an agreement. It was agreed that an Independent Advisory Review Body (IARB) would be established which would not only deal with the Willoughby case but deal with all cases where senior UPW representatives were either dismissed or compulsory transferred following a conduct case. Willoughby, who had been on paid leave whilst these negotiations had taken place, would be its first case. It was agreed that the IARB would be chaired by Sir John Wordie a practising barrister with wide experience of industrial relations and there would be two other Review Body members. The Post Office and the Union were both asked to nominate an IARB member each. The Post Office proposed Norman Singleton who was a retired senior Civil Servant but the Union objected to him on the basis that because of his previous connections with the industry he could not be trusted to be objective. The Union proposed Hugh Scanlon, President of the Amalgamated Union of Engineering Workers (AUEW) who it is understood the Post Office was not happy with. In the end they both agreed on Bob Ramsey the retired Director of Labour for the Ford Motor Company and Bill Kendall General Secretary of the Council of Civil Service Unions. The hearing was scheduled for 29 January 1982 and it was agreed that both sides would provide their evidence to the IARB by 23 December 1981. On 31 December the Union and the Post Office exchanged documents containing their respective evidence.

The Union's case was presented in a 40 page document by Tom Jackson and the Post Office set out their case in an 80 page document. On 17 February

1982 both sides attended a meeting with the IARB where they were informed by Wordie that Willoughby's original penalty had been overturned and it would be reduced to a suspended dismissal plus a Serious Offence. Bill Willoughby would return to work at the Western District Office and could continue as Branch Chairman. A Special Branch Circular on 19 February reported the outcome to the wider Union and Bill Willoughby and his Branch thanked the union for their assistance in bringing the case to a satisfactory conclusion. Tom Jackson placed on record the thanks of the Executive Council to those Branches and officials who lent their support to the action proposed by the National Union and it was quite clear that the Union had achieved a major victory.

Despite the show of unity in support of Willoughby the internal conflict within the District Council continued and neither side missed an opportunity to raise the issue or criticise their opponents at the monthly Council 3 meetings. The arguments continued at the Union's Annual Conference where those Branches in support of the agreement supported propositions that extended or improved the scheme and those in opposition fought a rear-guard action to reverse the decision or restrict the scheme's development. Inevitably however, the number of Branches involved in the scheme increased as time went by. The pressures on those Branches that remained outside of the scheme or chose to minimise their involvement increased considerably and a number of unofficial disputes took place during this period that resulted in disciplinary action being taken against Dave Percival, Secretary of the Croydon Branch and Norman Candy, Secretary of the West Central No. 1 Branch.

On 16 November 1982 another incident took place at WDO which resulted in management taking further disciplinary action against Bill Willoughby. As a result of this, and although Willoughby was only awarded a Serious Offence and suspended from duty without pay for three days, his suspended dismissal from the previous case was activated and he was dismissed. Bill Willoughby telephoned the LDC 3 Office and spoke to the District Organiser Derek Walsh on the day of the suspension and to let the LDC know of his pending dismissal. Walsh asked him what had happened and he explained that he had gone to the canteen Manager's office on his own and had spoken to Griffiths and the Assistant Manager. It was a friendly meeting and Bill had left the Manager's office without any idea that a day or so later he would receive his suspension letter. Walsh asked him why he had taken the chance of going to the canteen Manager's office on his own with the Assistant Manager being present and Willoughby replied (something to the effect) – if he had known what they were going to do he would have 'covered his back'. Walsh was annoyed about this and there was little doubt in his mind that Bill Willoughby was telling the truth and he had been set up by the canteen Manager. There was a short unofficial strike at the Western District Office but this was called off following intervention from Union Headquarters.

Tom Jackson had retired as General Secretary in February 1982 and was replaced by Alan Tuffin. Tuffin presented Willoughby's appeal to the Post Office's Director of Personnel on 11 May 1982 a few weeks before the Union's Annual Conference. Over the next few weeks a number of unofficial meetings were held amongst London activists in an attempt to shore up support for Willoughby. Some of those involved were concerned that Tuffin's support for Willoughby would not be as robust as Jacksons who had made it quite clear at the meeting of the London District Council that he believed the Post Office's case against Willoughby 'was pure victimisation'. There was also a view that the activists in London who had opposed IWM were being targeted by management for dismissal.

It was agreed that a motion would be submitted to the Union's Annual Conference in Douglas, Isle of Man, aimed at raising the profile of the Willoughby case and establishing better protection for Union representatives threated with discipline. The motion was moved by Norman Candy of the WCDO No. 1 Branch and seconded by Dave Percival Chairman of the Croydon Branch. It read: 'Conference agrees that in view of the recent discipline case against Branch Officers in the London Postal Region (LPR), should a Branch Representative be disciplined as a result of carrying out the instructions of the Branch membership, or should he/she be disciplined whilst carrying out his/her responsibilities as a Branch Representative, the Executive Council is instructed to remove such cases from the realms of the normal discipline procedure, and any complaint regarding the actions of a representative acting in their representative capacity should be subject to direct negotiation between the Union and Management.'

The mover and seconder argued that the motion was essential to protect the Union's representatives against victimisation and provided examples of where they believed this had already occurred in the London Postal Region. Support came from a number of London postal Branches but also two Telecoms Branches who identified a similar situation in British Telecoms. Tuffin told the Conference that there was no evidence to suggest either British Telecoms or the Post Office were deliberately harassing or victimising union officials in either London or elsewhere. He went on to argue that if the procedures for dealing with Union representatives was different from that which applied to the ordinary member then this would place a wedge between the representatives and the rest of the membership. He also argued that it would result in the Union taking on a disciplinary role which was something that he did not want to do. When the vote was taken the motion was defeated by 6,317 votes to 9,481 votes.

On 28 June 1983, a month after the end of the Annual Conference, the Union received notice that Bill Willoughby had lost his appeal. Branches were informed of the decision in a Special Branch Circular on 18 July. It also explained that Willoughby would have no recourse to an Independent Advisory Review Body hearing because his dismissal had not arisen from the incident in November 1982 but as a consequence of his earlier suspended dismissal. Shift meetings were held at the Western District Office where Frank Osie-Tutu the Branch Secretary and Executive Council member addressed the members. This did not result in the expected unofficial industrial action and on Friday 8 July the General Secretary, Alan Tuffin, Deputy General Secretary Tony Clarke and Frank Osie-Tutu Executive Council member met with senior Post Office management to try and resolve the problem. The outcome was a draft agreement that would keep Willoughby in Post Office employment but would result in his transfer to an unspecified office in the South East London area. This formula was not automatically accepted by the Union's negotiators because they were not prepared to accept the proposal until they had an opportunity to discuss the outcome with both Bill Willoughby and the Executive Council. Details of the draft agreement were put to Willoughby who asked for time to consider the proposal. He was asked by Tuffin to give his decision before 13 July, the day the Executive were due to discuss the case. On 12 July Willoughby informed him that he found the terms unacceptable. The next day the Executive Council made the decision that 'after considering the position in relation to the advice of the IARB, in February 1982, and the agreement which exists between the Union and the Post Office to deal in certain circumstances, with cases involving disciplinary award to UCW senior representatives, decided that the terms of the negotiated agreement should be accepted'. They noted Willoughby's decision to reject the deal and agreed that no further action would be taken on the matter. The Post Office confirmed that Bill Willoughby's last day of service would be 23 July 1983.

Willoughby's dismissal was a major blow to the anti-IWM camp. He had been a leading figure in the campaign and his dismissal removed an articulate and skilled advocate from the opposition and from the District Council. In November the Branch Officers Bulletin reported that Alan Tuffin on behalf of the Union had written to Willoughby regarding a report that he was due to speak at a meeting of the Communication Workers Broad Left (CWBL) in Coventry. The report claimed that a leaflet advertising the meeting was suggesting that he would be giving 'an account of his work and the treacherous role played by our Union's leadership in his victimisation'. In the letter, which was published in full, Tuffin informed Willoughby that 'if the report, published in the CWBL Newsletter is reliable, and you intend to go ahead to publicly castigate the Union for alleged treachery, then I will have no alternative but to terminate any further correspondence or contact with you'. Willoughby had decided to take his case to an Industrial Tribunal. He was doing this without the financial support of the Union and Tuffin's threat would obviously impact on his ability to prepare his case. Although the case went ahead Willoughby was not successful in his attempt to be re-instated.

Shepherds Bush Dispute

At its 1983 Conference the Union decided that changes needed to be made to the IWM Bonus Scheme. In particular to the clause that allowed management to abate a full week's core bonus, in the event of the service being disrupted because of industrial action. Discussions took place at the highest level involving Alan Tuffin and senior Post Office managers. The union argued that any stoppage of pay due to industrial action should be pro-rata to the length of the stoppage but following a meeting on September 1983 the Union received a letter from the Director Postal Pay and Grading rejecting the Union's claim.

In 1983 there had been a number of unofficial disputes in IWM offices.

These included Southampton, Reading and Bedford and in all these offices the Post Office had conceded the principle of the pro-rata stoppage of bonus payments in the locally agreed resolutions. In November 1983 a dispute over an imposed delivery revision occurred at the Shepherds Bush Delivery Office in West London. Work in the office began to accumulate and the local manager response to this situation was to cancel the second delivery and the 9.15 a.m. collection. Within a few days the backlog had built up and this resulted in management cancelling all the collections in the W12 area. Unable to accept that the backlog of work was as a consequence of the loss of five duties removed when the revision was imposed, management informed the Branch that their IWM bonus payments would be withheld for two weeks on the pretext that the staff were taking industrial action. The Branch was also informed that they would not be able to take the dispute through the agreed disagreement procedure. This resulted in 58 members of the Branch taking unofficial industrial action on Thursday 1 December.

Several attempts were made by the LDC Officers to resolve the problem and a meeting was held with the Director of the London Postal Region. The Director refused to intervene on the basis that IWM was a national agreement and he had no authority to amend the industrial action clause. This was despite the fact that management had already conceded this point in a number of other Regions. Following this the LDC Officers referred the issue to the Union's Headquarters. In the meantime an emergency meeting of the London District Council 3 was called where the District Officers Derek Saunders, Mike Hogan and Don Failes gave a report on the situation. The meeting agreed to establish a fund, based on a levy of £1 per member a week, to financially support the 58 strikers for the duration of the dispute. This raised a considerable amount of money from the 30,000 London members with both pro- and anti-IWM offices contributing to the fund equally. This financial support proved to be essential because it was two weeks before the General Secretary and a delegation of senior national officers met with the Post Office.

The meeting with the Director for Industrial Relations took place on 15 December, and despite the meeting lasting five and a half hours the Union were unable to persuade management to change their position. On 19 December the Union received a letter from the Director rejecting the Union's claim and on 21 December Tuffin called the Executive Council together to discuss the Union's next move. Tuffin gave the Executive a detailed report of the negotiations and proposed that the Union make the dispute official and that each member on strike would be given a hardship payment of £70 per week. The Executive decided at this stage not to extend the strike to the rest of London but to seek an urgent meeting with Ron Dearing, Chairman of the Post Office, in a last ditch attempt to resolve the dispute. A meeting with Dearing took place that afternoon where the Union was represented by Alan Tuffin and four of the Union's national officials including John Taylor. Dearing warned the Union that the dispute threatened the letter monopoly and would result in a loss of major business contracts. It was only four days before Christmas and even if the dispute was settled that day it was unlikely that the customers in the W12 area would receive their Christmas mail. The Union's view was that the disruption was the result of London management's refusal to act reasonably. After several hours of fruitless discussions, and to avoid a breakdown, it was agreed that the negotiations would continue under the chairmanship of the Board Member for Personnel and Industrial Relations. At this meeting management offered to amend the industrial action clause if the Union agreed to accept other changes to the agreement. This was rejected by the Union and after a further four hours of discussions both sides agreed to refer the issue to the Advisory, Conciliation and Arbitration Service (ACAS). ACAS met with the Post Office and the Union that evening but although the discussions continued until 3.30 a.m. the next morning no agreement was reached. A further meeting took place with the Post Office Chairman, Ron Dearing and finally it was agreed that the dispute would be referred to binding arbitration. This was a risky strategy for both sides but the Executive supported the proposal and on Thursday 22 December the London officials and the LPR negotiated a return to work agreement for the W12 office. The Shepherds Bush members accepted the formula at a meeting addressed by the General Secretary, John Taylor. Derek Saunders, Mike Hogan and Don Failes returned to work at 6.00 a.m. on Friday 23 December 1983.

ACAS proposed a number of possible candidates for Chairman of the Arbitration Board and both sides were happy to accept Ian Buchanan, Senior Lecturer in Economics at Dundee University for the role. Eric Hammond, General Secretary Elect of the EETPU was chosen to represent the Union and R.L. Worsfold CBE was nominated by the Post Office.

There was a certain amount of apprehension in London regarding the decision to go to binding arbitration and also concern at the choice of the Union's nomination for the Board. Hammond was considered by many London activists to be a poor choice, even before his infamous involvement in the 'News International Dispute in 1986'. However this concern proved to be unfounded. The Arbitration Board hearing began on 2 February 1984 at ACAS's London Headquarters and on 21 February the Union received the Board's judgement. The unanimous decision was 'That the industrial action clause in paragraph 2 of both the main and interpretive National IWM Agreement between the parties should be modified so that the bonuses are stopped pro-rata to the days on which any industrial action takes place as the Union claims'. This was a complete vindication of the Union's position and within a few days a new Postal Instruction was issued not only reflecting the change to paragraph 2 but also giving the Union the right to challenge management's decisions through the disagreements procedure in the event that any future bonus payments were abated. This was widely recognised as an important victory for the Union that benefited members far beyond the London District Council.

Chapter 16

NEW TECHNOLOGY
AND THE 1984 TRADE UNION ACT

In the 1980s Britain went to war with Argentina in a dispute over the Falkland Islands. The Windows program was invented by Microsoft, digital mobile phones were invented and the World Wide Webb was proposed by Timothy Berners-Lee. There were riots in Brixton in 1981 and 1985 and the Kings Cross fire killed 31 people in 1987. Print workers employed by News International went on strike in 1986 in the long running and bitter 'Wapping Dispute'. The 'Big Bang' in 1986 relaxed regulations on share dealing, banking and financial services. London's financial and banking services grew at an astonishing rate between 1981 and 1991. During this period financial services grew by 30% but by 1990 London's manufacturing had been decimated with its share of the London economy falling from 40% to 12% when compared to the 1950s.

Industrial and trade union life in the 1980s was dominated by the threatened miners' strike in 1981 and the actual miners' strike in 1984. It was widely accepted that in the 1970s the National Union of Mineworkers had brought down Edward Heath's Conservative Government. When Margaret Thatcher backed down from a confrontation with the NUM in 1981, over the closure of 20 pits, it was seen by many in the Labour Movement as a sign of weakness rather than a tactical retreat by the Government in preparation for a bigger fight three years later. In the wake of the 1984 Miner's strike the Conservatives accelerated the introduction of their anti-trade union laws and the de-industrialisation of the country in the knowledge that they were up against a wounded and weakened opposition. Thatcher's election had provided employers with the confidence to take on the big battalions of the trade union movement and Post Office management took the opportunity to accelerate the introduction of a number of projects that the Union were obstructing. The Monopolies and Mergers Commission (MMC) produced its second report in July 1984. It was critical of the pace of change and the failure of the Post Office to press ahead with the introduction of new technology and changes to work practices.

In 1979 the Union commissioned the Science Policy Research Unit (SPRU) at the University of Sussex to produce a report designed to assess the impact of new technology and its effect on the Union's members over the next 10 to 15 years. The Report concluded that the Union faced massive job losses in both the Postal and Telecommunications sectors and that if the Union refused to co-operate then this would simply damage the service to customers and damage the Post Office's position compared to its competitors. They suggested two possible strategies that the Union could employ to deal with the problem. In exchange for the Union's co-operation with its introduction they could negotiate higher wages for those that remained in the business and increased redundancy payments for those that left. Alternatively, and in exchange for the maintenance of higher employment levels, they could reduce hours, seek longer holidays, improve maternity and paternity leave, and negotiate retraining packages and sabbatical leave for staff wishing to take up adult education. The Union received the Report from SPRU in January 1980 and it was published and circulated to Branches in September 1980. In the same month the Executive Council published and circulated the Union's initial response to the Report and asked Branches to submit their comments and views on the Report in time for the Executive's November meeting. A commentary on the Report, produced by the Post Office, was also circulated. It was very critical, suggesting that the report contained 'a combination of misunderstandings, factual errors, selectively presented evidence and unsupported assertions' which 'in the view of the postal business must cast doubt on the credibility of the Report and its status as a piece of academic research'. Only 36 Branches responded despite the deadline being extended to December.

The first opportunity for the Union to debate the SPRU Report took place at the 1981 Annual Conference in Brighton. An amendment to the Annual Report, moved by Arthur McGuiness on behalf of the Liverpool Counter and Clerical Branch, instructed the Executive to produce a Special Report for discussion at a Special or General Conference no later than the 1982 Annual

Conference. It was vigorously, but unsuccessfully, opposed by Alan Tuffin the Deputy General Secretary, who argued that the Union could not afford to wait until 1982.

An Emergency Special Report on New Technology was presented to the 1982 Annual Conference in Bournemouth on Wednesday 26 May. It was moved by the Union's Assistant Secretary responsible for new technology, Les Hewitt. Hewitt was a postman from South East London and before his election to the Executive in 1967 he had been the Branch Secretary of the South East District Office (SEDO) No. 1 Branch. In 1981 he became a National Officer and his election took place against a background of considerable controversy. He had been unable to obtain a nomination for the Executive Council elections from his Branch because of his support for the 1979 pay deal which a sizeable number of his Branches members had opposed. However, presumably with the help of the National Union, he managed to arrange a transfer to the Woking Branch where he obtained a nomination. A letter headed 'To our Colleagues at Woking' and signed ' Yours in Solidarity, Rank and File Members UPW, SEDO' was circulated in the Woking Office urging them not to support Hewitt's nomination. A complaint to UPW Headquarters by the Woking Branch led to an inquiry by the Deputy General Secretary Norman Stagg but the authors were never identified and he received his nomination.

The Special Report detailed the terms of the Union's conditions for co-operating with the introduction of new technology. It included a claim for a 13 hour reduction in the working week introduced over seven years, early retirement, sabbaticals and various other improvements to terms and conditions. It was pointed out that the shorter working week alone would add £342 million to the total wage bill but nevertheless the Union was determined to get an agreement. The Special Report was endorsed with little change and for a number of years New Technology took a backseat to the more immediate and controversial issue of IWM. However this changed in 1984 after IWM had become established and the Post Office committed itself to introducing radical changes to working practices and a new generation of technology. In 1984 the Post Office made an attempt to link its pay offer to the Union agreeing a number of changes. These included co-operation with the introduction of new technology, agreement to IWM becoming mandatory in every office and an increase in the level of part-timers. There had been a proposition agreed by delegates at the 1983 Conference, under the slogan of 'no strings attached to the 1984 pay deal' that restricted the ability of the Executive Council to negotiate on these issues. Although the final 1984 pay settlement had no 'strings' attached, it did commit the Union to hold separate talks on a 'range of pay issues which had been deadlocked for a number of years'.

The Post Office had been testing an Optical Character Recognition (OCR) machine at the Mount Pleasant sorting office for some time. The OCR was capable of coding letters without the need for machine operators and the Union had a Conference policy of refusing to operate it with live mail until the Post Office conceded on a number of issues including a shorter working week. They had been unable to persuade successive Conferences to allow them more flexibility in negotiations and they were coming under increasing pressure from the Post Office to change their position. The second Monopolies and Mergers Commission Report noted that 'The Post Office's fundamental view is that progress can be maintained and the desired ends eventually achieved, if it persists in its present endeavours to introduce change with the co-operation of the unions, while being prepared to take executive action if that proves necessary in the end'.

Following the acceptance of the 1984 pay agreement talks began on the outstanding issues and although a number of meetings took place in between September and October, amounting to over 100 hours of negotiations, little progress was made. The Post Office issued a statement claiming that whilst differences existed on a number of issues progress had been 'thwarted' by the union's demand for a 3 hour reduction in the working week. They claimed that the 43 hours postmen and PHGs worked was equivalent to 39.5 hours if paid meal breaks were taken into consideration and that at a time when the 'New Earnings Survey' indicated a national average of 39.2 for manual workers the Union's claim was unreasonable. On 12 September 1984 the Post Office Chairman took the unusual step of sending a personal letter to all members of staff outlining their position. The Union countered this by arguing that the claim for less hours had been with the Post Office since 1974 and, whilst they had irrefutable evidence of significant progress towards a shorter working week in other industries, the last reduction in hours for UCW members was in 1965. They insisted that their claim was wholly justified and that a substantial reduction in the working week would be required if the Executive Council were to recommend an agreement to the membership.

On 23 November 1984 the Union received a letter from K.M. Young, on behalf of the Post Office, outlining their position and threatening to implement a range of changes because of the failure of the discussions to make any progress. On 28 November 1985 the Postal Group Management Committee (PGMC) met to consider their response. They came to the conclusion that the Union had to change direction, move away from confrontation, ditch its previous policies and negotiate a deal with the Post Office. A Special Conference of the Unions Postal Group was called where the Executive recommended that 'there would be a re-assessment of all previous Conference decisions relating to the issues under discussion'. Alan Tuffin wrote to the Post Office on 30 November informing them that the Conference would be held on 4 and 5 March 1985 and the Executive would be recommending a change of policy. He asked them to reconsider their position, continue the negotiations and give the Union's Conference time to debate the issue before they implemented any changes. In his reply K.M. Young acknowledged the efforts of the negotiators to find a settlement, but warned that the Union's response would force the business to proceed without the Union's agreement. On 17 December 1984 the Union dispatched special issues of *The Post* to Branches that contained a detailed report of all the discussion that had taken place and those issues that had made it impossible to reach an agreement. It was entitled 'Special Report on Postal Business Efficiency: Conditions of Employment' and on 4 March the Union assembled in Bournemouth to debate the Report.

In his introductory speech Alan Tuffin urged the Conference 'to give the Executive Council flexibility in the negotiations we want with the Post Office' and went on to say, 'The issues posed by the Report and the decisions we take are likely to have a profound and lasting impact for our membership in the Post Office. The choice is stark and let none of us run away from it. On the one hand the Report by the Executive Council offers opportunities, on the other hand, it poses the possibility of confrontation'. He went on to tell the Conference that in a hundred hours of negotiations the Union had failed to achieve an agreement with the employer and that the Union should have the courage to re-assess its priorities and that he was confident that the Union could meet the challenge.

The first four amendments called for either the rejection of the Report, industrial action or the censure of the Executive Council and these came from

Branches ranging from as far apart as Portsmouth and Glasgow. Les Hewitt, John Taylor and Alan Tuffin opposed them on behalf of the Executive and after lengthy debates, in which most speakers supported the Executive, they were all defeated on a show of hands.

Although London was as divided on this issue as they were over IWM a number of Branches had got together and agreed an amendment which was moved by Charlie Scully, SEDO No. 1 Branch and Seconded by Norman Candy, WCDO No. 1 Branch. It asked the Conference to defend its current policies on part-time labour, no operational use of OCR, inward code sorting, mandatory IWM, and retirement at 55 until the Post Office moved its position on the shorter working week and several other issues in the Union's claim. The proposition was opposed by Les Hewitt who, in a hard hitting contribution, urged the Conference to reassess its policies. The proposition was defeated in a card vote by 6,254 to 8,069 which was described in a later edition of *The Post* as 'a victory for realism'. The Croydon Amalgamated Branch, in an amendment moved by Dave Percival, made a last ditch attempt to phase out existing IWM schemes and replace them with lump sum payments but the amendment was defeated although the London Stations Amalgamated Branch in an amendment moved by Hughie Bowles convinced the Conference that the IWM scheme should remain voluntary. The Conference went on to agree that there would be no agreement to the extension of part-timers and agreed an amendment moved by Aubrey Beyer, ADO LDC 3 that OCRs would not be accepted operationally until the Post Office had identified the precise number of jobs that would be lost. Although the Executive had managed to convince the Conference to allow them more flexibility they were still restricted on a number of major issues. Those Branches that had opposed the Executive's policy felt that they had done enough to push them into taking a stronger line in the negotiations.

Immediately following the Special Conference the Union contacted the Post Office and a meeting was arranged for 12 March. The negotiating team informed management that they were now in a position to re-assess all previous policies except on the issues of part-time and casual staff and the introduction of a mandatory IWM scheme. Tuffin explained that they were now in a position to negotiate on a wide range of subjects provided the Post Office was prepared to negotiate on improved terms and conditions of employment. The Post Office's view was that the Conference's decisions were a major setback and that the decisions effectively wrecked the chances of getting an agreement. They made it absolutely clear that they had no intention of withdrawing their threat of executive action, informed the Union that they would confirm their position in writing and asked the Union to reflect on the situation. Further meetings took place on 20 and 25 March when it was agreed that they would try to produce a draft agreement by 31 March. On Saturday 30 March they met in a last ditch attempt to reach an agreement but although progress had been made in a number of areas they could still not agree on increasing the level of part-time and casual staff. Negotiations broke down on Saturday evening at 8.30 p.m. when it was agreed that the Union's negotiators would report back to the PGMC on Tuesday 2 April.

On Sunday 31 March, Alan Tuffin was informed that the Post Office intended to call a press conference and announce the breakdown of negotiations and it was also their intention to introduce the changes by executive action, including the use of the OCR machine at Mount Pleasant. The Union had previously agreed to assist with the trials of the OCR but the agreement covering this was due to expire on 31 March. Representatives from the two Mount Pleasant Branches, the Inland Section Postal (postmen/women) and the Inland Section Amalgamated (PHG's) were summoned to UCW Headquarters on Monday 1 April and informed that the Executive had made a decision to instruct their members not to operate the OCR's from 4.00 p.m. that evening. They were handed a written instruction dated 29 March confirming this. In the meantime the Post Office had been to the High Court and obtained an injunction under the 1984 Trade Union Act declaring that the Union's actions were unlawful and ordering the Union to cease its intended industrial action. The Executive Council, faced with the possible sequestration of the Union's funds, agreed to abide by the terms of the injunction and dispatched John Taylor, Assistant Secretary to Mount Pleasant to explain the situation to the members. However, whilst Taylor was making his way there, four UCW members were suspended, after refusing to work on the OCR in support of the earlier instruction. The rest of the Mount Pleasant membership had walked out in support and Alan Tuffin had appeared on the BBC and ITV Evening News urging the Mount Pleasant members to return to work. This resulted in a great deal of confusion because the Mount Pleasant members had walked out in support of the Executives earlier instruction and it was only when Taylor arrived and explained why the Union was now telling them to work normally that the members returned to work.

The Executive made a decision to ballot the Mount Pleasant members, in line with the new legislation, with a recommendation that they vote for industrial action. The Post Office contacted the Union inviting them to further discussions on 2 April 1985. At the meeting, both sides agreed to take a step back, and a provisional agreement on all the outstanding issues was reached, which the Executive Council at a meeting on 4 April agreed, would be put as a Special Report before the Union's May Conference.

The Chairman Derek Hodgson opened the Post Office Group Conference at 2.15 p.m. on Sunday 19 May at Bournemouth. The Special Report 'Safeguarding Jobs and the Mail Service', amongst other things, represented a complete change to the process for negotiating and agreeing staffing levels. Previously the agreed method used was based on the study and manual testing of duties. This involved the physical counting of the offices mails traffic and the use of the guidelines contained in Head Postmasters Manuals (W) to agree and construct duties. The new agreement proposed the introduction of 'Revised Revision Procedures' based on a rate per item of traffic set by independent work measurement techniques. It also accepted the introduction of an increased level of part-time workers (Associate Grades) and casuals, scheduled attendance (contracted overtime), new technology and code sorting keying rates, mandatory IWM and various other changes to long standing work practices. In exchange for this staff would receive a guarantee on no compulsory redundancies, involvement and consultation on the introduction and planning of new technology, improvements to bonus payments and a lump sum payment of £275 paid in two stages. A similar deal was proposed for catering staff, cleaners, liftmen and doorkeepers. The Special Report was moved by the General Secretary and in his opening address he warned Conference that the Union was in grave danger. The enemy was not the Post Office Board or the District Postmasters but the Government hell bent on privatisation and attacking the public sector he argued. The Executive believed it was essential that the Union changed its policies to avoid conflict and play into the hands of those in Government who were in favour of the Post Office losing its monopoly and privatising the industry.

In the period between the Special Conference and the Annual Conference the national leadership had been able to convince a significant number of

Branches that a change in policy was necessary. Those activists and Branches who wanted the Union to take a stronger line had only informal contact with each other although the 'Broad Left' and *The Post Office Worker* had attempted to co-ordinate opposition. London had no unified policy and the Branches were still broadly divided along the lines established during the IWM debate.

The opposition in London, who generally speaking were not opposed to the Union reaching an agreement, felt that the national leadership had conceded too much in return for very little from the Post Office. They moved away from total rejection and instead tabled a number of amendments designed to force more concessions from the Post Office, limit the scope of IWM, and restrict the increase in part-timers and casuals. Liverpool Amalgamated Branch however, moved an amendment seconded by Northampton PHG Branch, to reject the report and this received some support from London Branches. It was moved by Billy Hayes who urged the delegates to reject the report and challenged the General Secretary to take the Post Office on. 'The only time the Post Office listen is when we've got them by the throat' he argued. 'The only time they were prepared to listen was when those magnificent men in the Mount said we're going home'. He went on to ask Tuffin when he was going to start fighting and sat down to rapturous applause and a standing ovation. However, it was clear that the Union's machinery had been hard at work. Hayes was followed to the rostrum by a well-orchestrated line-up of District Organisers who all urged the Conference to reject the Liverpool proposition. These included DOs from Northern Ireland, the North West, Anglia and London. Tuffin in a hard hitting reply told the Conference 'It was not a matter of being chicken. The Liverpool Branch want you to stand still but if we do stand still we will be knocked over and the injuries will be fatal'. In an equally ardent reply, Hayes urged the Conference to reject the Special Report: 'Sooner or later we are going to have to take them on, if you say that now is not the time, when is the time? When will it be? Tell me'. The amendment was defeated in a show of hands as were all the propositions calling for the report to be rejected.

An attempt to limit the scope of the Report and establish more control over its application was tried when Lionel Sampson, Secretary of the Dartford Amalgamated Branch, moved an amendment instructing the Executive to ensure that work rates and work measurement techniques were agreed with the Union before their implementation. 'Our members demand and deserve more from these systems. If we are not careful we will become the sacrificial lamb to those two important goals – lower unit costs and increased productivity', he argued. Sampson went on to say that the Conference should not accept a new procedure without understanding what it involved and although it received strong support from those Branches that entered the debate it was not carried. The Leeds office was taking part in a trial of the new procedures and they made it clear that they opposed the amendment. The Widnes Branch moved an amendment to reject IWM becoming mandatory but this was also defeated. The Executive had achieved their objective. By the end of the Conference the Special Report was un-amended except for those changes that they had supported. John Taylor summed up the view of the Executive: 'I have to warn you that if delegates do not vote to go into IWM mandatory, those small branches that have been referred to in this debate will be mutilated. We are going to have part-timers with or without this agreement. We are going to have new revision procedures introduced with or without this agreement. Under the new revision procedures we get 75% of the savings – non staff hours we get 75% for a three year period. I am totally committed to IWM; because this is the only way we are going to protect our member's take home pay. If you do not grasp this nettle and believe that you are not able to negotiate locally, you will destroy our member's take home pay'.

In the aftermath of the Conference there was a heightening of tension as management pressed Branches to implement the agreement. The two sides met following Conference, and a number of changes to the agreement were made. In July 1985 the Union held a Branch ballot on the final settlement and the result was 7,284 in favour and 5,314 against. When Alan Tuffin wrote to the Post Office to inform them of the outcome he made the following comment: 'I do hope that in implementing these revised arrangements and procedures due account will be taken of the fact that many of our Branches will find it difficult to assimilate the changes and I hope, therefore, that your Managers will exercise tact and understanding in applying the agreement'. Full details of the new agreement, now called 'Safeguarding the Future of the Mails Business', were circulated to Branches in an 88 page handbook. Some Branches took the view that whilst accepting the outcome of the Conference they would restrict their involvement and co-operation with the agreement to the absolute minimum. Within a few months this resulted in a number of disagreements and unofficial disputes in various offices in the District including WDO, Croydon, and Greenwich where the Branch Secretary, Mark Palfrey held out until they forced in.

Trade Union Legislation 1980 to 1990

The Conservatives had introduced their first trade union legislation in 1980 and 1982 and two years later they built on this with the 1984 Trade Union Act. This legislation forced unions to change their election procedures and introduce secret ballots before they took industrial action. Before 1981 the Union elected its National Officers by Branch ballots and once elected they held the position until they retired, or resigned. Many members, activists and Branches were unhappy with this situation and attempts had been made to make the process more democratic over the years. At the 1982 Rules Revision Conference a New Rule was proposed that read 'that General Officers shall be elected for a term of office not exceeding five years'. The motion was moved by Eric Lovett and seconded by Phil Waker both from the East London Counters Branch. The proposition was vigorously opposed by Alan Tuffin, who accused the supporters of using the same arguments as Margaret Thatcher and *The Daily Telegraph* to attack the Union's rule book. Lovett and others who supported the new rule argued that it was nothing to do with the Tories or Thatcher but a question of democracy. Following a lively debate the motion was carried and the rule book revised to reflect the change although the election was still conducted by Branch Ballot and not an individual secret ballot.

The 1984 legislation changed this because it forced all trade unions to hold individual secret ballots of not only their National Officers but all voting Executive Council members. They would also have to stand for election every five years and failure to implement the changes would result in the Union losing its financial immunity. The Act also required unions to hold a secret ballot of all those members affected before calling a strike. Before the 1984 Act the Union's Rule 19 gave the Executive Council the sole authority to call industrial action, although the Union's Annual Conferences could instruct the Executive to hold a ballot if it chose to. The third part of the Act required unions to hold a secret ballot if they wished to maintain a Political Fund. This would have to be validated by the membership every ten years. It also required unions to hold a register of its member's names and addresses which had to be updated on a regular basis. This forced unions to keep accurate records and to routinely contact their members to check their information was correct. Ironically this led to the UCW recruiting hundreds of new members who had slipped through the net of the normal recruiting procedures.

In May 1985 the Union announced that in response to the new legislation they would be conducting a member's workplace ballot to allow them to maintain a Political Fund. The Union urged the membership to retain the fund to allow the Union to conduct political campaigns and influence political decisions, not simply finance the Labour Party. The ballot was held on Thursday 6 June and the result was an overwhelming vote to retain the fund. When Tony Clarke, Deputy General Secretary announced the result, it showed that in a 69.4% turnout, 102,546 had voted to keep the fund and 33,337 against. It was a resounding victory for the Union and because the UCW was amongst the first of the unions nationally to hold a ballot, in the words of Tony Clarke 'It was a great result, heart-warming and encouraging – a fitting conclusion to the UCW's hard fought campaign for the 'Yes' vote'.

The 1984 legislation allowed unions the time to amend their rule books in order to comply with the requirements of the Act. The UCW formalised this at the 1985 Rules Revision Conference and the Special Conference on the Trade Union Act held in Bournemouth in May 1986. In December 1986 a member of the Birmingham Head Office Amalgamated Branch, Ken Jarrett complained to the Certification Office that the Union's 1986 Executive Council elections were not conducted in line with the 1984 Trade Union Act. Representatives of the Union met with the Certification Officer who ruled that the 1986 elections should have been conducted on the basis of an individual secret ballot and therefore did not comply with the new Act. However, he also noted that the Union had subsequently changed its rules and had fully co-operated with his investigation. As a consequence the Union was not penalised but was instructed to bring its next round of elections forward to January 1987.

Thatcher's Governments strategy was to use the legislation to shackle the trade unions whilst at the same time destroying the Labour Movement's industrial base by transforming Britain from an industrial nation to one dependent on financial services, banking, insurance and the service industries. This strategy was largely successful and one of the consequences was that the level of industrial action in the country declined from the middle of the 1980s onwards. However, the number of strikes in the Post Office increased throughout the early 1980s with much of this due to unofficial strike action. In 1980/1 there were 47 strikes, involving 1,200 workers resulting in 2,000 lost working days, and this steadily increased until it hit a peak in 1988-9 of 323 strikes, involving 277,000 workers with the loss of 1,100,000 working days. Whatever the general effect of Thatcher's policies on worker's willingness to take industrial action it clearly did not affect postal workers in the same way. In fact it is clear that the new legislation introduced to reduce the level of unofficial action was ignored by large sections of postal workers and rather than a decrease in the level of unofficial industrial action it increased.

In July 1986 Mike Hogan, a member of the ECDO No. 1 Branch and London District Organiser joined the Executive Council to replace John Griffiths who had become Chairman of the Post Office Union's Council (POUC). The Union and London lost two prominent figures in 1987, Frank Osie-Tutu and John Taylor. They had been the leading protagonists for the opposing sides in the battles over IWM on the London District Council for almost a decade. In February 1987, Alan Tuffin announced that Frank Osie-Tutu had ceased to be a member of the Union and as a consequence he was no longer a member of the Executive Council. The Post Office had taken the view that Osie-Tutu had 'abandoned service' and he ceased to be employed by them from November 1986. Osie-Tutu had written to the General Secretary saying that he was seriously ill but further attempts to contact him were unsuccessful. In July 1987 Alan Tuffin announced the early retirement of Assistant Secretary, John Taylor, whose long struggle with alcoholism had reached the stage where he could no longer cope with the responsibilities of his job. In a communication to Branches Tuffin said 'that this decision will be received with some sadness, as well as concern in that we all wish to see the end of the deterioration in John's health and some improvements where possible'.They had both worked hard for the Union for many years and friends and opponents of both men recognised that whatever their differences they had both made a considerable contribution to the strength and development of the organisation.

Chapter 17

SHORTER WORKING WEEK 1987

In 1987 the Union's claim for a shorter working week was 13 years old and there had not been a reduction for 22 years. The Union's Annual Conference had rejected an opportunity for a two hour reduction in 1980 because the conditions the Post Office had linked to the offer were unacceptable. In 1987 several meetings had taken place in an attempt to resolve the issue but without any significant progress being made. The Union was represented in the negotiations by Les Hewitt, Harry Jones, Ernie Dudley and Derek Walsh. The first meeting had taken place in January 1987 and they continued right up until the Union's Annual Conference in May. At the final meeting the Post Office offered an hours reduction but his was rejected because management insisted on it being self-financing. It was formally rejected by the Postal Group Management Committee (PGMC) and an Oral Supplementary Report was placed on the agenda of the Annual Conference with a recommendation that the Executive be given the authority to ballot the membership for industrial action. Les Hewitt moved the report and emphasized the Executive's view that they should be given the flexibility to choose the timing and method of industrial action should it become necessary. Hewitt explained that the negotiations had been long and difficult and he urged the Conference to reject any of the numerous amendments that had been submitted against the report claiming that if they 'tied the hands' of the negotiators or set deadlines for resolving the dispute it would make it more difficult to reach an agreement. The Executive, he added, were prepared to ballot for industrial action but it needed to be at their discretion and when they felt that the negotiations had been exhausted.

A number of amendments rejecting the Executive's recommendation and replacing it with a tougher line had been submitted. The first was a Composite Amendment moved by the Liverpool Amalgamated Branch and seconded by the Croydon Amalgamated Branch. Billy Hayes moved the amendment and argued that a stronger recommendation was needed if the Union was to make a breakthrough after 13 years without any progress. He proposed a strategy that included a claim for a 3 hour reduction in the working week, at no cost to the membership, with a deadline of 1 September 1987 for its introduction. He went on to argue that if there was no progress then the Union should ballot the membership for industrial action and finished by saying that any subsequent agreement had to be agreed by a Conference of the Union. Dave Percival seconded the amendment and emphasized the long history of the Union's struggle to reduce working hours and the need to have a firm deadline for the completion of the negotiations. Hewitt when he replied to the debate insisted that if the amendment was carried, it would be more difficult for the negotiators to reach an agreement and urged the Conference to reject the amendment. However when the Chairman put the proposition to the vote Hewitt's arguments were rejected and the amendment was carried. The decision was significant for a number of reasons. Firstly it was the first time since 1971 that the Union's Conference had agreed to confront the employer on an issue relating to terms and conditions backed up by the threat of industrial action. It was also the first time since the end of the miner's strike in 1985 and the introduction of the new trade union legislation that a major union had been prepared to challenge a major company and ballot its members for strike action

On 24 September 1987 the Union dispatched a Special Branch Circular informing the membership that the negotiations that had been ongoing since the Annual Conference had now broken down. In early October Branches were informed that the Union was making preparation for a ballot and in the following weeks a special edition of *The Post* and several leaflets were distributed to Branches urging the members to vote for industrial action. The legislation in 1987 allowed unions to hold workplace ballots and on Thursday 29 October Branches began distributing individual ballot papers to their members. The result was announced a few weeks later and it showed that there were 73,349 votes for industrial action and 58,917 against. This represented a 55.46% vote in favour of action and a clear mandate for the

Executive to authorize a strike. During the next few weeks the two sides held five more meetings in an attempt to find a resolution and at the end of these discussions a draft agreement had been reached which the Executive felt was good enough to recommend to the members.

On 8 January 1988 a special issue of *The Post* was circulated containing a detailed report of the negotiations and the proposed agreement. The deal gave postmen, PHG's, cleaners and doorkeepers a 1.5 hour reduction in the working week and catering grades 1 hour plus a £100 lump sum payment. There was no reduction for the clerical grades who already worked less hours per week that the manual grades. It also promised an increase in the number of 5 day weeks (most uniformed grades still worked 6 days) but the most important element of the agreement, and the most controversial, was the proposal to cease IWM. It was proposed that this would be done by buying-out the existing scheme and replacing it with a new scheme based on Real Unit Labour Costs. This would result in many of those Branches that had embraced the scheme losing a considerable amount of money from their weekly pay packets. However there were 22,000 members who had never received any bonus payments from the scheme and 53% received less than £10 per week. The Executive explained why they had not been able to achieve any reduction for the clerical grades which they said was as a result of Government interference. They also claimed that during the negotiations the Post Office had attempted to divert IWM savings towards those areas of the country where they were finding it difficult to recruit staff and that this had been rejected by the Executive. The final settlement involved a minimum weekly supplement of £7.50 and a maximum of £20. Offices or units earning more than this would be subject to a buy-out formula which provided considerable lump sum payments over a two or three year period as compensation. The deal gave a large number of members an increase in take home pay and the first reduction in the working week for 22 years.

Opposition to the deal was strongest in the high IWM bonus earning areas and many of these were in the London District. There was also some disappointment that the negotiators had not managed to achieve any element of consolidation. The Executive argued that the Post Office had taken a decision to terminate the scheme and had written to the General Secretary in October 1987 stating that 'IWM had become a costly and ineffective mechanism for promoting greater efficiency. As such it cannot continue'. To convince the membership to accept the agreement, the Executive had to turn many of the arguments they used to encourage branches to join the IWM scheme on their heads. They argued that the membership was disenchanted with the scheme, quoting Conference debates and numerous letters to Union Headquarters. Payments bore no resemblance to levels of productivity and the national pay structure had become distorted. They also said that management audits indicated widespread overpayments and that further investigation would lead to the loss of payments particularly regarding locally negotiated 'authorized variations' to the scheme.

The opposition in London was considerable and many of those offices that had previously been the most loyal to the Union's promotion of IWM now found themselves at the forefront of the opposition to its replacement and many of those offices that had entered the scheme reluctantly felt that the terms for its removal were not good enough. Faced with a possible revolt against the national leadership Alan Tuffin, General Secretary and Alan Johnson, Assistant Secretary felt it necessary to address a meeting of the London District Council 3 held at the Mount Pleasant Staff Hall. Tuffin told the meeting that there was no alternative to the agreement. A national postal strike had been averted and it was the first reduction in hours for 22 years. He urged the Council to support the deal. Representatives from several of the large branches went to the rostrum and argued that they felt let down by the Executive's support for the agreement and that many of their members had threatened to resign from the Union if it was accepted in the national ballot. They made it clear that they would not be supporting the agreement and would be campaigning against it. The voting papers were dispatched on 15 January 1989 and the result was announced on 2 February with 61,778 (57%) voting for the agreement and 46,523 (43%) opposing it. There were no reports of any members resigning from the Union.

18 Speaking Fred Jepson London DO, National Chairman CWU, Hughie Lenaghan (far right)

19 South West Branch march to Central Hall Westminster

20 London members rally outside Central Hall Westminster Employee Agenda
Dispute 15 August 1996*

21 Employee Agenda Dispute 1996*

22 (L to R) Derek Walsh, John Taylor and Colin Maloney leading Grunwick Dispute march of London members 1976

23 WDCO No. 1 Branch members march to Mount Pleasant Staff Meeting Hall 1987 Dispute

24 Employee Agenda Rally London Regional/Divisional Officers (L to R) Dave Ward, Norman Candy, Andy Curran (speaking) and John Denton*

25 Employee Agenda Strike Leaflet

26 (L to R) Employee Agenda Dispute 1996 Tam McGee (National Executive), John Denton, Norman Candy, Bob McGuire (National Executive)*

27 London Employee Agenda Rally 1996*

28 Picket line, Mount Pleasant, Employee Agenda Dispute 1996*

29 Employee Agenda Rally 1996*

30 Tony Clark, London postal workers leader and 'Post' Editor 1979–1981, UCW Deputy General Secretary 1981–1993

31 Les Hewitt, SEDO No. 1 Branch Secretary and National Officer 1981–1990

32 John Keggie Scotland No. 2 Branch, CWU National Executive Council
1992–1998, Deputy General Secretary 1998–2003

33 Billy Hayes Liverpool Branch, CWU National Executive Council 1992, Assistant
Secretary 1992–2001, General Secretary 2001 to date

Chapter 18

THE DRAS DISPUTE 1988

Within a few months of the Shorter Working Week dispute being resolved and the IWM Bonus Scheme being wound up another crisis arose. For some time rumours had been circulating that the Post Office had plans to move away from national pay bargaining and introduce regional pay. Encouraged by the Government a number of large employers in the public sector had already moved in this direction. The recruitment of postmen and women was a serious problem in several parts of the country and although unemployment was above 7% nationally, in parts of the UK the Post Office could not attract and retain staff. The areas particularly affected were London, the Home Counties and the Thames Valley. Turnover was high and retention was difficult throughout the London district but it was a particular problem in the mail centres. It had been a problem since the 1960s and all previous attempts to resolve it had failed.

Every day London's regional and local newspapers carried large advertisements encouraging people to apply for the numerous vacancies for postmen and women in the capital. Agreements increasing the level of part-timers and casuals had failed. Introducing 'flexible' shift patterns had also failed. As management increased the pressure on Branches to accept more casuals and part-timers there was a corresponding increase in the level of unofficial industrial action. In particular the West Central District Office (WCDO) went through a long period of industrial conflict in 1987 and 1988. Turnover of staff was very high in WCDO and recruitment was difficult. The permanent staff, many of whom travelled some considerable distances to work each day, had come to rely on a fairly high level of regular overtime and local agreements provided generous 'end of duty concession' and tea breaks. In an attempt to encourage the acceptance of casual and part-time duties local management attacked these local agreements and this resulted in several bitter unofficial disputes. However, although management were successful in increasing the use of part-time workers in particular, the levels of overtime remained high and the recruitment difficulties remained.

Management at one stage floated the idea of recruiting staff from areas of the country where unemployment was high, bringing them to London and housing them in makeshift sleeping accommodation in various Post Office buildings including the Staff Halls at Mount Pleasant and Essavian House in Holborn. Although the idea never got off the ground it was under serious consideration and was discussed at London District Council meetings. Post Office management also argued that because seniority gave long service staff the first choice in the selection of duties, this disadvantaged new recruits and contributed to the high levels of staff turnover resulting in several unsuccessful attacks on seniority.

In early 1988 stories began to circulate that Post Office management intended to introduce a 'Difficult Recruitment Supplement (DRAS). On 29 April 1988 Alan Tuffin informed Branches that the Union had been informed by letter that they intended to introduce a pay supplement for new postmen/women, doorkeepers and cleaner recruits in certain areas of the country in an attempt to attract and retain staff. Les Hewitt informed the Postal Group Management Committee (PGMC) on 3 May that following confidential advice from Royal Mail Letters (RML) a few weeks earlier that they were considering this move, he had now received a letter from Euan Morrow, Head of Pay, RML on 21 April confirming that it was their intention to introduce this on 1 May 1988. Hewitt had also obtained a copy of an internal Telex to District Head Postmasters advising them of the Post Offices plans. Following representation from the Union, Hewitt subsequently received an apology from Royal Mail Director Brian Roberts, explaining that the introduction of the supplements on 1 May had been withdrawn, and that it had always been their intention to discuss the matter with the Union, although he went on to say that it was not their intention to seek the Union's agreement for this. Hewitt, in his correspondence to the PGMC, made the comment: 'Obviously, we need to talk to RML even though our formal agreement is not being sought, if only to ensure we are able to answer properly, questions from Branches which will undoubtedly come flooding in'. In his letter, Euan Morrow explained management's criteria for paying the supplement. They would pay it in areas where the unemployment levels average in 1987 was less than 6% and where wastage, other than that due to normal retirement, was over 16% in the same year. They went on to say that whilst they would only pay it in those 'provincial' offices that met both criteria the supplement would be paid to all offices in the London District. Another criterion was that those offices that met the unemployment criteria but not the wastage levels and where the former average previous IWM Bonus payment exceeded £25, would also receive it. In all cases the supplement would only be paid after six weeks of service and the letter also provided a list of those offices that would receive the payments and explained that the payments would vary between £7.50 and £20.00 depending on the ex-IWM supplements currently being paid in each office.

It is difficult to imagine a scheme that would infuriate the majority of UCW members more and make a fragile industrial relations climate worse. Offices within a short distance of each other would receive different payments and some none at all. Whatever Hewitt's view of the situation, the opposition was widespread and nationwide. The Union responded immediately to the proposals and a number of meetings were held with management prior to the Annual Conference where the Union emphasized their total opposition to the idea. In the Union's opinion the supplement was a direct breach of the Shorter Working Week Agreement, it would lead to 'dissension in offices and between offices and would not alleviate the recruitment and retention problems in the areas that it was intended to help'.

At the Union's 1988 Annual Conference on 25 May an Emergency Motion was moved by Tam McGee from the Edinburgh Outdoor Branch: 'Conference agrees that the Post Office's proposals to introduce a pay supplement in difficult recruitment areas are not in the best interest of the membership. It further agrees that an urgent meeting be sought at the highest level, to gain an agreement with management to advertise uniform grade vacancies, via *The Gazette*, throughout the country to alleviate the problems in those areas. Should the Post Office attempt to implement the supplement by executive action, the executive council is instructed to invoke Rule 19 (ballot for industrial action) to defend our position'.

There was never any doubt that the Motion would be agreed and following a long debate during which delegates from around the country went to the rostrum to pledge their member's support for industrial action it was carried overwhelmingly.

Following his return from Conference, Tuffin informed the Post Office of the Union decision and on 15 June the PGMC met and agreed to hold an individual ballot of the membership to secure a 'Yes' vote for industrial action. On 29 June Alan Tuffin led a delegation that met with the Managing Director of RML, Bill Cockburn where he urged Cockburn to withdraw the supplement and negotiate an agreed resolution to the problem of recruitment and retention. Tuffin told Cockburn that unless the supplement was to be paid to all new recruits it was unacceptable to the Union and the meeting broke up with Tuffin informing Cockburn, who had rejected the Union's proposals, that he intended to raise the issue with the Post Office Chairman. On 30 June the PGMC meet again to agree arrangements for balloting the membership and on 5 July a Special Branch Circular was dispatched informing members of the decision. Leaflets and circulars were distributed around the country urging support for the Executives recommendation. Divisional Councils, Regional Councils, Branches and individual offices held meetings in work time and outside of work time to drum up support for industrial action. Ballot papers were dispatched on 12 July and the result was announced on 12 August. The result was 48,134 votes for the Executive's recommendation and 23,048 against, an overwhelming vote for industrial action. The members had voted by a majority of 2:1 to support the Executive Council's recommendation. It was reported that management believed that the Conference decision was a 'storm in a teacup'. Tuffin reported that they believed it was yet 'just another Conference Motion' and that 'only half of the Union's membership voted and anyway one third of them had said 'No'. Even if the Union takes action it will only split itself in two'.

When the Executive called a 24 hour strike on Wednesday 31 August the Post Office issued an almost dismissive statement claiming that the action was 'patchy' and that 'much of the countries mail is being delivered as normal'. The truth was that 97% of the Union's membership were on strike and postal services throughout the country had ground to a halt. Management's miscalculation of the strength of feeling was apparent and the next day this was compounded by another serious mishandling of the situation. When staff returned to work, in the belief that management would want to see the backlog cleared as quickly as possible following what many had seen as a 'shot across management's bowels', they were in for a rude awakening. The Post Office flooded offices with casuals, threatened to move staff from their normal offices and attempted to divert mail around the country without the normal discussions with the Union's local representatives. Whether or not this was deliberately calculated to antagonise the situation is not clear. However the staff's reaction was quick and widespread. Within a couple of days postal services throughout the country were once again at a standstill. This time it was unofficial and illegal, a clear breach of the trade union legislation but as so often happens in postal disputes the focus had gone away from the original issue and was now about 'clearing up arrangements', threats of discipline and accusations of bullying. Management counter attacked with talk of 'hot heads' and 'militants' but the fact was that as *The Post* reported, from one end of the country to the other postal workers were on strike. In an attempt to calm the situation Alan Tuffin called for an independent Government inquiry into the causes of the dispute and despite the fact that the dispute was clearly illegal neither the Post Office or the Government attempted a legal challenge and the Union continued to support those on strike as if the dispute was official.

The strike in London was solid and in some instances Post Office Counters members walked out on unofficial action in support of their uniformed colleagues. The District Council held regular meetings in the Staff Hall in King Edward Building where Mike Hogan and Aubrey Bayer, the London District Officers, gave updates on how the dispute and negotiations were progressing. Branches and offices held meetings in car parks and local meeting halls to pass on the information. Negotiations had begun during the first week of the dispute and were still in progress on 11 September when an agreement for a return to work was agreed with the Post Office. By the end of the strike there was a backlog of 150 million undelivered letters and parcels. The agreement was hailed as a 'major victory' by the Union and included a commitment from management to withdraw the DRAS payments and to replace them with a negotiated alternative.

The issues that had led to the unofficial dispute were resolved by management agreeing to remove any casuals employed during the dispute and to negotiate locally on a range of measures to clear the backlog. They also agreed that there would be no victimisation of anyone involved in the dispute and that any union members suspended from duty as a result of taking action would be returned to work. The London District Council met and agreed that no London office would return to work until every office had a 'return to work agreement'. This proved difficult because it was apparent that some Postmasters and local managers were not happy with the agreement which they believed was a 'climb-down' by their national negotiators. Tuffin also instructed the Union's solicitors to challenge the Post Office over the use of employment agency staff during the dispute which was considered by the Union's legal advisors to be a possible breach of the legislation covering agency staff employed during an industrial dispute. When a meeting of the District Council was called on Friday 16 September most offices and Branches had negotiated local 'return to work agreements'. However a number were still unable to get agreements. These included Croydon, Western District Office (W1) and the East Central District Office (ECDO 1-4) but by midday only ECDO remained without an agreement. Whilst the District Officers and the ECDO Branch officials negotiated with management more than 300 representatives of the London membership waited in the King Edward Building Staff Hall. To help pass the time the meeting was entertained by a few songs from one of the delegates and by the early afternoon an agreement was reached and London returned to work united. Across the country a number of offices were still unable to get agreements and remained on strike. These included Cardiff, Newport, Liverpool, Manchester, Bolton, Coventry, Chester and Hull. However within a few days they had all returned to work. The last to return to work were Liverpool and Coventry.

Negotiations on a replacement for DRAS began almost immediately and continued throughout October with what was described as a 'crunch' meeting taking place on Tuesday 1 November. It became clear that there was still a considerable distance between the two sides. Management were still insisting on 'flexible adult recruitment rates', flexible DRAS payments, changes to overtime arrangements and scheduled attendance rates and the 'extension of London Weighting boundaries'. They were also insisting on the right to reduce payments if the recruitment difficulties ceased, whilst the Union were still insisting that the supplement should be paid to all UCW member grades, that London Weighting should be increased, and the 18 year pay increment should be abolished.

The situation was made more difficult as a result of a letter that Alan Tuffin received on 31 October 1988. It was sent on behalf of the full London District Council and was signed by the LDC Secretary Bill Flaherty, who was also a member of the Executive Council. Flaherty made it clear that he was speaking on behalf of the 'postal side' of the Union as the British Telecomms management had not yet made a formal offer on the London Weighting claim. He advised Tuffin that although the London Weighting negotiations with the Post Office were still in progress they were refusing to negotiate on a corporate basis with each of the organisation's businesses proposing separate solutions. They were also taking the view that London Weighting was no longer recognised by the Post Office businesses as an allowance for living and working in the capital but as a monetary inducement to recruit and retain staff. At its Annual General Meeting held on 10 March 1988 the London District Council had endorsed a claim on behalf on its postal members for a substantial increase in the London allowance. At the half-yearly General Meeting Flaherty reported that there had been little progress in the negotiations that had been taking place with the Post Office. In 1988 the London Weighting discussion were not conducted by the individual Post Office trade unions but jointly by the Post Office Unions Council (POUC). Following a lengthy and angry debate the London Branches instructed Bill Flaherty to write directly to Alan Tuffin and inform him that they were not prepared to accept management position any longer. Tony Conway, Branch Secretary of the South East London PHG Branch who for sometime had been arguing within the LDC against the erosion of London Weighting, played the leading role in encouraging the Council to make a stand on the issue.

Flaherty's letter to Tuffin made the feelings of the District Council absolutely clear. It read:

I was instructed by the Branches at the half-yearly meeting however to write directly to you without delay to make the following comments.

1.   LDC consider the offer of 5%, which they fully understand has been rejected, an insult. When you recall the posturing of the Managing Director RML as he sought to justify his actions during the DRAS dispute on the basis that something had to be done to recruit and retain staff in London, the offer of 5% now demonstrates to all the hypocrisy of the man.

2.   LDC will never accept any form of 'top-up' London Weighting, over and above the percentage pensionable increase, if it means

that supplement will be paid to only selected grades in specifically identified offices. The Council will oppose any form of London Weighting in difficult recruitment areas. It is no more than a variation of DRAS. For the Union to pursue such a course, will be tantamount to embracing the Post Office contention that London Weighting is purely a recruitment inducement and no longer an allowance for working in the capital.

3.   LDC wants a substantial increase in London Weighting payable to all grades of the CWU, because whether they be cleaners, postmen or postal officers they all have to live and work in the capital. Housing costs are still prohibitive and fares are due to rise again in January by between 9% and 20%. Any settlement must recognise and reflect that fact and all grades must be treated equally.

4.   The LDC is determined this year to put a stop to the erosion of the London Weighting allowance, the Inner Area rate has not changed since 1986 and has only gone up by £100 in the last five years. The time has come to rectify that situation.

In finality, I must advise you as General Secretary, in my capacity as the Secretary in the full Council, that if any settlement is recommended by you, which has the effect of or can be construed as setting grade against grade and office against office, then it will be met with such hostility that the consequences for the Union in London will be too horrendous to contemplate. I am sure you have no wish to see such a situation arise, and I assure you that the London Branches support you in that regard. We must not allow the Post Office strategy to divide us to succeed. I should advise you that this letter is being circulated to all Branches as your reply will when it comes to hand.

Best wishes as always.

Yours sincerely
Bill Flaherty
Secretary LDC

On 1 November another meeting took place between the Union and RML where management presented new proposals for resolving the dispute. When Les Hewitt, who was leading the negotiations on behalf of the Union, recommended the rejection of RML's offer, he stated that his recommendation had been 'greatly influenced by a letter to the General Secretary from the LDC'. Later in November a public 'war of words' erupted between Alan Tuffin and Bill Coburn, Managing Director Letters. Coburn had taken exception to an article by Tuffin published in *The Post*. This prompted the Post Office Board to accuse Tuffin of 'inaccurate and unjustified' attacks on the Managing Director 'that were unworthy of the Union'. Tuffin responded by saying that he stood by the article and that he was quite prepared to defend every word, demanding that the Board either withdraw the allegations or be prepared to defend themselves. In early December 1988 Les Hewitt informed Branches that progress with the negotiations were taking longer than anticipated but that they were expected to be completed by 14 December. He thanked the members and the Branches for their patience explaining that 'it is vital that every avenue should be explored before further industrial action is contemplated'. By Christmas 1988 an agreement had still not been reached and negotiations went into the new year.

At the end of January 1989 Tuffin was able to announce that the negotiations had reached a conclusion in a statement declaring that 'A major agreement with Royal Mail has now been accepted for recommendation to our Postal Grades in a Rule 13 Branch Ballot'. Details of the agreement were published to Branches on 6 February. However the method for consulting the membership caused considerable controversy and opposition from some Branches. The Executive had decided to hold a Branch ballot rather than an individual ballot but they had also agreed to separate the ballot into two sections. Several Branches wrote to the National Chairman challenging the decision and it was necessary for the Union to obtain legal advice before the vote could go ahead.

Section 1 of the agreement was in two parts, the first contained those changes that effected resourcing, new recruit's terms and conditions, associate grades, and a commitment to negotiate a new national productivity scheme. The second part dealt with overtime, scheduled attendance and bank holiday credits. There were two separate recommendations which were subject to a ballot of all the postal Branches nationally. Section 2 contained a Recruitment and Retention Incentive Scheme for London and a defined surrounding area, covering much of the Home Counties and the Thames Valley but only the London members were to be balloted on this section. The Executive argued that the Draft Agreement represented a significant breakthrough for the Union. It dealt with the problem of recruitment and retention in London and the South East whilst also improving the terms and conditions conditions of the membership throughout the country and protecting national pay bargaining.

There was very little organised opposition to the agreement and ballot papers were dispatched on Thursday 16 February 1989 and voting closed on Tuesday 7 March 1989. The ballot only covered Section 1 of the agreement and Recommendation 1 was carried by 6,975 to 6,885, and Recommendation 2 was carried by 7,145 to 6,769 and although the Executive claimed that it was the highest ever recorded return for a Rule 13 Ballot the result was very close. The London Section of the agreement involved a weekly supplement of £6 for Inner London, £10 for Outer London and £15 for the defined areas outside London. The London membership were never balloted on Section 2 of the agreement. Following the 1989 Conference negotiations commenced on London Weighting and initially management, once again, proposed different increases for the separate corporate businesses. This was rejected by the London Branches and further negotiations took place that resulted in the London Branches accepting a deal covering all the businesses of £315 for Inner London and £185 for Outer London. The vote was 3,564 for the agreement and 738 against. In 1988/9 there were 1,100,000 days lost to industrial action in Royal Mail and on top of those lost during the DRAS dispute there were also just under 60 separate unofficial disputes covering offices in every part of the country.

Chapter 19

THE 1990s
– DECADE OF CONFLICT

Industrial Relations and a New Branch Structure

The 1990s began with a severe recession, a slump in the housing market and Britain's humiliating exit from the Exchange Rate Mechanism (ERM).

In 1990 the Government introduced the last and most draconian of their anti-trade union legislation. Amongst other things it was designed to discourage workers from taking un-balloted, unofficial industrial action. The Act included the following words: 'An employee has no right to complain of unfair dismissal if at the time of the dismissal he was on unofficial strike or other industrial action'. If this was intended to intimidate workers it had no effect on some postal workers. In response to the new legislation Alan Tuffin issued a circular warning Branches that 'If they took part in industrial action without a ballot and the Executive Council's authority, they could place their employment and that of their colleagues at risk. The Union cannot authorise any action to help them'.

On the same day that the law came into effect Alan Smith, West London Area Distribution Representative, contacted the London Division Officials to let them know that the UCW members at Kings Cross railway station, members of the London Stations Branch, had walked out on unofficial industrial action. In the early 1990s Royal Mail Letters began the trial of Trandos, a computer assisted vehicle routing system and further developed CADRA, a computer assisted delivery revisions package. Before 1980 postmen and postwomen's uniforms were both uncomfortable and impractical. In 1980 after several years of negotiations and consultation, and a trial in 1978, a new lightweight uniform was issued. In August 1990, after several 'flashpoints' they agreed that delivery staff could wear shorts for the first time. During a spell of particularly hot weather the issue of uniformed staff wearing shorts arose. In 1989 Royal Mail gave managers the discretion to reach local agreement on this issue. They specified that they must be of 'sober design' and 'in keeping with the general design of the uniform and coloured either black, navy blue or grey'. It was also stressed that 'normal shoes and socks must accompany the shorts'. However, some District Postmasters were reluctant to allow this and Branches were advised to resolve difficulties through the disagreements 'Procedural Agreement'. In London a problem occurred at the Sydenham Delivery Office, where the UCW representative, Jim Greenman and the local staff played an important role in convincing management to change their attitude towards more comfortable work-wear.

The TUC organised an anti-Poll Tax rally and lobby of Parliament which the Union encouraged its members to support. Later in the year the Union advised Branches that a leaflet announcing the launch of an organisation called 'Postal Workers Against the Poll Tax' had come to the attention of UCW Headquarters. They advised Branches that the group did not have the support of the Union and that its policy of non-payment was not in line with the Union's Annual Conference policy. In October 1990 the London membership rejected a proposed London Weighting agreement by 2,960 votes to 547 in a Branch ballot and in November the Union announced the outcome of the annual pay negotiations. The negotiators had achieved an increase of 10.4%. Alan Tuffin, whilst recognising that the increase was below the current rate of inflation of 10.9%, pointed out that it was the highest achieved that year in the public sector and that only the Motor Industry in the private sector had achieved more.

In 1989 the Union had participated in a Joint Working Party (JWP) dealing with industrial relations and during the 1990 pay discussions Royal Mail attempted to commit the Union to accepting a number of changes to the way industrial relations were conducted. Despite the involvement of Pat Lowry, former head of ACASS, the 1989 discussions had broken down over the issue of the role of Assistant District Officers (ADOs). Whilst for historic reasons, London always had formal recognition for District Officers, this was not the case elsewhere. In 1990 the Union announced that negotiations had begun on a 'Joint review of issues of concern to Royal Mail and the Union of

Communication Workers'. These issues included: Team working, Productivity, Automation and Industrial Relations and for the first time the jargon of Total Quality Management entered Royal Mail's industrial relations vocabulary.

Discussions continued until May 1991 when they broke down. They began again in June and during this period the Union began a process of consultation with Branches and District Officers. Negotiation continued throughout the summer but once again they came close to breaking down, and in December it was announced that the Union would be holding a Special Conference in February 1992 to debate a Special Report related to the issues under discussion.

Meanwhile the Post Office announced the introduction of 'Business Development' which involved the removal of over 6,000 supervisors jobs and the re-organisation of the management structures from top to bottom. Postal Districts, Head Postmasters Areas and Postmasters were removed and authority below national level was transferred to nine divisions. These new divisions were sub-divided in to three functions – processing, delivery and distribution – with managerial responsibility at local, area and divisional levels. Senior management claimed that one of its aims was to push down managerial responsibility to the 'lowest level'. Since the Monopolies Commissions report in the 1980s the business had been under pressure to change its management structure and increase the number of 'direct entrant' recruits to supervisory positions. Business Development gave the Post Office an opportunity to do this.

In January 1992 Alan Johnson beat a field of five other candidates to become the Union's new General Secretary (Elect), Derek Hodgson became the Deputy General Secretary

(Elect) and a Special Conference to discuss the outcome of the 'Joint Review' was held at the Winter Gardens Bournemouth on 26, 27 and 28 February 1992. The Executive Council produced two Special Reports for Conference to discuss. The first was a report on industrial relations and the second a report on the Union's structure. 'Industrial Relations in Royal Mail' was a 29 page report that proposed the most far reaching and radical changes to the industrial relations structure since the Union's inception in 1920. Before 1992 industrial relations were governed by the 'Facilities Agreement'. This detailed the interface between Union and management and established the Branch Secretary and Branch Chairman as the principle negotiators of the

Union at local level. Branches had a great deal of local autonomy and their size ranged from the smallest with 6 members to the largest with 2500. Most Branches had a committee that dealt with local issues ranging from duty revisions to holiday spread and a locally elected Treasurer was responsible for the Branch finances. These were allocated by UCW HQ according to the size of the Branch. Time off for trade union purposes was usually negotiated locally and in London this was often quite generous. If local agreement could not be reached on a particular issue then it would be referred up to a higher level. In London this was the District Officers and outside of London it was Union Headquarters. London's industrial relations structure was peculiar to the capital and on certain issues the LDC had a constitutional right, dating back to the Union's formation, to negotiate directly with London Management. Sectional committees were elected by the London Branches and the London Divisional Council 3 met every month to discuss and agree policy. For some time management had argued that the industrial relations structure was costly, incompatible with 'modern industrial relations' and did not meet the needs of the new management structure introduced with Business Development.

In January 1991 Royal Mail told the Union that they intended to withdraw all financial support for the Union structures and withdraw from the Facilities Agreement. Their proposals reflected this and in the early stages of negotiations they attempted to restrict the Union's future role in the industry to negotiating on contractual issues and 'adding value in supporting the businesses drive to achieve its missions'. Although during the course of negotiations they moderated their position, nevertheless the final proposal on a new industrial relations structure was a radical change to what had proceeded it. The role of the Branch Secretary and Branch Chairman as the lead negotiators was removed and the role of the Branch was replaced with an industrial relation interface based on functions (i.e. delivery, processing, distribution and administration). This introduced local, area and divisional representatives as the three levels in the new industrial relations framework. Although the Union outside London gained a divisional industrial relations interface from this new structure, London lost its ability to negotiate directly with London management.

The second report was called the 'Union Structure Towards 2000' and once again the proposed changes were radical and far reaching. The proposals included reducing the number of Branches from 790 to 80 and establishing 10 Regional Committees. This structure would be completely separate from the industrial relations structure and would deal with administering and organising the Union in all other aspects. The report on industrial relations attracted 227 Amendments and the report on the Union's structure attracted 225. An early attempt by Crew and District to reject both the industrial relations report and the Union structure report was defeated and by the end of Conference both reports were agreed with very few changes. The majority of London Branches reluctantly went along with both reports on the basis that it was felt that the Union had little alternative other than to agree the changes. However some Branches and activists welcomed the changes as an opportunity for the Union to build bigger and better organised Branches.

The District Council proposed a number of amendments aimed at improving the final outcome of the restructuring. Probably the most important was Composite Amendment QQ which firmly established Divisional Committees and the industrial organising role of Divisional Officers. It also established the right of Divisional Committees to submit motions and amendments to the Union's Conferences and although it was vigorously opposed by the Organising Secretary in was overwhelmingly supported by the delegates.

The loss of the London District Council and its Sectional Councils was a big blow to London and the task of amalgamating Branches and establishing the new Divisional Committee was a formidable one.

Although Royal Mail were determined to withdraw financial support from the Union they had agreed to a proposal by Tony Clarke, Deputy General Secretary, that for a transitional period they would continue to provide paid release for Branch Secretaries on the basis of 5 hours per week for each branch with at least 1,000 members, with an additional hour for each 200 members above 1,000 and this would not be reviewed before 1 April 1995. A 'bedding in' period was also agreed whilst the new structures were being introduced, elections held and negotiations on union facility time for industrial relations activities negotiated. It was also agreed that those Union officials displaced as a result of the introduction of these changes would be offered voluntary redundancy. As a result many long serving and experienced Branch officials left the industry and the Union.

There is no doubt that Royal Mail saw the introduction of these changes as part of a strategy aimed at weakening and disorientating the Union. Employers throughout the country, with the support of the Conservative Government, were de-recognising unions, imposing changes to worker's pay and conditions, dismissing activists and attacking collective bargaining. However, although the introduction of these changes were initially difficult and demanding for the Union, the final outcome caused no lasting damage to the organisation but they did have a lasting effect on the Union's relationship with Royal Mail and the balance of power within the Union. Until 1992 the Union's Executive had enjoyed an almost unassailable control over the Union and its Annual Conference. Although on occasions Conferences reject Executive Council's recommendation this was the exception rather than the rule. After 1992, and the changes introduced following the Special Conference, power shifted away from the Executive and towards the Branches and the Divisional Committees. In the next few years this would have a significant impact on the Union, Royal Mail and industrial relations.

London Mail Centre Rationalisation
Following the third successive Labour Party defeat in the 1992 General Election Neil Kinnock resigned as leader and was replaced by John Smith. Tony Clarke ex-Deputy General of the UCW was elected Party Chairman. Billy Hayes took on the responsibilities of Alan Johnson when Johnson replaced Alan Tuffin as General Secretary. Fred Jepson a leading member of the Mount Pleasant PHG Branch and Albert Merriman a postman and member of the South East London Postal Branch became the first London Divisional Representatives and Norman Candy and John Denton, both from the London West End Amalgamated took on the role of Substitute Divisional Representatives.

In October 1992 an article was published in *The Guardian* newspaper carrying the headlines '2000 Jobs to go in Post Office Cuts' and *The Daily Express* ran an article claiming '5000 face the sack as Post Office piles on the agony'. They both reported that the Post Office was about to announce plans to close 54 of the country's Mechanised Letter Offices (MLOs). UCW Headquarters quickly issued a Special Branch Circular assuring Branches that 'There has been no proposals at National level or indeed at Divisional or Area level, on a programme of closures and the figure of 54 MLOs to close is speculative nonsense', it went on to say, 'There is no question that new technology will have a substantial effect on jobs. What we as a Union will and must do is ensure that the pace of that change is designed and regulated with the emphasis on job security and customer service'. Another Special Branch Circular headed MLO Closures/New Technology/Code of Practice was issued explaining that following discussions with management at the 'New Technology Committee' Royal Mail had confirmed that 70 to 75 MLOs would be required to meet their outward sorting needs and that this was determined by the level of new technology introduced by the business. The circular went on to say that the Union had a policy agreed by the 1991 Annual Conference and they had advised Royal Mail that if they wished to have staff co-operation with the introduction of new technology a package of measures must be developed encompassing a new statement on compulsory redundancies, improved Early Retirement Terms (EVR) and a new relocation package. Management responded by publishing a document titled 'Code of Practice' and informed the Union that if they wished to negotiate an alternative to this then the negotiations must be completed within four weeks. The Union published a statement explaining that management documents 'contained some improvements on previous proposals but fell considerably short of what the Union considered their members deserved and what was well within the scope of Royal Mail to provide'. It concluded that although the Union had no difficulty with the Code of Practice it continued to press for improvements. It was apparent, however, that management felt the 'Code of Practice' was sufficient to deal with the changes resulting from the closures and within a few weeks it had been circulated to managers as a working document. It was clear that the two sides were on a collision course and the front-line was the London Division.

For some time rumours had circulated about the future of the London MLO network and the new Divisional Committee had begun to discuss the issue earlier in the year. It was obvious that a large number of jobs were under threat and it was also clear that the aspirations of the Committee regarding a package for dealing with the changes was more ambitious than those on offer from Royal Mail. On 3 December 1992 a Branch Circular was issued saying that the London Divisional Officials would be attending a meeting with the London Royal Mail Directors where proposals to close four MLOs and downgrade another to a delivery office would be made. At the same time the Post Office issued a press statement estimating that job losses for the project would be 2,100 in the first round of closures leading to a total reduction of about 5,300 jobs by March 1996. The Union responded by attacking the 'sensational stories' in the press that claimed 30,000 postal workers would be losing their jobs in the 'next few months'. The statement went on to say that the losses, including those from a separate review of Post Office Counters was expected to be three to four thousand, including management grades, and the Union would not countenance compulsory redundancies and any savings achieved by the introduction of new technology must be used to reduce working hours. Nevertheless the redundancies amounted to about 50% of the London processing workforce and at the meeting on 3 December 1992 management informed the Divisional Representatives that West Central, South East, North West and King Edward Building would be closed and Western District Office downgraded to a delivery office. From the outset London management made it absolutely clear that in their view compulsory redundancies could only be avoided if there was total co-operation from the Union and the workforce, including the compulsory transfer of staff to offices both inside and outside of the Division. They also informed the Divisional Representatives that management would select those suitable for redundancy based on cost and suitability. They went on to say that the only compensation package, regarding allowances and loss of pay was that which had already been published in the 'Code of Practice'.

The Divisional Committee met several times during the next few weeks and after a great deal of discussion and debate agreed a policy which they would ask the London membership to support. In the first place they were opposed to the closure plan and wanted the opportunity to examine in detail management's proposals and where appropriate suggest alternatives. Secondly they believed the 'Code of Practice' was insufficient to deal with such a large movement of staff. Only a package that included a clear commitment to no compulsory redundancies or transfers, voluntary retirement and voluntary redundancies based on seniority, improved compensation and pay protection for those that volunteered to transfer would be acceptable. They also demanded pay protection for those employed in the offices that remained open and a lump sum payment for all staff affected by the closure plan. Their main priority would be to ensure that those who remained employed by Royal Mail would have decent terms and conditions, whilst those that left would do so voluntarily and with the best terms possible. The Committee informed both UCW Headquarters and London management of their position and following the intervention on Mike Hogan, the National Officer responsible for MLOs and new technology, it was agreed that the Division would have complete access to the rationalisation plans and the opportunity to propose alternatives. A series of meetings, to discuss the details of the package and the closure plans was also agreed. The Divisional Committee did not believe that London management had any intention of listening to the Union's arguments for keeping offices open. The central London site was worth a huge amount of money and the rationalisation plan also gave management an opportunity to close a number of problem offices that had been a thorn in their side for some time. The effects of new technology and the decline in postal traffic within the capital could not be ignored either. However the Union were convinced that the size and scope of the closure plan would lead to serious quality of service problems if it went ahead in its proposed form. Work on examining management's plans started almost immediately and Denton and Candy, the sub-Divisional Representatives began the task of drawing up the Union's counter-proposals.

Discussions began on 16 March and there were a further six meetings between then and 17 May. The meetings were held at the West Central District Office in New Oxford Street WC1 and the Western District Office in Rathbone Place W1. The Union was represented by Mike Hogan, Fred Jepson, Albert Merriman, John Denton and Norman Candy. Royal Mail London was represented by Peter Forest, David Legge, Jennifer Thorne, Alan Eccleston and Howard Levinson. At the first meeting management outlined their proposals and the grounds for their proposals which they argued were demographic, financial and structural. A key factor they said, was the Government's policy of encouraging companies to relocate out of Central London which they said had already resulted in a 60,000 job reduction in Greater London and a 7% fall in residential population. Additionally they claimed that companies had left London in response to the high cost of operating in the capital. As an illustration of this they claimed that postings in the West Central area had declined from 600,000 per day to 350,000 per day and that furthermore London's offices had been designed for a manual operation when the business needed to make greater use of new technology.

The Union responded by arguing that in their view management's plans were short sighted and presented a clear threat to London's quality of service. Reducing capacity by 50% in 15 months was reckless and that if it was necessary to reduce capacity then it should be done without the risk to quality that management's proposals threatened. As the talks progressed the differences between the two sides on the 'manpower plan' began to emerge. The Union asked for guarantees that there would be no compulsory redundancies or transfers. Management replied that they wished to avoid compulsion but it could not be guaranteed. They also asked for an assurance that staff would be compensated for loss of pay and bonuses, in particular they argued for 'bulk transfer terms' to compensate staff that transferred from Inner London to Outer London and from Outer London to provisional offices for loss of London Weighting payments. Although the Union were able to provide evidence that this had been paid on previous occasions when staff had been forced to transfer, management refused to accept this and by the meeting on 17 May it was clear that negotiations were on the verge of breakdown.

Management informed the Union that their detailed counter proposals had been rejected and at the meeting Fred Jepson responded by reading out the following statement: 'From the commencement of negotiations we have been of the opinion that management have been of the view that improved compensation was not an item for consideration. Management have continued with their stance that they would not or could not make an improved offer even though Royal Mail stand to make vast savings on the proposed closures. From these savings we were seeking justified compensation. We have offered co-operation on voluntary movement of staff and therefore find it hard to accept management's inflexible approach on improved compensation or an incentive scheme. We have made reports to the Area Representatives, who have relayed the information to the members. We would inform you that if management maintain their rigid approach on any improvement to compensation then the London membership will be seeking authority for a Rule 19 ballot (industrial action)'.

The meeting concluded with both sides accepting that they had taken the discussions as far as they could and that the outstanding issues could only be concluded 'elsewhere'. Both sides reported the breakdown to their respective headquarters and in early June the Union issued a press statement headed

'London Strike Ballot'. The Union announced that it would be balloting its 21,000 London, Royal Mail Letters staff for industrial action and that the dispute concerned Royal Mail's refusal to negotiate an appropriate personnel package to deal with the proposed closure of five Mechanised Letter Offices with the loss of up to 6,000 jobs against the background of the Post Office announcing a record £283 a million year profit, the 17th in succession. The decision by the Divisional Committee to request a ballot was a calculated risk. The majority of London's members were not directly affected by the changes. In fact some offices would gain work from the implementation of the plan and the majority of delivery offices were not directly affected. On 2 July 1993 the Union announced that 8,624 had voted for industrial action and 7,105 had voted against. Within a few days the Union announced that the Royal Mail had asked to meet their national representatives and that pending the outcome of those meetings industrial action would be deferred.

A series of meetings began on 5 July 1993 and lasted for four days. The Union was represented by Alan Johnson and Mike Hogan and the Post Office was represented by the London General Manager, Brian Thompson and his London team. At the end of the negotiations, on 9 July, an agreement on London MLO restructuring was placed before the Postal Group Management Committee (PGMC). The PGMC agreed the new package and on the morning of Saturday 10 July, at a meeting held at the Union's Clapham Headquarters, the agreement was endorsed by the London Divisional Committee. On 14 July details of the agreement were published in a special issue of *The Post* and distributed to the London membership. It was a vast improvement on the 'Code of Practice' and there were agreed mechanisms for avoiding compulsory transfers and redundancies, improved protection for take home pay and bonus payments, and importantly, 'bulk transfers' terms were agreed. This provided payments of £2,700 for those moving from Inner to Outer London, £3,200 for moving from Outer to National and £6,000 for moving from Inner to National. The agreement represented a significant achievement for the Division. It was the first time that the whole of London had ever balloted for industrial action and the Divisional Committee had only been functioning for a few months. Many of the Representatives and Branch Officials had only been in office for a short period following the national re-organisation of the Union's structures. The outcome of the ballot was by no means certain and it was due to the hard work and commitment of those activists that the Union's national negotiators were able to achieve the changes that resulted in the restructuring plan being implemented without any compulsory redundancies or transfers.

The first stage of the rationalisation plan was the closure of the West Central District Office where on 22 June 1993 unofficial industrial action took place a few days before it was due to close. Royal Mail, believing it related to the implementation of the plan, obtained a High Court Injunction prohibiting further strikes, not just at West Central, but across the whole Division. This was not discharged until January 1994 and later in 1993, the Union was served with another injunction following an alleged overtime ban at the Mount Pleasant office. On this occasion the injunction was nationwide and covered every UCW member working for Royal Mail in Britain. The injunction was served on 8 October 1993 and was lifted on 13 October 1993.

London Weighting had continued to fall behind the increase in the London cost of living and the campaign for an increase in London Weighting had been maintained since the DRAS dispute in 1988. In 1993 the Union in London took a big step forward when Mike Hogan negotiated a deal that produced a change to the way that the allowance was calculated. Since the 1950s recruitment had been a major problem and in the 1980s Royal Mail had only reluctantly agreed to increase the allowance. The 1993 deal represented a significant advance for London postal workers. Instead of yearly negotiations the allowance would be automatically increased each year in line with the national pay increase. From November 1993 the term London Weighting was replaced by the name London Pay Range when the agreement was accepted in a Branch ballot by a comfortable majority.

In December 1994 the Dartford Amalgamated Branch launched a campaign to save the Dartford MLO from closure. Although no longer part of the London Division the links between London and the Dartford Branch remained. Lionel Sampson, had been a London District Officer before the Union's re-organisation and was now the Divisional Representative for the South East. The Branch had a number of experienced and capable officials who led a well organised and skilful campaign to save the office. On 18 December the Branch came out on strike and on 22 December the leadership, Terry Pullinger, Martin Akerman, Chris Bennett and Lionel Sampson were able to tell their members that they had been successful. They had worked hard to gain the support of

Dartford Council, the local Chamber of Commerce and many people in the local community including Bob Dunn, Dartford's Conservative Member of Parliament. The membership remained solid during the dispute, despite the strike taking place just before the Christmas holiday, convincing Royal Mail to change their plans.

In December 1992 Michael Heseltine, President of the Board of Trade had announced that Parcelforce was to be privatised and in March 1993 the Union launched the second phase of the 'Stand by Your Post' campaign in defence of a publicly owned Post Office. The Union announced in April 1993 that the campaign against the dismissal of the 'REM 11', Postal Officers dismissed by Post Office Counters Ltd (POCL) in 1991 for an alleged overtime fraud in the Cash Remittance Unit in South East London, had been brought to a successful conclusion. The REM 11 were offered the option of either their jobs back and financial compensation for their lost pay or larger financial compensation if they decided they did not want to continue working for POCL. This success was largely due to the efforts of Moss Haley, Branch Secretary of the South East London Counter and Clerical Branch who led a tireless campaign in support of his members for nearly three years, and Alan Tuffin, General Secretary had supported the campaign and negotiated the final agreement that offered them re-instatement. However, the support of thousands of UCW members who helped financially throughout their ordeal was also crucial.

In December 1994 the Union announced the result of the ballot for the merger of the Union of Communications Workers and the National Communications Union. The UCW vote was 53,800 for amalgamation and 6,539 against and the NCU vote was 41,539 for and 6,957 against the merger, giving the two Executive Councils an overwhelming endorsement of their recommendations to support the new merged union the Communication Workers Union (CWU). Norman Candy was elected Divisional Representative in 1994 to replace Albert Merriman who had taken voluntary redundancy the previous year.

Computer Assisted Delivery Revisions (CADRA) Dispute 1995

In 1995 the industrial spotlight moved away from the MLOs and onto the delivery side of the business. Before the 1960s major revisions of staffing levels were carried out to a fixed timetable using an exercise known as the

'Quinquennial Review'. This involved a study of the duties, walks and collections in each office and the physical counting of the offices traffic. This information and whatever other statistical and operational data was available were then used to establish the required staffing levels. It was carried out every five years, as the name implies, and was abandoned in the mid-1960s. It was replaced by 'Interim and Sectional Revisions' which were designed 'to cater for the rapidly changing conditions, that are more economic, result in improved efficiency and are more satisfactory from a staff point of view'. To assist branches and representatives to carry out revisions the Union produced a detailed 68 page booklet titled 'Postal Revision Procedures' which provided agreed guidelines on duty revisions and copies of the relevant Postal Instructions and sections of the Head Postmasters Manuals (known as Manual W). In 1983 this was jointly reviewed and updated to take into consideration the changes produced by the introduction of Improved Working Methods (IWM) and other agreements.

Branches were informed in 1986 that the Union was co-operating with the trial of a new delivery revisions method involving the use of a 'Computer Assisted Letter Delivery Revisions (CADRA)' package. It was described as a 'simple and flexible planning tool for carrying out delivery revisions. It enables revisions to be done more quickly, which will help to maintain standards in the light of current traffic growth and also facilitates the testing of alternative work patterns. Once all this basic information is held on computer file, future revisions become easier and can therefore be undertaken more often to provide for changing circumstances'.

In 1989 the Union published details of an agreement for the wider use of CADRA and by 1994 its use had grown considerably as it began to replace the traditional Manual W method of carrying out duty revisions. In 1993/4 it was introduced into selected London offices and almost immediately problems began to arise concerning its application. Its initial introduction into East London was fairly innocuous and Derek Cooper the East London Area Delivery Representative reported to the Divisional Committee, that the early revisions had actually produced an increase in duties, although he qualified this by saying that this was in areas where mail levels were increasing. Within a short time it became a regular item on the agenda at Divisional meetings and the Committee began to develop a policy of opposing it in its current form and replacing it with an agreement that was less easily manipulated by management to meet their budgetary targets. In line with this policy the Committee submitted a motion to the 1994 Annual conference which was an eight point proposition aimed at giving local representatives a bigger input into the process, including guarantees on take home pay, delivery standards, meal reliefs, duty patterns and productivity savings. The motion was moved by Norman Candy and seconded by Fred Jepson. A number of London delegates supported the proposition including Fred Carpenter, London North West who explained how management were using the agreement to impose savage job cuts. Chris Tymco, Western District Office explained that management were misusing the process and the Union needed to control the input of information into the package. Dave Ward, Branch Secretary of the London South West Branch told the Conference that management were attempting to use CADRA to remove five day duties and in some offices impose 25% job cuts. Lionel Sampson, South East Divisional Representative supported the motion pointing out the dangers of the erosion of delivery standards. However there was strong opposition to the motion from some Branches who argued that their experience with CADRA had been positive and in some cases it had resulted in an increase in duties. Although York, Coventry, Shropshire and Mid-Wales all entered the debate to oppose the motion, Billy Hayes on behalf of the Executive supported the motion and it was carried overwhelmingly.

Following the Conference there was little progress on the issue although it was reported to Branches that negotiations on CADRA were expected to 'resume shortly' and a further report informed Branches that a meeting on the issue was due on 18 January 1995. In the meantime the situation in the London Division was deteriorating. Managers in some areas were quite clearly attempting to manipulate the information being fed into the package to cut duties and worsen conditions. North West and South West London were the areas where the problem was greatest with delivery offices 'registering' disagreements one after the other. Management were threatening to implement delivery revisions by Executive Action and in response the Divisional Committee agreed a policy to co-ordinate industrial action. This proved to be difficult because local negotiations were at different stages. Some areas were more advanced with their negotiations than others and some were reaching agreements. However the Committee had agreed to support the principles in the Conference Motion and support any London Branch that came under attack.

In the months leading to Christmas 1994 the Divisional Committee prepared the membership for a possible confrontation in the New Year and in the weeks before Christmas the South West Area obtained a 7 to 1 vote for industrial action and the North West Delivery Office voted 5 to 1 for action. Meetings with the members in both areas were held and John Keggie representing the National Executive addressed a large member's meeting at the Battersea Arts Centre. The Divisional Committee's policy was to avoid being provoked into unofficial industrial action, maintain discipline and not give Royal Mail an opportunity to use the anti-trade union legislation to stop the Union balloting. However as Christmas approached it became increasingly difficult to maintain this position.

The North West Branch had written to the Executive Council requesting their authority to take strike action but this had not yet been agreed. Management made it clear that following the Christmas break they intended to introduce un-agreed duty changes in the North West Delivery Office in St Pancras Way by Executive Action. This involved imposing a set of un-agreed delivery duties, the allocation of duties without a re-sign, and the introduction of 'simplified sorting'. The Divisional Representatives held a number of meetings with senior London Management in an attempt to persuade them to give the Union's National Officers the opportunity to deal with the matter in line with the Disagreements Procedures. However, they pushed ahead with their plans confident that the trade union legislation could be used to force the Union into accepting the changes. The scene was set for a major confrontation in the New Year and when the North West London staff returned to work after the Christmas break they were faced with unfamiliar walks, a new sorting system (ALFA) and a large reduction in the number of delivery duties. Those who were due to be taken to their deliveries in Royal Mail vehicles discovered that some vans were not available and those that were lacked the necessary seating arrangements. The members of staff considered the new vehicle arrangements to be unsafe and this view was supported by the local CWU Health and Safety Representative. As far as management were concerned this amounted to unofficial industrial action. Individuals who refused to travel in the vehicles were interviewed by supervisors and if they still refused were suspended from duty. Before the end of the day several members of staff had been suspended and Royal Mail wrote to the Union demanding that they 'repudiate' the alleged industrial action.

On 4 January the Union informed Branches that the Post Office had obtained an injunction prohibiting the 'unlawful and un-balloted action at NW1 MLO and that there would be a further court hearing on 6 January at which the Union would have an opportunity to put its case forward regarding the health and safety issues. The circular also instruct other CWU branches not to 'become embroiled' in the dispute and that 'it was only by obeying the law and pursuing the terms of the order placed against the Union that the issues at the heart of the walk-out can be dealt with lawfully and through the proper procedures'. The Union did not repudiate the action, as management were demanding, but sought an urgent meeting with London management to try and resolve the issues. It soon became apparent that Royal Mail had no intention of negotiating and were intent on using the courts to force the Union to accept the imposed changes. On 6 January 1995 a further Branch Circular was issued informing Branches that: 'As a result of the hearing, Deputy Judge Maway granted an injunction to Royal Mail which ordered that all UCW members in the London NW1 office should forthwith work in accordance with their contracts of employment, the injunction is continuous until discharged by further order of the court'. The circular went on to warn that 'any inducement by Branch Officials which could be seen as persuading UCW members not to work in accordance with their contracts of employment may lead the Union into Contempt of Court proceedings'. Although there were a number of meetings involving National and Divisional Officers meeting with senior London managers, a resolution could not be found because management refused to discuss the underlying problems until the Union stopped the industrial action. From the Union's point of view this was not possible because the cause of the dispute was a health and safety issue not an industrial relations issue.

Within a few days over 30 members had been suspended and Andy Curran the local Area Processing Representative and London's Sub-Divisional Representative informed the Divisional Officers that the situation was becoming more difficult to control and he was unsure how long he could continue to keep the members from walking out. The Divisional Officers, still determined to keep the dispute legal, urged the Branch to do whatever it could to keep its members in work. Other ballots were in progress and it was important to avoid any legal challenge that might place those ballots in jeopardy. An urgent Divisional Committee meeting was called and a decision was taken to establish a fund to pay the wages of those members suspended. Union Headquarters dispatched Tam McGee, the Executive Council member with responsibility for London, to the North West Office to try and find a way forward and assist the Branch in keeping the dispute legal. This was initially successful but the following week the number suspended had increased to over 140 and it became clear that the strategy would be impossible to maintain. The division did not have enough resources to pay an ever increasing number of suspended members and it was also felt that management might use the dispute to selectively dismiss the leading activists involved in the dispute.

A further meeting of the Divisional Committee, Chaired by Peter Donaghy, was held at Swinton House in Gray's Inn Road, WC1 where Billy Hayes provided the meeting with a report on the national situation and Norman Candy updated the meeting on the situation in North West London. A long discussion took place on the options available and although some delegates expressed the view that the Union might be walking into a trap aimed at stopping other Branches from balloting, all were convinced that the Committee could not allow management to progressively suspend all the NW1 delivery members and then selectively dismiss the activists. The focus now had moved away from CADR and was now on the re-instatement of the suspended members. Billy Hayes left the meeting and the Committee continued their discussion on how best to resolve the dispute and insure that the North West London Branch and its members were not left isolated.

The following day the Union issued another Special Branch Circular saying: 'The action which began at North West London MLO has now spread to virtually the whole of London. North West delivery staff are the only ones who have been balloted. All other action is illegal and unconstitutional. Last night the Post Office obtained a further High Court injunction. This injunction specifically requires:

(a) all employees to carry out tasks which they are lawfully required to perform

(b) all mail to be handled, sorted, processed and distributed normally

(c) that there be no picketing.

This is the extension of the Injunction granted last week. Illegal action exposes the Union and the individuals to punishment for Contempt of Court.

The circular went on to urge Branches outside London not to become involved.

The first office to walk out had been the West End Delivery Office where the distribution staff walked out in the early afternoon, followed by all the main central London offices. Within 24 hours a steady stream of offices had hit the streets and the majority of London's 20,000 CWU members were on unofficial strike. Union Headquarters issued another Branch Circular informing Branches that on Friday 27 January 1995 a writ would be moved at the Royal Courts of Justice seeking to: 'Sequester all the real and personal property of the defendants, the Union of Communication Workers, for their contempt of court in wilfully committing a breach of the following injunction made by order of Mr. Richard Morey QC dated January 13 1995 of which the defendants had due notice'.

The dispute was now taking the Union into uncharted waters but nevertheless it began to spread outside the Division with some Branches in the Home Counties, including the Northern Home Counties Distribution Centre and Romford Mail Centre refusing to handle diverted mail. London management finally agreed to negotiate and after several days of talks an agreement was reached that ensured that all those members suspended were re-instated and that there would be no disciplinary action taken against them or anyone involved in the unofficial strike. Discussions would begin to resolve the health and safety issues, the CADR related issues and the imposed revision. The agreement was placed before the Divisional Committee and, although there was some disappointment that the settlement included an agreement to withdraw all current notices for industrial action, affecting South West London delivery offices and the W1 delivery office, the general view was that the unofficial action had been necessary and the outcome satisfactory. Following a meeting held at the Irish Centre in Murray Grove, Camden, addressed by Alan Johnson, Billy Hayes and Norman Candy the North West London members agreed to return to work and although problems relating to CADR continued to dominate industrial relations into 1996, management became very cautious about imposing delivery revisions in London by executive action.

The legal consequences of the strike however were not over and on 27 January the Union appeared at the Royal Courts of Justice in the Strand, before Mr. Justice Drake, to face a charge of contempt of court.

In the court case that followed Royal Mail attempted to prove that the

Divisional Committee had broken the terms of 6 January injunction by calling a London wide unofficial strike. The Union denied these allegations and argued that the strike had been a spontaneous reaction to the suspensions and management diverting mail without agreement. Alan Johnson, Billy Hayes, several local officials and a number of lay Branch members gave evidence.

The Post Office's QC, in an attempt to discredit the Branch, asked Johnson if it was true that they were known in Union circles as the 'Martini Branch' because of their reputation for taking unofficial industrial action. Johnson pointed out that the Branch had not been involved in unofficial industrial action for several years and the Judge asked the QC to explain what he meant by the term 'Martini Branch'. The QC explained that a 1970s Martini advert had made famous the catch phrase, 'Any time, Any place, Anywhere' and that this alluded to their reputation for taking unofficial industrial action. Justice Drake responded that given their recent strike record 'that did not seem like a very strong Martini to me'.

A Royal Mail witness complained to the court that CWU members sitting at the back of the court were intimidating him with their attitude and body language and Justice Drake warned those present to be careful about their behaviour. The Post Office QC argued that the London Division had orchestrated the unofficial action and cited a conversation between Andy Curran, Area Processing Representative and Gary Delue, the North West London Processing Manager who had alleged that Curran had threatened to escalate the dispute across London unless they re-instated the suspended members. Curran denied this under oath but nevertheless the Judge chose to believe Royal Mail. They also argued that the National Union had failed to repudiate the industrial action as they were required to do under the Trade Union legislation and once again the Judge accepted Royal Mail's arguments. In his summing up the Judge made the point that Contempt of Court was particularly serious because it was an act against the Court. When he announced that the Union would be fined £7,500 there was a considerable amount of relief amongst the CWU members present but when Royal Mail asked for costs and he awarded them over £100,000 this turned to shock. However, before the end of the proceedings the Judge also gave the following advice to both sides, 'Experience has shown that management and unions resorting to the Courts is not always the best way to resolve industrial disputes'.

In Johnson's report to the Executive in late February 1995 he informed them that 'the fact is that the same judgement has left the Union totally exposed to attacks through the Court' and that the 'Union now had previous'. He went on to argue that the Union had no choice other than to change its policy towards 'repudiation'. He explained that between 1992 and 1994 there had been 78 unofficial stoppages in Royal Mail, 5 in Parcelforce and 1 in Post Office Counters and within a few days of the North West London judgement there had been another unofficial dispute in London at the Willesden Delivery Office (NW10) and staff had also walked out at the Cardiff MLO.

Court action was pending in respect of claims for damages in relation to disputes in Liverpool and Bristol and in addition the Union had a 'check off' agreement with Royal Mail, which allowed them to withdraw this facility by giving six months' notice, if un-balloted industrial action occurred. Johnson told the Executive that in his view it was clear that the future of the Union and its financial survival were a stake. He recommended that the Union undertake a review of its proceedings when dealing with unofficial industrial action and that they issue new guidelines to Branches, underlining the responsibilities of Branch Officials during disputes. He went on to argue that the Union should introduce a new procedure for 'fast-tracking' ballots and in future the Union would have to 'repudiate' unofficial industrial action if it was believed that the organisation and its funds were in jeopardy. However when it came to the vote Johnson's proposal for a change in the policy for dealing with unofficial industrial action was rejected by the Executive but nevertheless the change was introduced for all subsequent disputes.

Royal Mail Productivity and the 'Chalk-up' Dispute

In 1994 the Union issued a number of Special Branch Circulars dealing with 'Royal Mail productivity and remuneration'. They dealt specifically with savings that had been accumulated and 'chalked-up' for payment once a new productivity scheme had been agreed. Discussions on a new productivity deal had been going on for some time and in April 1995 Branches were informed that negotiations had broken down and they should not become involved in discussing productivity at a local level. This presented a serious problem in London because a large number of offices had chalked up savings and the discussions on the issues outstanding from the London CADR dispute, including savings, had still not been resolved. On 7 March the Divisional Reps wrote to Alan Johnson.

Dear Alan,

London Delivery Revisions – Savings

You are aware of the numerous problems that we have in the London Division regarding the twin issues of CADR and savings resulting from delivery revision activity. For some time now, we have been attempting, with the assistance of Billy Hayes to resolve these problems (CADR and savings resulting from delivery revisions activity). Indeed, the recent London dispute resolution agreement, committed both sides to finding a way forward on these two issues. Unfortunately, these discussions have not been successful. Considerable savings have been made in the Division, and management have now informed the Union that a deadline of 31 March 1995 has been placed on protecting these savings for a future national scheme. This matter was discussed at a recent meeting of the London Division Area Delivery Reps, with the result that in the absence of a national agreement on remuneration, we shall have no alternative other than to seek a Divisional agreement on this issue. As a Division we are not prepared to see these savings lost to our members. We have explained this situation to Billy, and needless to say, he was not happy with this decision.

We feel, however that it is the correct decision, and that it is in the interest of all our members to ensure that these savings are not lost. Consequently, we are writing to let you know it is our intention to seek a Divisional agreement on this issue before 31 March 31.

Yours sincerely

Norman Candy and Fred Jepson
London Divisional Representatives

On 23 March the London Director, Delivery Services, David Legge wrote to Union Headquarters reiterating management's position and at the same time he wrote to London delivery staff informing them that unless an agreement was reached by 31 March they stood to lose all the accumulated savings resulting from local delivery staff revisions. The Divisional Representatives informed Johnson that if the National Union could not give them the authority to sign a Divisional agreement then they would be requesting a ballot for industrial action as the only way of protecting the accumulated savings. There were numerous other issues facing the Division and once again the Committee began preparations for a major dispute with the employer. Ballot requests had been submitted relating to the concentration of North West's traffic into North London MLO and the loss of various local agreements and bonuses. Both North West deliveries and South West deliveries had live ballots connected to CADR revisions. The NW1 delivery revision had still not been resolved three months after the dispute and there were several disciplinary cases pending against Union Representatives. These involved the North West Branch Secretary, Tony Davis, who management alleged went into work whilst on sick leave to call his own office, NW10, out on strike during the January dispute and Martin Walsh, a Unit Representative at the SW1 delivery office who was facing a charge related to the same dispute and a Unit Representative at NWDO accused of using 'abusive language' on the picket line.

It was against this background and following an approach to Royal Mail by Alan Johnson that a series of meetings, beginning on 15 March and ending on 23 March, took place. The Union was represented by Alan Johnson, Mike Hogan and Billy Hayes and after 30 hours of negotiations they had reached a position where they could recommend an agreement to the Executive. The proposal was that London would be given the 'green light' to sign up to an agreement that would not only to protect pay and weekly bonus for the 'chalked-up' savings but for all savings that had been brought in by agreement pre-1994 and this would hold the field until a national agreement was reached. When the Executive met to discuss the proposal they rejected the agreement but instructed Johnson to ensure that London had the same facilities as the rest of the UK to chalk-up savings and protect these savings beyond 31 March 1995. This would have meant that thousands of pounds in bonus payments would have been lost across London because management were still insisting that the 31 March deadline would be implemented.

On 4 March the London Divisional Committee met to discuss the Executive's decision and unanimously decided to recommend to Branches that they make local agreements to protect savings until a national agreement was reached. In May 1995 London Divisional Representative, Fred Jepson was elected Vice-Chair of the Postal Executive and in October 1995 Dave Ward, Branch Secretary, London South West Postal Branch, was elected London Regional Secretary.

Cricklewood Dispute

A year after the 1995 strike another dispute occurred in North West London. On 5 January 1996 CWU members at the Cricklewood Delivery Office walked out following the suspension of a local Union representative who it was alleged had been involved in an altercation with another member of staff. Following a meeting between local management and the Divisional Representatives, a return to work agreement was reached following assurance from management regarding the treatment of the case. Further problems erupted on 10 January when management began disciplinary proceedings against another two Cricklewood representatives regarding their alleged conduct during the earlier dispute and the office walked out again. The dispute quickly spread to the rest of North West London and a hastily arranged meeting of the Divisional Committee was called to discuss the situation. The response from other London Branches was more restrained on this occasion. Understandably some Branches were not very enthusiastic about becoming involved in another North West London dispute. When evidence emerged that management might have a 'hit list' of London CWU Representatives who they intended to dismiss the dispute gained momentum and by Friday 12 January over 6,000 London postal workers were on unofficial strike. The Divisional Representatives held a number of meetings with management and a settlement, acceptable to the individuals involved and the North West London Committee was reached. On Saturday 13 January a mass meeting of the branch accepted the agreement and they returned to work followed by the other offices that had also taken action.

The Employee Agenda Dispute

Discussions on Total Quality Management (TQM) and team working began in 1994 however several unsuccessful attempts to introduce TQM styled initiatives had been attempted dating back to the 1980s. Successive Conferences had established clear opposition to any involvement with what was often referred to as 'Japanese style management techniques' when the negotiations restarted in 1994. TQM was seen by many as a strategy to undermine the Union in the workplace. Its introduction in many UK industries, including what remained of the motor industry and manufacturing in general had seen trade unions marginalised and severely weakened at the shop-floor level.

In August 1994 several Branch Officials, Steve Bell, John Ireland, Kevin Slocombe and Executive Council members Andy Furey, John Keggie, Tony Kearns and Pat O'Hara, with the support of Billy Hayes, Assistant Secretary Outdoor produced a document exposing the dangers of TQM. It was called 'The Postal Workers Next Steps' and was circulated to Branches throughout the country. This provoked on angry response from Alan Johnson, the General Secretary who on 1 November 1994 dispatched a Special Branch Circular (SBC) urging Branch Secretaries to ensure that it was made available to 'all relevant officials, particularly those that received the Next Steps document'. The Circular included a report, drawn up by Johnson on behalf of the Executive Council, re-stating the Unions position, a document headed 'Royal Mail Staffing Arrangements – Negotiators Brief' and a letter addressed to Eric Lovett from Dr. John Fisher an academic from the Department of Education Studies at the University of Surrey who was advising the Union on TQM issues. The letter was a strong defence of his strategy for dealing with TQM and Johnson was particularly annoyed at what he considered to be an unwarranted attack on Dr. Fisher contained in the Next Steps. Johnson made it very clear that he considered the 'uncompromising opposition' to TQM taken in the Next Steps was not the right strategy for the Union and the Executive Council members who had associated themselves with the document had made an 'error of judgement'. The Executive's position, he made clear, was a 'defence and involvement' strategy which was in line with the strategies already adopted by the Transport and General Workers Union (TGWU) and the Amalgamated Electrical and Engineering Union (AEEU) in the car industry and our National Communication Union (NCU) colleagues in British Telecoms. Special Branch Circulars, keeping Branches informed of progress with the negotiations, were dispatched in May, August and October 1995, and in November the Union circulated a further report which included copies of the exchanges of correspondence between the General Secretary, Alan Johnson and Royal

Mail's Head of Remuneration and Employment, Mark Callanan outlining their respective positions. Area Representatives, Branch Secretaries, Divisional and Regional Representatives were regularly updated at National Briefings and this was supplemented with information leaked from Union Headquarters by dissident members of the Executive Council. Meanwhile in London TQM became a regular item on the Divisional Committee's agenda and as details of the negotiations emerged the opposition hardened. The London Branches kept their members informed of the latest developments through staff meetings and circulars. A solid body of opposition was building up and it became apparent that even the traditional loyalists were distancing themselves from the direction the negotiations were taking. It became clear that the only member of the Union's leadership enthusiastic about the Employee Agenda was Alan Johnson. It was also clear to many activists that the Union's Conference policy on TQM and associated issues was being ignored as the negotiations moved towards a possible agreement. Concessions on team working and team leaders were being traded off in exchange for promises of improvements in other areas.

Throughout this period the Divisional Committee held several meetings to discuss the way the situation was developing and came to the conclusion that there was very little in the deal for members and that management's aim was to relegate the Union to the role of an ineffective staff association, restricted to dealing with health and safety issues, individual representation and national bargaining, with collective bargaining in the work place being undermined by 'teams' competing with each other, undermining local deals and terms and conditions. The London Divisional Representative's and the Regional Secretary were in regular contact with other Divisions and Regions. The Union held Divisional Representative's meetings and these became a regular vehicle for discussing the 'Employee Agenda' across Divisional boundaries. Other unofficial meetings involving Divisional and Regional Representatives and Branch officials from London, Anglia, South East, South Central and the South West Divisions met on a regular basis. Meetings with leading members of the Executive and the authors of 'Next Steps' to discuss and co-ordinate the opposition were also held on a regular basis in a West London public house called 'The Pride of Paddington'.

On Sunday 14 January 1996 *The Independent* ran an article headed 'Postal Strike Looms': 'The threat of nationwide postal strikes moved a step nearer yesterday in the wake of a wildcat stoppage which brought widespread disruption to mail services in London – senior union officials warned that a national walkout was now virtually inevitable – an increasing number of CWU officers are predicting that official action will begin by the end of February – Mr. Johnson is facing a groundswell of opinion on UCW's powerful national postal committee which wants to take management on'.

The prediction of a strike by the 'end of February' was premature but it was an indication of the pressure building up on the Executive. Branches and Divisions were making it clear that Executive Council members who supported any deal that included 'team working' would not receive their support in future elections. The Union's long standing claims for a shorter working week, improved holidays and improved pay were marginalised by the groundswell of opposition to the Employee Agenda, TQM and in particular team working and team leaders. When it became apparent that the proposed 'new benefits', emerging from the talks, would be self-financing the limited support for the deal that existed in some areas of the country began to evaporate.

A meeting of the 'opposition' took place and it was agreed that it was the right time to hold a national meeting. The organisers were very careful to avoid allegations that they were breaking the Union's Rules and the large hall at the TUC was booked in the name of the London Region. Invitations for the meeting, to be held on Saturday 2 March 1996, were sent out in the name of over 30 sponsoring Branches from across the UK. These included Manchester, Liverpool, Milton Keynes, Watford, Edinburgh, Bristol, Cardiff, Oxford and all of the London Postal Branches. The invitations were sent to all the Union's Postal Branches, Postal Executive members, Regional Secretaries, Divisional Representatives and National Officers.

The General Secretary, Alan Johnson responded by warning Branches that: 'The meeting is unconstitutional and Branches have no authority to spend Union money on either organising or attending such a gathering arranged by a self-appointed clique, faction or gathering'.

However this clearly had no effect on the attendance, and some observers have even argued that it guaranteed a larger turnout than would have normally been expected. Several Executive Council members, Divisional Representatives, Regional Secretary's and approximately 150 individuals attendanded representing over 40 Postal Branches. It was agreed by the organisers, that to reduce the possibility of disciplinary action following Johnson's letter to Branches, all contributions would be made from the floor. Only Norman Candy, London Divisional Representative, who acted as Chair for the meeting, sat on the platform. Speakers included PEC members, Divisional Representatives and Regional Secretaries, Branch Secretaries and Area Reps and individual members. It was clear that those present represented a solid block of Branches and individuals from across the UK who were prepared to work and organise to defeat the 'Agenda'. In the following months both sides stepped up the propaganda war. Posters, leaflets and booklets attacking the 'Agenda' were distributed and Dave Ward, London Region Secretary organised a three day TQM School in Birmingham which activists from around the country attended to discuss tactics and strategies for opposing its introduction. Guest speakers included representatives from an American Labour organisation called 'Labour Notes' who had considerable experience in opposing TQM in the USA and promoted a different strategy to that advocated by Dr. John Fisher that was based on 'organised opposition' rather than 'defence and involvement'.

Management used their staff journal *The Courier* to promote the alleged benefits available for employees if they embraced TQM and letters were sent directly to their home addresses with the same message. In March 1996 management threatened to introduce the 'Agenda' with or without the agreement of the Union who responded with leaflets to members urging opposition to any un-agreed imposition of TQM. Management needed a deal with the Union to bring in the changes but this was looking more and more unlikely and the reports from CWU Headquarters were that the Executive were holding firm and that Johnson was becoming increasingly isolated.

In May 1996 the PEC took a decision to authorise a ballot for industrial action. Members were asked to vote for a strike in support of the Union's long standing claims on a whole range of issues and designed to rally the members around a negotiated resolution to the impasse the Union found itself in. Management responded with a direct mailing to staffs home addresses promoting the benefits of the 'Employee Agenda' and including a dire warning of the consequences for the industry if they voted for industrial action. The National Union urged the membership to deliver an overwhelming 'Yes' vote and Divisions, Regions and Branches throughout the country produced thousands of leaflets, badges and posters urging members to support the Executive's recommendation. When the result was announced at the Union's 1966 Annual Conference, 67,311 had voted for industrial action and 31,528 against.

An article in the 3 June edition of *The Independent* made the following comments: 'The Royal Mail is to table a new pay and productivity package after leaders of 138,000 postal workers yesterday announced a vote of more than two to one for a national strike. Leaders of the Communication Workers Union and management agreed to meet next week in an attempt to avert what would be the first national strike for eight years – Alan Johnson, joint General Secretary of the CWU, warned that staff would not simply be bought off. Key demands for greater efficiency would also have to be withdrawn – The CWU leader said the Union wanted quick answers. 'My members will take this action with great reluctance but they are at the end of their tether. We want a five day week before the end of the millennium'. A Royal Mail spokesman said more money would be put on the table so that no postal workers would lose out. 'There is a very strong will at the Royal Mail to reach agreement. A strike is in no one's interest', he went on to say'.

Armed with a 68% vote for action the Union began further negotiations with management on 10 June but management's 'new pay and productivity package' proved to be a watered-down version of their earlier proposals. On 12 June the PEC rejected the offer and announced industrial action for 20 and 27 June. In a late attempt to avert the strike the negotiators met on 17 June but the momentum for action was too strong and the inability of Royal Mail to improve their offer ensured the inevitability of the strike going ahead on 20 June. The following day the Union announced that the response across the country had been almost 100% despite the fact that management had pulled out all the stops to encourage staff to go into work. The second strike went ahead on 27 June and once again support remained solid. Nationally the Union reported that support was better than on the first day. That week the Government announced plans to lift the monopoly if the strikes continued and further negotiations took place on 1 July. The Union circulated details of the discussions which suggested a possible deal involving a trial of team working, the introduction of a uni-grade and various other changes including 'personal development plans'. Talks at ACAS resumed on 8 July but collapsed the next day and on 11 July the Executive announced instructions for further action to take place on 18, 26 and 31 July and 6 August. The strike on 18 July went ahead, but on the basis that progress was being made in negotiations, the strikes set for 26 and 31 July were called off. Alan Johnson, on behalf of the negotiating team, put a new document 'Proposed Settlement of Royal Mail/CWU Dispute' to the PEC at a Special Meeting held on Monday 29 July 1996 but this was rejected and the strike on 6 August went ahead.

Management stepped up their campaign to undermine support for the strike by sending another letter directly to member's home addresses with details of the offer and urging them to demand a ballot on the new proposal. Staff who wished to work on strike days were urged to make contact with their local manager and meet at a secret location where secure transport would be provided to take then through picket lines. They informed any member of staff wishing to take up the offer that their confidentiality would be assured. However the number that accepted the offer was very small and in fact, during the course of the dispute, the Union actually recruited 6,000 new members. Articles appeared in the press attacking the Postal Executive and accusing the 'militants and extremists' orchestrating the dispute of 'holding the country to economic ransom'.

On 9 August a Divisional Representatives meeting was held in Birmingham to gauge national support for the on-going industrial action with every Division reporting that support remained very strong.

On 14 August 1996, the day announced for the fifth strike, the London Region organised a rally in central London at Central Hall, Westminster. Some central London Branches marched from their picket lines to the hall where over a thousand striking CWU members from across the Region and beyond were addressed by the Regional Secretary Dave Ward, Andy Curran Sub-Divisional Representative, and Norman Candy Divisional Representative. Various speakers addressed the meeting from the floor including Fred Jepson the Union's Vice-Chair. The room was decked with CWU Branch banners from London and other parts of the country. A full size imitation coffin with 'RIP Employee Agenda' was placed at the front of the stage and to great applause it was taken from the hall and delivered to Royal Mail's London Headquarters in Old Street.

A speaker from the floor, Brian Pammet, Area Delivery Representative, North West London, proposed that following the end of the meeting all those present should march from the hall to Old Street. This was rejected by the platform but it was agreed a march and rally be arranged for the day of the next strike when the London officials would have an opportunity to organise it properly. On 16 August and against the wishes of the General Secretary, the Union announced that unless an agreement was reached before, four days of continuous action would take place from 30 August to 2 September. Royal Mail produced a press statement calling the decision irresponsible and once again urged the Union to ballot its members on the latest deal on offer. The Government threatened a three month suspension of the 'monopoly' and *The Daily Mirror* attacked the Union, declaring: 'A four day strike is absurd to the point of self-destruction. These strikes and the language the Union uses have all the hallmarks of old-fashioned, bone-headed confrontation. The result will be a disaster for the Union and its members'.

The sixth strike took place on 22 August and the London Branches once again reported that the action was solid despite attempts by management to convince members to go into work. Talks resumed on 27 August and on the same day the Union's Divisional Representatives were called to a meeting at CWU Headquarters for an update on the progress being made with the negotiations. Although it was reported that some progress had been made it was felt that this was insufficient and although the four days of continuous action were cancelled, Friday 30 August and Monday 2 September were named as two more 24 hour strikes. It was 106 years since London members of the Postmen's Union had braved Police and Post Office provocation to assemble in Clerkenwell Green to hear Keir Hardy and John Mahon speak in support of building the Postmen's Union and it was in Clerkenwell Green that over a thousand CWU members assembled to march to Royal Mail Headquarters in Old Street on 30 August 1996. The march, led by a Musicians Union jazz band, set off along Clerkenwell Road to the junction where it continued along Old street to the roundabout at the junction with City Road and then came back on itself to return along Old Street again, pausing for a few minutes outside Royal Mail Headquarters whilst the band played 'Colonel Boggie'.

Support for the eighth strike on 2 September was almost 100% and the mood in London remained positive. The PEC discussed the possibility of escalating the dispute but this did not materialise. The view in London was that TQM/team working could not be introduced without the active support of the Union and if they tried to introduce it without agreement it would be a failure. It was felt that the concept behind TQM required the compliance and co-operation of at least a majority of the workforce and this was further away than ever. London's main aim was to defend workplace trade union organisation and protect existing terms and conditions. The delivery issue, shorter working week and five day weeks were important but secondary to workplace organisation which they felt must be defended at all costs. At this stage in the dispute it began to emerge that the objectives of London were not necessarily the same as some of the opposition leaders on the PEC who felt that a deal acceptable to the members, which did not include TQM could still be achieved. London's view was that any deal at this stage would inevitably lead to a watered-down compromise involving some form of team working and as a consequence a weaker role for the Union in the workplace.

The issue of re-balloting became an issue again and this time it came from within the Union. Johnson clearly saw re-balloting as a way out of the dispute and there was some support for this in the North East Division where one prominent Division Rep publicly called on the Union to hold another ballot. Some in London felt that a re-ballot was unnecessary and a sign of weakness whilst others felt that a re-ballot would confirm the member's rejection of team working/TQM and strengthen the Union's hand. Reports in the media appeared suggesting that Royal Mail were attempting to recruit an 'Army of Casual Employees' to use in the event of strike action being stepped up. On 9 September another Divisional Representative's meeting was called at CWU Headquarters to gauge support for the strike and on 10 September the PEC voted to call two further days of action on 20 and 22 September. Royal Mail responded by threatening to withdraw the package already on the table, but this was not seen as much of a threat as it was exactly what most activists wanted them to do. The TUC and the Labour Party attempted to bring pressure on the Union to reach an agreement and Labour's employment spokesman David Blunkett accused those opposed to re-balloting of being 'Armchair revolutionaries whose only interest is disruption'. John Monks, TUC General Secretary, asked to address the PEC on the disputes implications for the future of the wider trade union movement.

A national briefing held at Central Hall, Westminster on Tuesday 17

September was addressed by Monks who was listened to with respect but with little effect on those present, who remained committed to continuing the dispute, until they achieved on acceptable resolution. On 19 September the PEC met again and it was expected that they would call further industrial action but this did not happen and within days it was announced that Royal Mail were attempting to have the strike declared illegal. They had been threatening this for some time and they were now claiming that in the notification for industrial action on 2 June the Union has failed to notify them of the number of spoilt ballot papers, which they claimed contravened trade union legislation. Apparently the figure had been inadvertently 'tippexed' out and legal advice to the Union was that ignoring the challenge could lead to a possible £1 million fine and unlimited claims from those Royal Mail customers affected by the strike. A re-ballot became inevitable and notification was sent out advising Branches that this would begin on 11 October and close on 29 October with a strong recommendation from the Executive to continue the dispute. The general view amongst the activists was that it was a 'stitch up' but if one thing could guarantee another 'Yes' vote it was this.

London began a massive campaign to re-affirm support for the strike. Mass meetings were held across the country and when the result was announced it was 64,919 to 40,581 in support of further action. The result was slightly less than the 68% majority in the first ballot but nevertheless a massive endorsement of the Executive's recommendation. Royal Mail, the media and the Government had launched a huge propaganda campaign to convince members to vote 'No'. This included adverts in national newspapers, threats to the monopoly and letters sent directly to member's home addresses. When the vote was announced Royal Mail, who for several months had been urging the Union to re-ballot, bizarrely insisted that – 'the ballot result doesn't take us anywhere. The central problem of the need for a new way of working cannot be wished away'. Effectively the dispute was now over and Royal Mail's attempt to impose TQM on their unwilling workforce had been defeated. The only thing left to discuss was how the issue could be brought to a conclusion in a way that satisfied both sides. Johnson consulted a number of people involved in the dispute and this included the London Divisional Representatives and the Regional Secretary. At a meeting held at the Union's Clapham Headquarters, Divisional Officers Norman Candy, Andy Curran, John Denton and the Regional Secretary, Dave Ward met with Alan Johnson. A number of ideas were discussed on how the dispute could be brought to a conclusion.

Negotiations re-started on 1 November 1996 and it was agreed that a number of Joint Working Parties (JWPs) would be established to explore possible ways forward on 'team working', 'delivery issues' and various other issues that were stopping agreement being reached. A pay and allowances increase of 3% was also agreed which, when put out to ballot on 18 December 1996 was accepted by 55,955 votes to 16,199. Although some activists were disappointment with the final settlement it was absolutely clear that it represented a major victory for the Union. The delivery issues were to be dealt with separately and TQM/team working was effectively buried.

Importantly the Union's workplace structures and organisation remained intact. The CWU was the only union to successfully defeat a major national employer on the issue of team working/TQM, and significantly their Royal Mail workplace organisation continues to be significantly stronger than most other unions in the UK.

1996-2000 Industrial Action

There was no let-up in London's deteriorating industrial relations climate and on 10 December 1996 there was another unofficial dispute at the North West DO. Richard Bruce, Branch Secretary, Mount Pleasant Branch and Bob McGuire, East London Parcels Branch were both elected onto the Executive Council and John Keggie, who had been prominent in opposing the Employee Agenda, challenged Mike Hogan for the position of Assistant Secretary Indoors, a position Hogan had held since 1990. Keggie mounted a strong challenge and the London Branches were equally divided between the two candidates. When the result was announced at the 1996 Annual Conference, Hogan received 19,808 votes and Keggie received 18,503 votes. In the same year Dave Ward, who had previously been the London Regional Secretary, was elected to the position of Divisional Representatives left vacant when Fred Jepson was elected as the Union's National Vice-Chair. John Denton replaced Dave Ward as Regional Secretary in 1998.

In January 1997 a problem arose at the London Distribution Centre (later to be re-named the Princess Royal Distribution Centre). The Hub had been created by an amalgamation of all the London station hubs into what was called at the time a 'state of the art' distribution centre. Trains from around the country went directly into the Willesden Centre, where mail was loaded and unloaded, large articulated vehicles then distributed it around London and the Home Counties. It was an extremely important part of Royal Mail's national network handling up to 7,000 York containers daily, representing 60% of the nation's distant traffic and 20% of all mails traffic. When it was originally established, groups of CWU members who had previously been employed at various railway stations across the capital came together at the Centre. When John Denton and Andy Curran negotiated the agreement that set the Centre up they managed to maintain most of the local agreements and practices enjoyed at the previous workplaces. In January 1997 management attempted to remove some of these practices and a series of negotiations involving Mike Hogan, the Divisional Representatives and Paul O'Donnell, Tony Wilkins and Steve Cook senior representatives from the local Branch took place. It was agreed that the previous work practices would be removed and the staff would receive financial compensation in exchange for accepting and co-operating with the changes. This was endorsed in a secret ballot of the 400 CWU members employed at the Distribution Centre. On 21 February 1997 there was another dispute at the Princess Royal Distribution Centre when staff walked out over staffing levels. This was resolved after four days when staff accepted an agreement to increase the number of full-time staff.

As the 1997 General Election approached the Union produced its own policy document on the future of the Post Office called 'Freedom to Deliver – Posting the way to Greater Success'. It contained 12 proposals which included transforming the Post Office into 'an independent corporation within the public sector', and the introduction of an 'Independent Regulator' to oversee the industry. The election was held on 1 May and it was a landslide victory for the Labour Party led by Tony Blair who polled 13,518,167 votes to obtain 418 seats against the Conservatives led by John Major who won 165 seats having polled 9,600,943 votes. Three weeks before the election Alan Johnson was offered the safe Labour seat of Hull West and Hessle when the previous MP Stuart Randall stood down suddenly and was subsequently elevated to the House of Lords. In the same year the European Union adopted the 1997 Postal Services Directive (amended in 2000) aimed at opening up the member states postal markets to competition by 2009.

On the day that Blair entered Downing Street there was another dispute at the NW1 Delivery Office which was now housed in the basement of the North London Mail Centre. This was resolved on 6 May and the members returned to work the following day. In the 1997 Executive Council elections Richard Bruce and Bob McGuire were re-elected and Fred Jepson retained his position as Vice-Chair. Another dispute occurred at the NW1 Delivery Office when CWU members walked out over staffing levels that again was resolved following an agreement to provide ten part-time workers at the Mail Centre with full-time jobs in the North West 1 delivery office. On 9 May 1997 the ex-Branch Secretary of the London West End Amalgamated Branch was dismissed as a result of an alleged breach of the attendance procedures. The Branch believed that his sickness record was being used to victimise him for his previous trade union activities. Following an overwhelming vote for industrial action the Branch embarked on a long, protracted period of industrial action which took place between 16 June and 22 August 1997. The Branch leadership Alan Smith, Dave Morson, Steve Turner, John Simkins, John Hart and Jim Logan called five separate strikes covering 12 days. Following the intervention of John Keggie, who was Acting Assistant Secretary (Outdoor) at the time, an agreement was reached to refer the case to the 'Independent Advisory Review Body (IARB)'. This was unusual because Tymkow was no longer a union official and the IARB agreement specifically referred to 'senior union officials' and Royal Mail's submission to the review body included the following statement: 'It would not be normal Royal Mail policy to go so far beyond the terms of a negotiated agreement, in this case the Independent Advisory Review Body agreement, were it not evident that the disruption of the mail service at the West End Delivery Centre showed no sign of coming to an end'.

After several days of deliberation the Review Body agreed that Tymkow's dismissal was unfair and he returned to work at the West End office.

There was a strike at the E1 Delivery Office on 3 July in a dispute over workloads, Alpha Sorting and staff flexibility which was resolved after two days. The election to replace Alan Johnson took place in April 1998. There were three candidates, Derek Hodgson (Deputy General Secretary), Billy Hayes (Assistant Secretary Indoors) and Tony Young (Joint General Secretary). The result was Hodgson 26,127, Hayes 17,105 and Young 16,780 votes. A number of changes also took place in the Division when Mark Baulch and Martin Walsh were elected as Sub-Divisional and Assistant Divisional Representatives respectively. At national level John Keggie was elected Deputy General Secretary from a field of five candidates receiving 12,712 votes against his closest rival Martin Collins who received 7,299 votes. Keggie was popular in London and had strong support in the London Division, following his involvement in several high profile London disputes and the Employee Agenda. This was reflected in the number of votes he received from London where the Divisional Officers actively campaigned for his election. Although Keggie won the election comfortably, a number of complaints were received from unsuccessful candidates and Branches which reflected the hostility that had surrounded the campaign.

Another dispute at PRDC occurred in February 1998 following the accusation that a number of code sorters were deliberately working slow and mis-sorting mail. The 13 code sorters were all subsequently exonerated when the cases were processed through the conduct code. However, there was another unofficial dispute at PRDC in March 1998 when three postmen were suspended from duty for allegedly refusing to carry out a manager's instruction. It was apparent to the London Divisional Committee that the industrial relations problems that had dogged the centre since it opened would not be resolved without a strategy to support the members at PRDC and resolve the underlying issues causing the disputes. The dispute quickly escalated across the capital when other London offices refused to handle work destined for the Centre. Within a short period of time over 20,000 London postal workers, including distribution and delivery staff were on unofficial strike. After several days of negotiations involving the Divisional Representatives, local representatives and Ernie Dudley, Assistant Secretary, an agreement to settle the dispute was agreed by a mass meeting of the Distribution Centre's members.

Between 1998 and 2000 the Union dealt with a number of issues unresolved following the Employee Agenda dispute. The 'Interim Delivery Agreement' was debated at the 1998 Blackpool Annual Conference and although it was considerably amended, following further negotiations with Royal Mail a revised agreement was accepted in an individual member's ballot. The result was 25,640 votes for the agreement and 4,910 against. It resolved a number of long standing issues and introduced a new 12 step Revision

Process. It also introduced, amongst other things a new approach to maximising 5 day weeks, a commitment from Royal Mail to remain 'primarily a full-time employer', manageable workloads and an in principled agreement to the cessation of the use of private cars on delivery. The agreement also committed both sides to ensuring that wherever possible available mail should be delivered on the first delivery. In February 1999 the Union agreed, in an individual ballot by 40,732 votes to 27,889, a new productivity deal, the 'Performance Bonus Scheme'. It was a compulsory scheme and was based on providing different levels of reward depending on the level of productivity (EP) in a particular work unit. There were three grades of payment 'High Performance Quality Bonus', 'Improvement Scheme' and 'Main Gainshare Scheme'. The scheme was also designed to generate funds that could be deployed nationally and which might be used to enhance pay, terms and conditions and it included a 12 stage revision procedure in line with the delivery agreement. It resulted in numerous disagreements but generated very little in terms of increased earnings or improvements in productivity within the Division.

The differences between London and the Union nationally, which had first emerged in the final stages of the Employee Agenda dispute began to re-emerged in 1999 as a consequence of the pressure that branches and members in the Division were now coming under. When, following lengthy national negotiations, a new national agreement surfaced in September 1999 many London activists felt that it was simply the 'Employee Agenda' minus the team leaders and that the proposed changes would create 'winners and losers', including reducing some member's pensionable pay. A shorter working week was offered in exchange for 'flexibility' and changes to seniority. The introduction of a single grade replacing postmen/women and PHGs was unpopular in central London where there was a high proportion of PHGs. The Executive argued that the agreement provided £93 million in new money and considerable benefits for the members. Unlike the campaign against the Employee Agenda there was no organised opposition to the agreement just a general view in some parts of the country that the agreement was not good enough. These differences strained the relationship between London and the Union's national leadership, particularly John Keggie who was now the National Officer with overall responsibility for postal matters. Keggie had received considerable support from London during his election campaign for Deputy General Secretary and this developing rift would have a lasting effect on the future politics of the Union. In an individual ballot with a 65% turnout the agreement was rejected by 39,903 to 49,581 with all the London Branches recommended a 'No' vote. However it was not just in London that concern was growing about the direction that the Union was taking industrially and activists around the country began to talk about the need for a change in direction.

The decade ended as it began. There was a dispute at the Poplar Delivery Office (E14) in April 1999 and on 2 November 1999 staff at the North London Mail Centre walked out over the dismissal of a distribution driver, resuming work on 4 November following negotiations at Divisional level. Industrial relations at the Princess Royal Distribution Centre finally began to settle down in February 1999 when, following several months of negotiations, involving Divisional Representatives and Local Representatives, the PRDC Productivity Agreement was accepted by the Centre's membership in an individual ballot. In 1999 meetings between the Divisions in the South of England became more frequent and the foundations of what was to become known as the 'Southern Alliance' become firmly established.

ABOUT THE SOURCES

I first took an interest in the history of the London Postal Workers in the late 1970s when I found a dog-eared copy of a pamphlet on the subject at the bottom of a filing cabinet in the Union Room at the Western Central District Office. In particular it interested me because there was a chapter titled the 'Battle of Mount Pleasant'. My paternal grandfather had started work there straight from school and spent his entire working life there other than when he fought with the Post Office Rifles during the Great War.

In 1984 Alan Clinton produced his mammoth study 'Post Office Workers – a trade union and social history'. Originally the UPW had commissioned Dr. J.E. Williams of Leeds University to produce a history of Post Office trade unionism. Unfortunately he died before it hardly got of the ground and Clinton, his research assistant was asked to take over the task. Over a number of years I gradually worked my way through its 713 pages. The book is packed with information, statistics and facts probably unparalleled in any study of a section of organised workers.

From reading his book I learnt that an earlier study called 'A History of Postal Agitation' had been produced by H.G. Swift in 1899. I have been unable to discover much about Swift other than he was the Editor of the Fawcett Association's journal from 1895 until 1899 and again in 1904. From that I assume he previously worked as a sorter and would have had personal knowledge of many of the events and people that he wrote about. According to Clinton, Swift's account was 'incomplete and often inaccurate', although he does not qualify this. Thirty years later Swift was asked to produce an updated edition of his earlier study and indeed a new edition was produced in 1929. However, when I managed to get my hands on a copy of the second edition it seemed to me identical to the first. I have not been able to discover what has happened to the extra unpublished chapters covering the period to 1929.

I found another book hidden away in a cupboard at the Western Central District Office in the mid-1980s. This was a copy of a book containing a verbatim report of the evidence provided to the 'Tweedmouth Committee' in 1896 by representatives of the Postman's Federation'. It is titled 'The Postmen's Case for Enquiry' and contains numerous photographs of the individuals involved in giving evidence. The first chapter is called 'Postal Service History' and is a short 15 page history of trade union activity between 1860 and 1869.

In 1992 I noticed a copy of an edition of the 1932 year book of *The Post* in the library at the South Eastern District Office' just before the office closed. Tony Conway, the Branch Secretary was kind enough to let me borrow it. When I began reading it I discovered that it contained details of negotiation, agreements including an early recognition agreement for local UPW officials and it added a bit more to the information that I was beginning to accumulate.

I also read M.J. Daunton's 'Royal Mail – The Post Office since 1840'. Commissioned by the Post Office Board and published in 1985. It is a surprisingly objective study of the industry and the individuals who administered it during this period.

In 2003 Gregor Gall, at that time Professor of Industrial Relations at Stirling University and now at Bradford University, published 'The Meaning of Militancy' a detailed and invaluable study of the dynamics of industrial relations in the Post Office during the 1980s and 1990s.

'The Victorian Workhouse' by Trevor May published in 1997 and 'Poverty and Poor Law Reform in 19th Century Britain 1834 – 1939' by David Englander provide an illuminating insight into the worst aspects of Liberal reform in 19th Century Britain.

'The Book of London' edited by Michael Leapman and published in 1989 is a mine of information on the development of London as a world city and financial centre and 'London in the 19th Century' written by Jerry White and published in 2008 is essential reading for any student of London history as is Peter Ackroyd's 'London the Biography'.

'The Rise of the Labour Party 1880 – 1945' (Seminar Studies in History) by Paul Adelman and published in 1972 provides a short but precise history of the early Labour Party.

'The First Industrial Nation – an Economic History of Britain 1700-1914' by

Peter Mathias published in 1969, 'British Economic and Social History 1700-1964' by C.P. Hill first published in 1957 and William Ashworth's 'An Economic History of England' published in 1960 are essential reading.

'Blackshirt – Sir Oswald Mosley and British Fascism' published in 2006 and written by Stephen Dorril and 'Sir Oswald Mosley' written by Robert Skidelskey and published in 1975 are both brilliant studies of the one time Labour politician and later fascist leader.

'The Great Stink of London' by Stephen Halliday, published in 1999 is a fascinating study not just of the subject but also a social and political insight into 19th Century London.

'A History of British Trade Unions since 1889' by H.A. Clegg, Alan Fox and A.F. Thompson, published in 1964 is essential reading for any student of trade unionism as is David Goodman's, 'London Chartism 1838-1848' for anyone wishing to understand the development of Chartism in the capital city.

'A History of the Deficiency in the Fund of the Post Office Staff Superannuation Scheme 1969-1984' by G.P. Olver is the best and most detailed study of the Fund available and I would like to thank Lionel Sampson, Senior Policy Advisor, Postal Department, for providing me with a copy of this.

I have to thank Derek Walsh retired CWU National Officer for his assistance particularly with the sections dealing with the Grunwick dispute and the Improved Working Methods but also his assistance in checking the book and correcting some of the detail. I would also like to thank Dave Percival, retired CWU Policy Advisor, for his assistance and help in correcting some aspects of the book particularly relating to the Improved Working Methods section and the chapter relating to Bill Willoughby. Thanks also to Billy Hayes and John Denton for reading a draft copy of the book and providing me with some valuable guidance on its contents.

Thanks also go to Ian Cook, CWU Research Department for his assistance and help in giving me access to the numerous historical documents from the Union's archives and library and thanks to John Colbert for his help in getting the book printed. I also need to thank Lloyd Harris Secretary of the Mount Pleasant Branch for allowing me to borrow and study several bound copies of *The London Post* covering the period 1939 to 1952.

I have obtained useful information from the Trades Union Congress Archives and the Post Office Archives. Numerous CWU activists have provided me with information and photographs which have been invaluable. In particular I would like to thank Brian Lee and Lee Wenborne for allowing me to study historical documents from their Branch archives. Two booklets produced by the Union of Post Office Workers 'How We Began' and 'Official Recognition' were short histories of the Union and I believe were published in the 1950s.

Access to the bound editions of the Branch Bulletins 1976 to 1990 were invaluable particularly when checking my own recollection of times and events. Last but not least I must thank Pauline Hinchliffe and Pam Riordian, Secretaries in the LDC offices for helping me with the typing.

The rest is all my own work.

INDEX

B

D

E

F

H

I

J

K

L

S

T

U

Y